Absolute Beginner's Guide

to

eBay

(handwritten notes)

1 $ RED ROSE

.4,
.516
.125
———
.641

Fourth Edition

Michael Miller

800 East 96th Street
Indianapolis, Indiana 46240

Associate Publisher
Greg Wiegand

Acquisitions Editor
Michelle Newcomb

Development Editors
Sean Dixon
Rick Kughen

Managing Editor
Charlotte Clapp

Project Editor
Mandie Frank

Indexer
Ken Johnson

Proofreader
Paula Lowell

Technical Editor
Jenna Lloyd

Publishing Coordinator
Sharry Lee Gregory

Book Designer
Anne Jones

Page Layout
Julie Parks

Contents at a Glance

Table of Contents

About the Author

Michael Miller is a a successful and prolific author, and a top eBay seller. He has a reputation for practical, real-world advice and an unerring empathy for the needs of his readers.

Mr. Miller has written more than 75 nonfiction books over the past 17 years, for Que and other major publishers. His books for Que include *Easy eBay, eBay Auction Templates Starter Kit, Tricks of the eBay Masters, Making a Living from Your eBay Business,* and *Absolute Beginner's Guide to Computer Basics.* He is known for his casual, easy-to-read writing style and his ability to explain a wide variety of complex topics to an everyday audience.

You can e-mail Mr. Miller directly at abg-ebay@molehillgroup.com. His website is located at www.molehillgroup.com, and his eBay user ID is trapperjohn2000.

Dedication

To Sherry. Finally.

Acknowledgments

Thanks to the usual suspects at Que, including but not limited to Greg Wiegand, Michelle Newcomb, Sean Dixon, Mandie Frank, Charlotte Clapp, Rick Kughen, and Jenna Lloyd.

We Want to Hear from You!

As the reader of this book, *you* are our most important critic and commentator. We value your opinion and want to know what we're doing right, what we could do better, what areas you'd like to see us publish in, and any other words of wisdom you're willing to pass our way.

As an associate publisher for Que, I welcome your comments. You can e-mail or write me directly to let me know what you did or didn't like about this book—as well as what we can do to make our books better.

Please note that I cannot help you with technical problems related to the topic of this book. We do have a User Services group, however, where I will forward specific technical questions related to the book.

When you write, please be sure to include this book's title and author, as well as your name, e-mail address, and phone number. I will carefully review your comments and share them with the author and editors who worked on the book.

Email: feedback@quepublishing.com

Mail: Greg Wiegand
Que Publishing
800 East 96th Street
Indianapolis, IN 46240 USA

Reader Services

Visit our website and register this book at www.quepublishing.com/register for convenient access to any updates, downloads, or errata that might be available for this book.

INTRODUCTION

eBay is a true phenomenon.

In 2005, eBay transactions defined a new economy worth more than $44 billion. Read that number again; it's not a misprint. *Forty-four billion dollars.* That's $44 billion in sales that didn't exist before eBay. Forty-four billion dollars of transactions that appeared seemingly out of thin air. Forty-four billion dollars in merchandise that wouldn't have been sold otherwise.

Where did that $44 billion come from? It came from you and from me and from 180 million other people around the world who log on to the eBay site to buy and to sell all manner of merchandise. Before eBay, there was no global marketplace for the 180 million of us; there was no way to buy and to sell that $44 billion of merchandise, except for small local garage sales and flea markets.

eBay made that $44 billion happen. eBay brought 180 million of us together.

In doing so, eBay became one of the first—and maybe the only—of the online businesses to make a profit from day one of its existence. eBay kept its costs low by not actually handling any of the merchandise traded on its site, and generated revenue by charging listing fees and sales commissions on every transaction.

Smart people, with a smart concept.

And here's somebody else who's smart about eBay:

You.

You're smart because you bought this book to help you learn how to buy and sell merchandise on the eBay site. You know that you need to learn how eBay works before you can start buying and selling, and you also know that a little extra knowledge can give you the edge you need to be a real auction winner.

Absolute Beginner's Guide to eBay, 4th Edition, will help you get started with eBay auctions—even if you've never bought anything online in your life. Read this book and you'll learn how to bid and how to sell, and what to do when the auction ends.

More important, you'll learn how to maximize your chances of winning important eBay auctions—without paying through the nose. And if you're a seller, you'll learn how to stand out from the crowd and generate more bids—and higher selling prices.

You'll also learn that buying and selling on eBay isn't that hard, and that it can be a lot of fun. You'll even discover that you can actually make a living from your eBay activities, if you don't mind a little hard work.

Really!

How This Book Is Organized

This book is organized into five main parts:

- **Part I, "Welcome to eBay,"** shows you how the eBay marketplace works, as well as how to sign up for eBay membership and find your way around the eBay site.

- **Part II, "Using eBay's Essential Tools,"** is all about the features and tools necessary to get the most out of buying and selling on eBay. You'll discover how to track your auctions in My eBay, create a personal About Me page, read and create product reviews and guides, and utilize eBay's post-auction feedback.

- **Part III, "Buying Merchandise on eBay,"** tells you everything you need to know about bidding for items in eBay auctions, as well as buying fixed-price items in the eBay marketplace. You'll learn how to search for items to buy, how to bid in online auctions, how to find and purchase fixed-priced items from eBay Stores and Half.com, how to pay for your purchases, how to place last-second "snipes" to win eBay auctions, and how to avoid getting ripped off by unscrupulous sellers.

- **Part IV, "Selling Merchandise on eBay,"** is the flip side of the coin. This section tells you everything you need to know about selling on eBay; you'll learn how to create auction listings, sell items for a fixed price, determine what payment methods to accept, pack and ship your merchandise, and best manage all your selling activity.

- **Part V, "Becoming a Power Seller,"** is for the really ambitious eBay user. You'll learn how to manage your auctions with third-party software and services, sell and ship internationally, open a Trading Assistant Business, and how to turn your hobby into a full-time profession—and make a real living from your eBay auctions.

Taken together, the 30 chapters in this book will help you get the most from your eBay experience. By the time you get to the end of the final chapter, you'll be buying and selling online just like a pro!

Conventions Used in This Book

I hope that this book is easy enough to figure out on its own, without requiring its own instruction manual. As you read through the pages, however, it helps to know precisely how I've presented specific types of information.

Web Page Addresses

There are a lot of Web page addresses in this book—including addresses for specific pages on the eBay site. They're noted as such:

www.molehillgroup.com

Technically, a Web page address is supposed to start with http:// (as in http://www. molehillgroup.com). Because Internet Explorer and other Web browsers automatically insert this piece of the address, however, you don't have to type it—and I haven't included it in any of the addresses in this book.

Special Elements

This book also includes a few special elements that provide additional information not included in the basic text. These elements are designed to supplement the text to make your learning faster, easier, and more efficient.

Finally, in various parts of this book you'll find big *checklists*. Use these checklists to prepare for the upcoming task—just check off the items on the list, and you'll be ready to go.

note

A *note* is designed to provide information that is generally useful but not specifically necessary for what you're doing at the moment. Some notes are like extended tips—interesting, but not essential.

caution

A *caution* will tell you to beware of a potentially dangerous act or situation. In some cases, ignoring a caution could cause you significant problems—so pay attention to them!

" Mike Sez "

This element is my personal opinion or recommendation regarding the topic at hand. Remember—I might not always be right, but I'll always have an opinion!

tip

A *tip* is a piece of advice—a little trick, actually—that helps you use your computer more effectively or maneuver around problems or limitations.

Further Reading

I'd be somewhat remiss if I didn't point you to further reading on the subject of eBay—in particular, books you can read after this one to help you be even more successful with your eBay auctions. To this end, I draw your attention to several other books I've written that you might find useful:

- *Easy eBay* (Que, 2005), a four-color, step-by-step guide for easily intimidated eBay newbies

- *eBay Auction Templates Starter Kit* (Que, 2006), a book-and-CD combo that shows you how to create eye-popping auction listings, by using either ready-to-use auction templates or by creating your own templates with HTML.

- *Tricks of the eBay Masters, 2nd Edition* (Que, 2006), which assembles 600 tricks and tips from almost two hundred successful eBay buyers and sellers—great advice that any eBayer can use.

- *Making a Living from Your eBay Business* (Que, 2005), which shows you how to turn your eBay hobby into a profitable business. (This one's more of a business book than an eBay book—just what you need to turn pro!)

Let Me Know What You Think

I always love to hear from readers. If you want to contact me, feel free to e-mail me at abg-ebay@molehillgroup.com. I can't promise that I'll answer every message, but I will promise that I'll read each one!

If you want to learn more about me and any new books I have cooking, check out my Molehill Group website at www.molehillgroup.com. Who knows—you might find some other books there that you'd like to read.

PART

i

WELCOME TO EBAY

1

UNDERSTANDING THE EBAY MARKETPLACE

What is it you need?

A new computer printer? A vintage German military helmet? An authentic prop from your favorite movie? A specific trading card or comic book or Barbie doll? How about some jewelry, or an antique desk, or a new winter coat, or maybe a DVD player? Or, perhaps, you have one of these items that you would like to sell?

Whatever you're buying or selling, there's one place to do it—eBay.

What eBay Is—And How It Came To Be

What is eBay? I think the site's official mission statement does a good job of summing up what eBay is all about:

eBay's mission is to provide a global trading platform where practically anyone can trade practically anything.

What eBay does is simple: It facilitates the buying and selling of merchandise between users, over the Internet. Most (but not all) of eBay's transactions take place using a type of online auction, where interested buyers bid on items that sellers have for sale. eBay itself doesn't buy or sell anything; it carries no inventory and collects no payments. eBay is just the middleman in the selling process, hooking up buyers and sellers around the world—and collecting fees for doing so.

The eBay Story

eBay was one of the first online auction sites on the Internet, launched way back on Labor Day of 1995. It almost single-handedly pioneered the concept of online auctions and, in doing so, carved out the dominant market share. (It also made a lot of money for those who invested in the firm—especially in the early years.)

As the official story goes, founder Pierre Omidyar launched eBay as the result of a conversation with his then-girlfriend (now wife), who was an avid collector of PEZ dispensers. She supposedly commented to Pierre about how great it would be if she were able to collect PEZ dispensers using the Internet. Pierre did her a favor and developed a small PEZ-dispenser trading site, originally called Auction Web.

This small site quickly became a big site. Pierre started charging users a small fee to list items, to help pay his expenses. The day that Pierre opened his mailbox and saw $10,000 worth of fees was the day he quit his day job and made eBay a full-time proposition.

Because of its fee-based model, eBay is that rare website that made money from day one. That made eBay an attractive candidate for venture capital investment and eventual IPO; the company did, in fact, go public in 1998, and it made a lot of people (including Pierre) a lot of money.

Today eBay is one of the most successful Internet businesses in the world, making a little bit of money on each of the millions of transactions that take place every day. It truly is the number-one place to buy and sell any type of item online.

How Big Is eBay?

How big is eBay? Just look at these statistics:

- On any given day, eBay has more than *36 million items* listed for auction.
- As of the end of 2005, eBay had more than *180 million registered users*—almost 72 million of whom are "active" users (having bid, bought, or sold something in the last twelve months).
- During the entire year of 2005, *$44.3 billion worth of merchandise* was traded over eBay—30% more than in the previous year.

All this activity makes eBay not only the biggest shopping site on the Internet, but also the largest online community of any type—bigger than Yahoo!, Google, or America Online.

And that's not small potatoes.

Different Ways to Buy and Sell on eBay

eBay started out as a pure online auction site; every transaction was conducted via the online auction format. While a majority of eBay's sales still come from online auctions, a growing percentage of transactions come from fixed-price sales, made from the eBay site itself or from the associated eBay Stores and Half.com websites. There's something for everyone—if you like the bidding game, the online auction format is for you; if you want your merchandise immediately, without the risk of losing an auction, then the various fixed-price formats may be to your liking. Here's a quick overview of the different ways to buy and sell on eBay:

- Online auctions, where the seller establishes a starting price and interested buyers bid higher and higher until the end of the auction, when the highest bidder wins.
- Buy It Now, which supplements the normal auction process; when a seller establishes a Buy It Now price (in addition to the normal auction starting price), a buyer can end the auction early by paying the fixed price.
- Fixed price listings, which enable sellers to offer items for sale to the first buyer willing to pay the fixed asking price.
- Want It Now, where buyers create a "wish list" of items they're interested in, and interested sellers contact them to arrange a transaction.
- eBay Stores, where sellers can offer a comprehensive inventory of fixed-price items for sale on an everyday basis.
- Half.com, which is a separate fixed-price marketplace for individuals and retailers selling books, CDs, DVDs, and video games.

If you're an interested buyer, you can place bids or make purchases on any of these marketplaces. If you have items to sell, you can choose whichever marketplace and format you think will provide the best results. Payment from buyer to seller is facilitated by eBay's PayPal service, which enables any individual seller to accept credit card payments from buyers. It's all quite versatile, quite slick, and quite easy to do—for both buyers and sellers. Anybody can do it!

How eBay Auctions Work

Of all these different types of transactions, the most unfamiliar to many users is the online auction. In fact, some new users get quite anxious about placing bids or trying to sell an item via online auction. Never fear; participating in an online auction is a piece of cake, something hundreds of millions of other users have done before you. That means you don't have to reinvent any wheels; the procedures you follow are well established and well documented.

Let's start with the basics. An eBay online auction is an Internet-based version of a traditional live auction—you know, the type where a fast-talking auctioneer stands in the front of the room, trying to coax potential buyers into bidding *just a little bit more* for the piece of merchandise up for bid. The big difference is that there's no fast-talking auctioneer online; instead, the bidding process is executed by special auction software on the eBay site. In addition, your fellow bidders aren't in the same room with you—in fact, they might be located anywhere in the world. Anyone anywhere can be a bidder, as long as they have Internet access.

We'll get into the detailed steps involved with buying and selling later in this book; for now, let's walk through the general operation of a typical eBay auction:

1. You begin (as either a buyer or a seller) by registering with eBay.

2. The seller creates a listing for a particular item and launches the auction on the eBay site. (eBay charges anywhere from $0.20 to $4.80 to list an item.) In the item listing, the seller specifies the length of the auction (1, 3, 5, 7, or 10 days) and the minimum bid he or she will accept for that item.

3. A potential buyer searching for a particular type of item (or just browsing through all the merchandise listed in a specific category) reads the item listing

note

Before you can list an item for sale or place a bid on an item, you first have to register with eBay. There's no fee to register, although eBay does charge the seller a small *insertion fee* (sometimes called a *listing fee*) to list an item for sale, and another small *transaction fee* when the item is sold. eBay doesn't charge any fees to buyers.

and decides to make a bid. The bidder specifies the maximum amount he or she is willing to pay; this amount has to be equal to or above the seller's minimum bid, or higher than any other existing bids from previous bidders.

4. eBay's built-in bidding software automatically places a bid for the bidder that bests the current bid by a specified amount. That is, the software bids only the minimum amount necessary to create a high bid, up to but never going over the maximum amount specified by the bidder. (In fact, the bidder's maximum bid is never revealed.)

   For example, let's say that the current bid on an item is $25. A bidder is willing to pay up to $40 for the item, and enters a maximum bid of $40. eBay's bidding software places a bid for the new bidder in the amount of $26—higher than the current $25 bid, but less than the specified maximum bid of $40. If there are no other bids, this bidder will win the auction with a $26 bid. Other potential buyers, however, can place additional bids; unless their maximum bids are more than the current bidder's $40 maximum, they are informed (by email) that they have been outbid—and the first bidder's current bid is automatically raised to match the new bids (up to the specified maximum bid price).

5. At the conclusion of an auction, eBay informs the high bidder of his or her winning bid, and the seller sends the winning bidder an invoice.

6. The winning bidder arranges payment for the item he or she just won. Payment can be immediate (via credit card), or the buyer can send a check or money order through the mail—whichever methods the seller offers.

7. When the seller receives the buyer's payment, he then ships the merchandise directly to the buyer.

8. Concurrent with the close of the auction, eBay bills the seller for a small percentage (starting at 5.25%) of the final bid price. This selling fee is directly billed to the seller's credit card.

> **note**
>
> eBay is kind of like a newspaper that runs classified ads—eBay isn't the actual seller, and isn't even really a "middleman." All eBay does is facilitate the transaction, and therefore it can't be held responsible for anything that goes wrong with any particular auction or sale. When you buy an item, you buy it from the individual who put it up for sale—you don't pay anything to eBay.

That's how it works, in general. For more detailed instructions on how to bid in an eBay auction, see Chapter 8, "Bidding in Online Auctions." For more detailed instructions on how to place an item for sale on eBay, see Chapter 15, "Selling Items via Online Auction."

What You Can—And Can't—Trade on eBay

As you can tell from eBay's mission statement, you should be able to trade practically anything you can think of on the eBay site. You can't trade literally everything, of course; there are some types of items that eBay refuses to deal with. Read on to learn more.

eBay's Product Categories

eBay organizes its listings by product category. There are a few dozen major categories, each of which is subdivided into dozens of more targeted subcategories. For example, the major category of Cameras & Photo is subdivided into a variety of smaller categories, such as Camcorders, Digital Cameras, Film Cameras, and so on. To make it easier to find specific items, these subcategories are further subdivided into even more targeted subcategories; for example, the Digital Cameras subcategory is subdivided into subcategories for Point & Shoot, Digital SLR, Parts & Repair, and so on.

When you're selling an item, you drill down through the categories and subcategories until you find the one that best fits the item you're selling. When you're looking to buy an item, you just keep clicking through the subcategories until you find the type of item you want to buy.

What You *Can't* Trade on eBay

Of course, you can't sell just *anything* on eBay—there are some items that eBay prohibits you from selling. This list of what you *can't* buy or sell on eBay makes a lot of sense; most of these items are illegal, are controversial, or could expose eBay to various legal actions.

eBay's list of prohibited items includes the following:

- Academic and beta software
- Alcohol
- Animals (except for tropical fish and domestic aquatic snails) and wildlife products
- Artifacts protected under federal laws
- Bootleg or counterfeit recordings of CDs, videos, computer software, or other items that infringe on someone else's copyright or trademark
- CDs, DVDs, and screen saver programs that contain multiple images of celebrities or models
- Catalog listings
- Counterfeit currency and stamps
- Drugs and drug paraphernalia

- Embargoed goods and goods from prohibited countries
- Firearms and ammunition
- Government and transit documents, IDs, licenses, and uniforms
- Hazardous materials
- Human body parts and remains
- Items that contain the image, likeness, name, or signature of a person, unless the person has authorized the product in question
- Law enforcement badges or equipment
- Lockpicking devices
- Lottery tickets
- Mailing lists and personal information
- Mod chips, game enhancers, and boot discs for video game systems
- Movies and music stored on recordable media, such as CD-R discs, DVD+/-R discs, videotapes, and so on
- Multi-level marketing, pyramid, and matrix programs
- OEM software originally included with a new PC
- Postage meters
- Prescription drugs and devices
- Recalled items
- Satellite and cable TV descramblers
- Slot machines
- Stocks and other securities
- Stolen property
- Surveillance equipment
- Teacher's edition textbooks
- Tobacco
- Used cosmetics

Other items, such as adult-oriented items, fall into the questionable category. If you're in doubt about a particular item, check out eBay's Prohibited and Restricted Items page at pages.ebay.com/help/policies/items-ov.html.

What's What (and What's Where) on eBay

Not even counting the millions of individual auction listings, eBay has a ton of content and community on its site—if you know where to find it. (And the home page isn't always the best place to find what you're looking for!)

eBay's Home Page—for New Users

On your first visit to the eBay site (www.ebay.com), you'll be prompted to register as a new user. The Welcome to eBay page provides some general overview information on using the site, and also provides a shortcut to registration. Just click the Register Now button, then follow the onscreen instructions. (Learn more about eBay registration in Chapter 2, "Joining Up and Getting Started.")

eBay's Home Page—for Registered Users

After you've registered with eBay, you see the site's normal home page, shown in Figure 1.1. From here, you can access eBay's most important features and services— as well as sign in to your eBay account, if you've already registered.

FIGURE 1.1

Access the most important parts of eBay from the home page (www.ebay.com).

The big chunk of space in the middle of the page is probably best ignored; it's nothing more than a big advertisement for the category or items du jour. Better to focus on the links along the top and left side of the page.

Across the top of the home page—across virtually every eBay page, as a matter of fact—is the Navigation Bar. This bar includes links to the major sections of the eBay site: Buy, Sell, My eBay, Community, and Help. When you click one of these links, you go to the main page for that section.

To the right of the Navigation Bar is the Search box. This is what you use to search for items you might want to buy; enter your query into the box and then click the Search button. More advanced search options are available by clicking the Advanced Search link. (Learn more about searching eBay in Chapter 7, "Searching for Items to Buy.")

Along the left side of the home page is a collection of links to specific eBay item categories and specialty sites. When you want to find an item on which to bid, it's easy to click through the categories listed on the left of the home page—or to search for items using the Search box.

For other key activities, refer to the information in Table 1.1, which shows you which links to click.

> **note**
>
> There are also several links *above* the Navigation Bar—Home, Pay, Register (if you're a new user or haven't yet logged in), and Site Map. Like the Navigation Bar, these links appear at the top of most eBay pages.

Table 1.1 Key Home Page Operations

To Do This	Click This Link
Sign up for eBay membership	Register
Sign into the eBay site (for buying and selling)	Sign In
Browse items for sale	Buy
Sell an item	Sell
Access your My eBay page	My eBay
Access message boards and discussion forums	Community
Read help files	Help
Get "live" help via instant messaging	Live Help
Pay for items you've purchased	Pay
Access other parts of eBay	Site Map

Where to Find Everything Else: eBay's Site Map

The good news is, there's a lot of great content on the eBay site. The bad news is, there's so much stuff—and it's so haphazardly organized—that most users never find some of eBay's most interesting and useful features. In fact, you simply can't access many features from the home page. To really dig down into the eBay site, you need a little help—which you can get from eBay's Site Map page.

You can access the Site Map page by clicking the Site Map link above the Navigation Bar. This page, shown in Figure 1.2, serves as the true access point to eBay's numerous and diverse features.

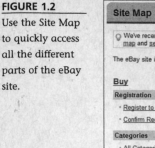

Site Map

We've recently reorganized our site map and services page. During this transition period, you can still access the original site map and services page.

The eBay site is organized into five sections: **Buy, Sell, My eBay, Community** and **Help**. Get an overview of each section below.

Buy

Registration
- Register to Buy
- Confirm Registration

Categories
- All Categories
- Antiques
- Art
- Automotive (eBay Motors)
- Baby
- Books
- Business & Industrial
- Cameras & Photo
- Cell Phones
- Clothing, Shoes & Accessories
- Coins
- Collectibles

Sell

Selling Activities
- Add to Your Item Description
- Block Bidder/Buyer List
- Buyer Block Exemption List
- Cancel Bids on Your Listing
- Change Your Item's Gallery Image
- End Your Listing
- Manage Your Counters
- Manage Your Store
- Pre-approved Bidder/Buyer List
- Promote Your Item
- Promote your listings with link buttons
- Relist Your Item
- Revise Your Item
- Search Want It Now
- View the Status of Your

Community

Feedback
- Feedback Forum
- Follow Up to Feedback You Left for Others
- Leave Feedback for a Member
- Leave Feedback for a Transaction
- Make Feedback Public or Private
- Reply to Feedback Received
- View a Member's Feedback

Connect
- About Me
- Chat Rooms
- Discussion Boards
- Find a Member
- Find Contact Information
- Groups

If you've never visited the Site Map page, I guarantee you'll be surprised at everything you'll find there. The Site Map offers direct links to a bunch of features and services that you probably didn't even know existed!

You can also use the links on the Site Map page to keep up with all the new features of the site—and keep up on the daily events and happenings. For example, if you're new to eBay, you might want to check out the links in the Community section of the Site Map. Or, to find out about any technical system updates (or planned outages), click the System Announcements link (in the News section).

Contacting eBay

Although you *could* use eBay's various discussion boards to try to contact eBay (as eBay suggests), you'll quickly discover that this method of communication often leaves something to be desired—like a fast response! Instead, try contacting eBay staff *directly* through the Web form support system. Start at the Contact Us page (shown in Figure 1.3), located at pages.ebay.com/help/contact_us/_base/. Select a topic, subtopic, and specific issue, and then click Continue. The following "instant help" page includes links that answer the most common questions. To continue through to contact eBay, click the Email link to display the Contact Us form. Enter your message or question then click the Send button.

FIGURE 1.3
Contact eBay
from the Contact
Us page.

You can also contact eBay by phone (800-322-9266 or 408-558-7400) or by postal
mail, at

> eBay Inc.
>
> 2145 Hamilton Avenue
>
> San Jose, CA 95125

THE ABSOLUTE MINIMUM

Here are the key points to remember from this chapter:

- eBay was founded in 1995 as a site for trading PEZ dispensers; today eBay is the world's largest online auction community, facilitating the trading of all sorts of items between buyers and sellers around the world.

- There are many different ways to buy and sell on eBay, including online auctions, fixed-price listings, eBay Stores, and Half.com.

- An eBay online auction is similar to a traditional auction, except that automated bidding software replaces the role of the human auctioneer.

- eBay's home page (www.ebay.com) lets you access the most important operations—although the Site Map page is better for finding all of eBay's features and services.

2

JOINING UP AND GETTING STARTED

You can browse through eBay's millions of listings anonymously (and without registering), but if you want to buy or sell something, you have to register with the eBay site. Registration involves telling eBay who you are, where you live, and how to contact you. If you're interested in selling on eBay, you'll also need to give eBay a valid credit card number—which won't be charged—and your checking account information. Don't worry; it's all in the name of security.

And, although eBay registration is free, selling an item isn't. You have to pay eBay a fee for every item you list for sale, and for every item you actually sell. You *don't* have to pay eBay when you buy an item; fees are charged exclusively to sellers.

Read on to learn more about eBay's registration process—and its fee structure.

Everybody Does It: Filling Out eBay's Registration Form

Registration is free, easy, and relatively quick. But before you register, you need to be prepared to enter some key information, as detailed in the following checklist:

Checklist: Before You Register

☐ Your name

☐ Your street address

☐ Your email address

☐ Your phone number

☐ Your date of birth

☐ Your credit card number (optional if you're only going to be bidding on items; mandatory if you're going to be selling items on auction)

☐ Your checking account number (not necessary if you're only going to be bidding on items; mandatory if you're going to be selling items on auction)

Signing Up for Basic Membership

With this information at hand, you register as an eBay user by following these steps:

1. From the Welcome to eBay page, click the Register Now button—or, from the eBay home page, click the Register link above the Navigation Bar.

2. When the Enter Information page appears (as shown in Figure 2.1), enter the following information:

    ■ First name and last name

    ■ Street address (including city, state, ZIP code, and country)

note

eBay asks all members to supply a valid physical address and telephone number. They don't disclose this info to any third parties outside the eBay site, although they will supply appropriate personal data to other eBay users on their request. (It's how they try to contact deadbeat bidders and sellers.) You can get more details from eBay's Privacy Policy, found at pages.ebay.com/help/policies/privacy-policy.html.

Your eBay user ID must be at least two characters long, and can contain letters, numbers, and/or certain symbols. It cannot contain spaces, web page URLs, or the following symbols: @, $, &, %, ', <, or > —and you can't use your email address as your user ID.

If you ever move, you'll need to change the address and phone number information eBay has on file. Just go to any My eBay page, click the Personal Information link (in the My Account section), and then click the Edit link next to the item you want to change: User ID, Password, Registered Name and Address, Registered Email Address, and so on.

■ Telephone numbers—primary (required) and secondary (optional)

■ Date of birth

■ Email address

FIGURE 2.1

Enter your name, address, phone number, and email address.

3. Still on the Enter Information page, scroll down and read the eBay User Agreement and Privacy Policy, check the box to agree to both agreements, and then click the Continue button.

4. When the Choose User ID and Password page appears (as shown in Figure 2.2), select one of the user names that eBay suggests for you, or create and enter your own user ID into the Create Your Own ID box.

5. Still on the same page, create and enter a password (at least six characters long, with no spaces) into the Create Password box. Enter the password again into the Re-Enter Password box.

6. Still on the same page, select a question from the Secret Question list, and then enter your answer in the Secret Answer box. (This is used if you ever forget your password.) Click Continue when done.

note

You may also be asked to provide a credit card number if you're a bidder using a free web-based email account, such as Hotmail, Yahoo! Mail, or Gmail.

FIGURE 2.2

Select a user
name and
password.

7. eBay now verifies your email address and sends you a confirmation message via email, like the one shown in Figure 2.3. When you receive the email, click the Activate Your eBay Membership link in the email message to finalize your registration.

FIGURE 2.3

eBay's confirma-
tion email.

Creating a Seller's Account

If you intend to sell items on eBay, you'll need to provide a little bit more information to eBay—in particular, your checking account number and either a credit or debit card number. The credit/debit card number is for billing purposes; your card is billed for all seller's fees you incur. (You can also choose to pay via checking account withdrawal; eBay bills your account once a month.) The checking account information is used to confirm that you are who you say you are, in an attempt to weed out fraudulent sellers from the system.

tip

Even if you're just a buyer, you still might want to enter your credit card information—not that eBay requires it, or will charge anything against it. Registering your card allows you to access eBay's adult areas and sets everything in place in case you do want to list items for sale in the future.

To set up your eBay account for selling, follow these steps:

1. After you've completed your normal registration, and see eBay's Congratulations screen, click the Start Selling link. (Alternately, you'll be prompted to create a seller's account the first time you try to sell something on eBay.)

2. When the Create Seller's Account page appears, as shown in Figure 2.4, click the Create Seller's Account button.

FIGURE 2.4

Getting ready to create your eBay seller's account.

3. You are now asked for a credit card to confirm your name and identity, as shown in Figure 2.5. Enter the requested information, then click Continue.

4. Now you have to enter your checking account information—bank name, bank routing number, and checking account number, as shown in Figure 2.6. Click Continue when ready.

Register: Confirm Identity   Help

1. Enter Information   2. Choose User ID & Password   3. Check Your Email

Registration is **free** . However, we require a credit or debit card to confirm your identity. This helps keep eBay a safe place to buy and sell.

👄 Live help - Chat online with a Customer Support representative.

Your card will **not** be charged or shared with eBay sellers. Your personal information is protected by eBay's Privacy Policy and encrypted by industry-standard software.

Credit or debit card number

Visa, Mastercard, American Express, or Discover

Card Identification Number

This is the 3-digit number on the back of your credit or debit card. For American Express this is the 4-digit number on the front of the card. Learn more

Expiration date
--Month--   --Year--

Cardholder information (change)
Marcus Miller

Carmel, Indiana 46032
United States

Continue >

Create Seller's Account: Enter Checking Account   👄 Live help

1. Enter Credit or Debit Card   2. Enter Checking Account   3. Select How to Pay Selling Fees

Please place your checking account on file. This assures us of your identity and keeps eBay a safe place to buy and sell . Funds will not be deducted unless you authorize us to do so to pay selling fees.

Account holder (Personal or business)
Michael Miller

Bank name

US bank accounts only

Your Name
Your Street
Your City, State, zip   1000

   Date

Pay to the
order of $

Dollars

Bank routing number   **Checking account number**   If you don't have these numbers, please call your bank for this information.

9 digits between the ⑆ symbols   1000 Ignore check number   Approximately 10 digits usually before the ⑈ symbol

Note: The bank routing, checking account, and check numbers may appear in a different order on your check.

Continue >

5. When the Select How to Pay Selling Fees page appears, select how you want to pay your eBay fees—as a debit from your checking account or via credit card. Click the Submit button when done.

Your credit card information will be applied to your eBay account within 12 to 24 hours—at which time you'll be able to participate fully in everything eBay has to offer.

The Costs of Using eBay

You don't have to pay eBay anything to browse through items on its site. You don't have to pay eBay anything to bid on an item. You don't even have to pay eBay anything if you actually buy an item (although you will be paying the seller directly, of course). But if you're listing an item for sale, you gotta pay.

eBay charges two main types of fees:

- **Insertion fees** (I prefer to call them *listing* fees) are what you pay every time you list an item for sale on eBay. These fees are based on the minimum bid or reserve price of the item listed. These fees are nonrefundable.

- **Final value fees** (I prefer to call them *selling* fees, or *commissions*) are what you pay when an item is actually sold to a buyer. These fees are based on the item's final selling price (the highest bid). If your item doesn't sell, you aren't charged a final value fee.

> **"Mike Sez"**
>
> While you have the option of using an automatic checking account withdrawal to pay your fees, I recommend that you go with credit card billing instead. I don't like the idea of eBay (or any other company) having automatic access to my checking account; who knows whether I'll have enough funds on tap the day they decide to make the automatic withdrawal? Credit card payment is easy and just as automatic, with few (if any) hassles.

eBay also charges various fees for different types of listing enhancements. Table 2.1 lists all the fees eBay charges, current as of March 2006. (Fees for items listed in the eBay Real Estate and eBay Motors categories are typically higher.)

Table 2.1 eBay Fees

Type of Fee	Explanation	Fee
Insertion fee	In a regular auction, based on the opening value or minimum bid amount. In a fixed-price auction, based on the Buy It Now price. In a reserve price auction, based on the reserve price. In a Dutch auction, based on the opening value or minimum bid—multiplied by the number of items offered, up to a maximum of $4.80.	Items priced $0.01–$0.99: $0.20 Items priced $1.00–$9.99: $0.35 Items priced $10.00–$24.99: $0.60 Items priced $25.00–$49.99: $1.20 Items priced $50.00–$199.99: $2.40 Items priced $200.00–$499.99: $3.60 Items priced $500 and up: $4.80

Table 2.1   (continued)

Type of Fee	Explanation	Fee
Final value fee	In regular auctions, fixed-price auctions, and successful reserve price auctions, based on the closing bid. In Dutch auctions, based on the lowest successful bid—multiplied by the number of items sold.	5.25% of the amount of the high bid to $25.00, *plus* 3% of that part of the high bid from $25.01 up to $1,000, *plus* 1.5% of the remaining amount of the high bid that is greater than $1,000.
		For example, if the item sold for $1,500, you'd pay 5.25% of the first $25 ($1.31) plus 3% of the next $975 ($29.25) plus 1.5% of the remaining $500 ($7.50), for a total fee of $38.06.
Reserve price auction	Additional fee for holding a reserve price auction.	Items priced $0.01–$49.99: $1.00 Items priced $50.00–$199.99: $2.00 Items priced $200 and up: 1% of the reserve price (maximum $100)
Buy It Now	Fee to use the Buy It Now instant purchase option in an auction listing (doesn't apply to fixed price auctions).	Items priced $0.01–$9.99: $0.05 Items priced $10.00–$24.99: $0.10 Items priced $25.00–$49.99: $0.20 Items priced $50.00 and up: $0.25
Scheduled listings	Schedules your item to be listed at a specific date and time, up to three weeks in advance.	$0.10
10-day auction	Additional fee for longer auctions.	$0.40
Gift Services	Adds a Gift icon to your listing and lets you offer gift wrap, express shipping, and shipping to the gift's recipient.	$0.25
Bold	Boldfaces the title of your item on the listing pages.	$1.00
Border	Puts a color border around your item on the listing page.	$3.00

Type of Fee	Explanation	Fee
Highlight	Puts a color shading behind your item on the listing pages.	$5.00
Item Subtitle	Adds a subtitle to your item listing.	$0.50
Listing Designer	Applies fancy templates to your listings.	$0.10
Gallery	Displays a thumbnail picture of your item in the Gallery section.	$0.35
Gallery Featured	Randomly displays your Gallery listing at the top of the category, at a larger size.	$19.95
Featured Plus!	Puts your listing at the top of the listing pages for that category, and also displays your listing (randomly) in the Featured Items section of the related category home page.	$19.95
Home Page Featured	Displays your listing (randomly) in the Featured area on eBay's home page and on the Featured section of the related category page.	$39.95

There's all manner of fine print associated with these fees. Here are some of the more important points to keep in mind:

- Insertion fees are nonrefundable—although if a buyer ends up not paying for an item, you can relist the item and request a credit for the second insertion fee.

- You will not be charged a final value fee if there were no bids on your item or (in a reserve price auction) if there were no bids that met the reserve price—that is, if your item didn't sell.

- It doesn't matter whether the buyer actually pays you (or how much he or she actually pays); you still owe eBay the full final value

note

View eBay's current fee structure at pages.ebay. com/help/sell/fees.html. These fees apply to its primary auction site; other specialty sites, such as eBay Stores and Half.com, have different fee structures.

fee. (You can, however, request a refund of this fee if the buyer punks out on you; see Chapter 24, "Dealing with Non-Paying Buyers," for more info.)

Invoicing on your account occurs once a month for all your activity for the prior month. (That is, you're not billed one auction at a time; all your fees are saved up for the monthly billing cycle.) You'll get an invoice by email detailing your charges for the month; if you've set up your account for automatic credit card billing, bank account withdrawal, or PayPal billing, your account will be charged at that time. (If you prefer to pay by check, now's the time to get out the old checkbook.)

> **tip**
>
> eBay also offers two "feature packs" that offer special combinations of listing enhancements for a discounted price. The Value Pack combines Gallery, Subtitle, and Listing Designer for $0.65 total; the Pro Pack combines Bold, Border, Highlight, Featured Plus, and Gallery Featured for $29.95.

Protecting Yourself from Phishing Scams

There's one last thing worth mentioning about your eBay account. eBay will never, ever send you emails asking you to update your account and then provide a link in the email for you to click for that purpose. While eBay will send you emails (and lots of them—either informational or promotional in nature), they don't send out the type of "instant account management" email shown in Figure 2.7.

FIGURE 2.7
A "phishing" email that looks like it's from eBay—but it's not.

If you receive this type of email, for either your eBay or PayPal account, you can be sure it's a scam—in particular, a "phishing" scam. If you click the link in the email (which looks like a real, honest-to-goodness eBay URL), you won't be taken to eBay. Instead, that fake URL will take you another site, run by the scammer, which will be tricked up to look like the eBay site. If you enter your personal information, as requested, you're actually delivering it to the scammer, and you're now a victim of identity theft. The scammer can use the information you provided to hack into your eBay account, make unauthorized charges on your credit card, and maybe even drain your banking account.

caution

Phishing emails come in all shapes and sizes, many of which look extremely official. If you receive one of these phony emails, you can report it to spoof@ebay.com.

It goes without saying that you should never respond to this type of email, no matter how official-looking it appears. If you want to make changes to your eBay or PayPal account, never do so from an email link. Instead, use your web browser to go directly to the official site, and make your changes there. No one from eBay or PayPal will ever ask you for this information via email. Be warned!

Also be warned that phishers are getting more sophisticated in the ability to spoof official-looking eBay emails. In recent months I've received spoof emails that purport to invite me to join eBay's PowerSeller program; that purport to be another user asking a question about an in-process auction (even when I wasn't running any auctions that week!), and that purport to warn me about unauthorized use of my PayPal account. When I clicked the links in these emails, I was presented with an official-looking but quite unofficial eBay log-in screen; were I to log in, the phishers would have been able to grab my eBay ID and password, and then do who knows what with my account.

The profusion of all these spoof emails has inspired eBay to add a My Messages section to the My eBay page. To access this feature, click the My eBay link at the top of any eBay page, and then scroll down to the My Messages section and click the "new messages" link. This displays the My Messages screen, shown in Figure 2.8, where all your recent messages are listed. These are official communications

note

Learn more about My eBay in Chapter 5, "Managing Your eBay Activity with My eBay."

from eBay, and from other eBay users. It's safe to read the messages listed here, because they've been confirmed authentic by eBay. Click any message subject to read the full message—and then ignore any spoof messages that end up in your email inbox!

FIGURE 2.8
My Messages—
the safe way to
access your eBay
messages.

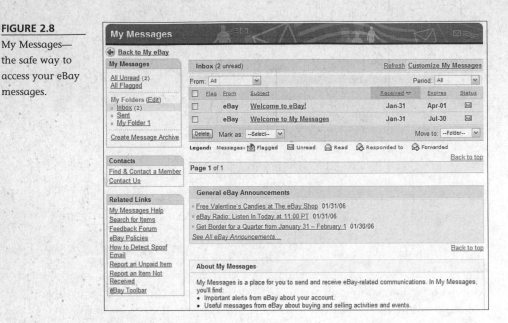

FIGURE 2.8
My Messages—
the safe way to
access your eBay
messages.

Getting Started

Now that you're all signed up (and aware of eBay's fee structure), you're ready to start bidding—and selling. The bidding process is fee-free; all you have to do is find something you want to buy, and start bidding. (This process is detailed in Chapter 8, "Bidding in Online Auctions.") The selling process is a little more involved and costs a little money. (This process is detailed in Chapter 15, "Selling Items via Online Auctions.") Whichever you choose, get ready for lots of action—and fun!

THE ABSOLUTE MINIMUM

Here are the key points to remember from this chapter:

- Before you can bid or sell on eBay, you need to create an eBay user account; registration is free.

- If you want to sell items on eBay, you'll have to leave a checking account and credit card or debit card number on file.

- Buyers are never charged any fees by eBay.

- eBay charges sellers various fees, including listing fees (nonrefundable) and final value fees (if your item actually sells).

- eBay will never send you emails asking you to click a link to update your account; if you get one of these spoof emails, it's a scam!

PART II

USING EBAY'S ESSENTIAL TOOLS

3

UNDERSTANDING AND USING FEEDBACK

How do you know if the buyer or seller you're dealing with is legitimate—and will pay on time or ship in a timely fashion? The best way to check up on potential trading partners is to find out what your fellow eBayers think about them—which is pretty easy to do, thanks to eBay's feedback system.

What Do All Those Stars and Numbers Mean?

Next to every buyer and seller's name on eBay are a number and (more often than not) a colored star. (Figure 3.1 shows my personal star and feedback number.) This number and star represent that user's feedback rating. The larger the number, the better the feedback—and the more transactions that user has participated in.

FIGURE 3.1

Check the feedback rating next to a member's name.

Seller information
trapperjohn2000 (815 ☆) **me**
Feedback Score: 815
Positive Feedback: 100%
Member since Aug-22-98 in
United States

How are feedback ratings calculated?

First, every new user starts with 0 points. (A clean slate!) For every positive feedback received, eBay adds 1 point to your feedback rating. For every negative feedback received, eBay subtracts 1 point. Neutral comments add 0 points to your rating.

Let's say you're a new user, starting with a 0 rating. On the first two items you buy, the sellers like the fact that you paid quickly and give you positive feedback. On the third transaction, however, you forgot to mail the check for a few weeks, and the seller left you negative feedback. After these three transactions, your feedback rating would be 1. (That's 0 + 1 + 1 – 1 = 1.)

If you build up a lot of positive feedback, you qualify for a star next to your name. Different colored stars represent different levels of positive feedback, as noted in Table 3.1.

Table 3.1 eBay Feedback Ratings

Color/Type	Points
Yellow star	10–49
Blue star	50–99
Turquoise star	100–499
Purple star	500–999
Red star	1,000–4,999
Green star	5,000–9,999
Yellow shooting star	10,000–24,999
Turquoise shooting star	25,000–49,999
Purple shooting star	50,000–99,999
Red shooting star	100,000 or more

Obviously, heavy users can build up positive feedback faster than occasional users. If you're dealing with a shooting-star user (of any color), you know you're dealing with a trustworthy—and extremely busy!—eBay pro.

Reading Feedback Comments—And Contacting Other Users

You can also read the individual comments left by other users by going to the user's Member Profile page. To access this page, just click the user's name or feedback number.

The Member Profile page, like the one shown in Figure 3.2, includes a lot of information you can use to judge the trustworthiness of other users. At the top of the page is the user's Feedback Score, followed by the Positive Feedback percentage. You'll also see the raw numbers—the number of members who left positive feedback, and the number who left negative feedback. Recent feedback ratings are summarized in the Recent Ratings table.

> **"Mike Sez"**
>
> eBay regards its feedback system as the best protection against fraudulent transactions. I certainly recommend that, whether a transaction went swell or went south, you leave feedback about your partner in every transaction. I know that I check the feedback rating of every seller I choose to deal with; it really is a good way to judge the quality of the other party in your eBay transactions.

FIGURE 3.2

A typical Member Profile page; hey, people like this guy!

Member Profile: trapperjohn2000 (815 ☆) me

| Feedback Score: | 815 |
| Positive Feedback: | 100% |

Members who left a positive:	816
Members who left a negative:	0
All positive feedback received:	999

Learn about what these numbers mean.

Recent Ratings:

	Past Month	Past 6 Months	Past 12 Months
⊕ positive	18	101	182
⊙ neutral	0	0	0
⊖ negative	0	0	0

Bid Retractions (Past 6 months): 0

Member since: Aug-22-98
Location: United States
- ID History
- Items for Sale
- Visit my Store
- Add to Favorite Sellers
- Learn more About Me
- View my Reviews & Guides

[Contact Member]

Feedback Received | **From Buyers** | **From Sellers** | **Left for Others**

999 feedback received by trapperjohn2000 (0 ratings mutually withdrawn)   Page 1 of 40

Comment	From	Date / Time	Item #
⊕ Excellent doing business with you. Thanks AAA +++	Buyer (142 ☆)	Jan-28-06 18:19	4577838306
⊕ Item delivered as promised. Great communication. Wonderful Seller!!!	Buyer (13 ☆)	Jan-26-06 18:36	6457774772
⊕ great item, quick ship, will buy again. AAA+++	Buyer (218 ☆)	Jan-26-06 04:47	6470222923
⊕ A+ Seller! THANKS!	Buyer (6119 ☆)	Jan-23-06 15:42	6470222905
⊕ Received book, very pleased with this transaction! Thank You	Buyer (51 ★)	Jan-23-06 13:37	4565858769
⊕ AN A+ EBAY DEALER	Buyer (47 ☆)	Jan-22-06 18:46	6026653557

To the right of the Recent Ratings Table are links you can use to find out even more about this user—his ID History, current Items for Sale, a link to his eBay Store (if he has one), and a similar link to his About Me page (again, if he has one). Below these links is a Contact Member button; click this to send an e-mail to this user.

Below the summary information is a list of all the feedback comments for this user. You can click a tab to view All Feedback Received, just those comments From Buyers or From Sellers, or comments that this user Left for Others.

tip

You can also use the Member Profile page to read feedback comments about you—just click your own member name on any page. (Even more convenient: Go to your My eBay Feedback page.)

How to Leave Feedback

You can leave feedback from any item listing page; just click the Leave Feedback link. When you see the Leave Feedback page, shown in Figure 3.3, you can choose to leave Positive, Negative, or Neutral feedback, along with a brief comment (80 characters maximum).

FIGURE 3.3

Leaving feedback comments for a transaction partner.

> **Feedback Forum: Leave Feedback**   help
>
> Rating other members by leaving feedback is a very important part of transactions on eBay.
>
> Please note:
> - Once left, you cannot edit or retract feedback; you are solely responsible for the content.
> - It's always best to keep your feedback factual; avoid making personal remarks.
> - Feedback can be left for at least 90 days following a transaction.
> - If you have a dispute, contact your trading partner to try and resolve the dispute before leaving feedback.
>
> User ID: xxxxxxxxx   Show all transactions
> Item Number: 6032140553
> Rating: ○ Positive ○ Neutral ○ Negative ⊙ I will leave feedback later
> Comment: [   ]
>   80 characters left.
>
> [Leave Feedback] Cancel

Make sure your feedback is accurate before you click the Leave Feedback button; you can't change your comments after they've been registered.

Figuring Out What Kind of Feedback to Leave

You should leave feedback at the end of every auction—whether it was a positive or a negative experience for you. Don't miss your chance to inform other eBay users about the quality of the person you just got done dealing with.

Table 3.2 offers some guidelines on when you should leave positive or negative feedback—and the types of comments you might use to embellish your feedback.

Table 3.2 Recommended eBay Feedback Comments.

Transaction	Feedback	Comments
Transaction transpires in a timely fashion.	Positive	"Great transaction. Fast payment/shipment. Recommended."
Transaction goes through, but buyer/seller is slow or you have to pester the other user to complete the transaction.	Positive	"Item received as described" or "Payment received," accompanied by "a little slow, but otherwise a good seller/buyer."
Transaction is very slow (over a month to completion).	Neutral	"Very slow payment/shipment;" if you're buying, follow by "item received as described."
Other user backs out of transaction, but with a good excuse.	Neutral	"Buyer/seller didn't follow through on sale but had a reasonable excuse."
Other user backs out of transaction without a good excuse, disappears off the face of the earth before paying/shipping, or bounces a check.	Negative	"Buyer/seller didn't complete transaction."
Transaction goes through, but item isn't what you expected or was damaged in transit; seller refunds your money.	Positive	"Inaccurate description of item" or "Item was damaged in shipping," followed by "seller refunded money."
Transaction goes through, but item isn't what you expected; seller won't refund your money.	Negative	"Item not as described and seller ignored my complaint."

As you can see, there's a proper feedback and response for every situation. Just be sure to think twice before leaving *any* feedback (particularly negative feedback). After you submit your feedback, you can't retract it.

tip

If you must leave negative feedback, avoid leaving personal comments. Keep to the facts as much as you can—you're only commenting on the transaction, not on the buyer/seller himself.

Dealing with Negative Feedback

Many eBay users are zealous about their feedback ratings. Although it's a good thing to want to build up a high rating, some users get quite obsessive about it.

For that reason, you want to be very sure of yourself before you leave negative feedback about a user. Some overly zealous users might retaliate by leaving negative feedback about you—even if it wasn't warranted.

Unfortunately, there's not much you can do if you receive negative feedback; under normal conditions, feedback comments cannot be retracted. (There have been some exceptions, when the feedback has been obscene or slanderous in nature.) What you *can* do is offer a response to the feedback, which you do by going to your Feedback Forum page then scrolling down to and clicking the Reply to Feedback Received link. When the feedback comments list appears, click the Reply link next to a particular comment and then enter your response, as shown in Figure 3.4. Your new comment is listed below the original feedback comment on the Feedback Profile page. Just try not to get defensive; the best response is one that is calm, clear, and well-reasoned.

" Mike Sez "

Don't get too upset if you receive the occasional negative feedback; it happens to the best of us—especially those who run a *lot* of auctions. You can't please everyone all the time, and sometimes you make mistakes that justify a negative feedback response. Just try to work out as many issues with other users as you can, and don't let the occasional negative feedback get to you.

note

If you and the other user work out your issues, you can agree to mutually withdraw any negative feedback. Complete the form at feedback.ebay. com/ws/eBayISAPI.dll?MFWRequest to initiate the removal process.

FIGURE 3.4

Replying to
feedback left
about you.

Feedback Forum: Reply to Feedback Received

An important part of the Feedback Forum is sharing with the community your experience with other members. In
addition to leaving feedback, there may be occasions when you want to reply to a comment another member has left in
your member profile; it will appear directly below that comment in your member profile.

Please note:
- You can reply only once to a comment. You cannot edit or retract your reply.
- It's always best to keep you feedback factual; avoid making personal remarks.
- Leaving a reply does not affect your feedback score or number of ratings.
- If you have a dispute, contact your trading partner to try and resolve the dispute before replying.

Buyer:	(142 ☆)
Item:	Making a Living from Your eBay Business - Autographed! (4577838306)
Date/Time left:	Jan-28-06 18:19:37 PST
Feedback:	Excellent doing business with you.Thanks.AAA +++
Reply:	

80 characters left.

[Leave Reply]

THE ABSOLUTE MINIMUM

Here are the key points to remember from this chapter:

- You can use feedback ratings and comments to judge the trustworthiness of other eBay users.

- For quick reference, different levels of feedback ratings are indicated by a different color and type of star.

- You can view other users' feedback by clicking on the feedback rating numbers next to their user names.

- At the end of every auction, you should take the time to leave feedback about the other user—although you should be cautious about leaving negative feedback.

4

RESEARCHING PRODUCTS WITH REVIEWS AND GUIDES

eBay has recently added two new features that help eBay members share their collective expertise. eBay Reviews are product reviews written by other eBay members; Guides are more detailed how-tos that help you buy particular types of items or complete specific tasks.

For example, you can find product reviews for CDs, home audio receivers, golf clubs, and so on. Guides are available for a number of different topics, and include both buying guides (Skis & Skiing Equipment Buying Guide, NASCAR Diecast Cars Buying Guide) and more informational guides (How to Identify a Powerbook G3, How to Plan the Perfect Vacation).

Read on to learn more.

Reading the Reviews and Guides

Not sure whether a particular CD is to your tastes? Then read the reviews before you buy. Don't know which PC games are best for your particular game system? Then look for a Guide on buying PC games. Your fellow eBay members are not short of opinions; use those opinions (and their experience) to your advantage.

All of eBay's Reviews and Guides are centralized at the Reviews & Guides page (reviews.ebay.com), shown in Figure 4.1. Finding what you want is relatively easy; you can browse through all available Reviews and Guides by category, or search for specific offerings.

FIGURE 4.1

The main page for eBay's Reviews & Guides.

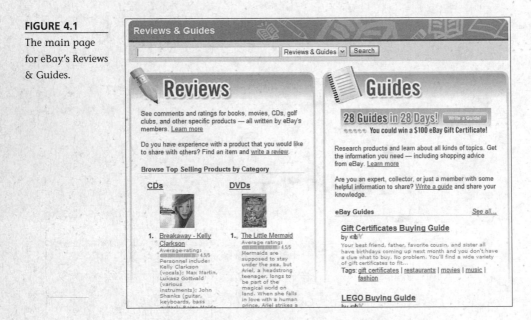

Browsing and Searching the Product Reviews

eBay's product reviews—written by your fellow eBay users—provide a great way to learn more about how specific products are received in the real world. eBay hosts tens of thousands of these reviews, which are organized into major product categories. You can browse through all the reviews in a given category, or search for specific reviews across all categories.

To browse through the reviews, scroll to the bottom of the Reviews & Guides page and click the appropriate category heading. Within each major category, as shown in Figure 4.2, products are further organized into appropriate subcategories. Depending on the category, there may be additional levels of subcategories; just keep clicking until you get to the list of products you're looking for. From there, click the heading for a specific product to read the available reviews.

FIGURE 4.2
Browsing the product reviews in a particular category.

To search for a review of a specific product, enter the name of the product (or appropriate keywords) into the search box at the top of the Reviews & Guides page. Then pull down the Reviews & Guides list and select Reviews; click the Search button and all matching reviews will be displayed.

As you can see in Figure 4.3, a typical review includes a photo of the item, a summary of important details, and a bar graph that represents the average rating of the item (on a scale of 1 to 5, with 5 being the highest rating). When you scroll down the page, you'll see the individual reviews in full. Reviews by eBay's most reliable and prolific reviewers are listed first, under the heading of Top Reviews, with all other reviews listed under these, in reverse chronological order (newest first).

caution

Many products are listed in the Reviews database, even though no reviews are yet available for the item. If you come across an item with the note to "Be the first to review it!", that means that no reviews exist yet for that item.

Some reviewers offer very detailed, very helpful reviews of the product. Others chip in with a short sentence or two. If you find a review particular helpful (or not), just click the Yes (or No) button. Your ratings of a review contribute to the rating of the reviewer; eBay's top reviewers are fond of jockeying for position among their peers.

If the reviews for a particular product are particularly convincing, eBay makes it easy for you to find one of these items to buy. At the top of each product review page is a big Buy One Like This button. Click this button and eBay automatically conducts a search for that item in its current auctions database. It's that easy!

Browsing and Searching the Guides

eBay's Guides are a bit different from its prod-uct reviews. Instead of focusing on specific products, they provide information about an entire category or activity. In fact, many of eBay's Guides don't have much if anything to do with the products being sold on eBay; many are guides to general activities or hob-bies. In any case, there's some good informa-tion here, if you hunt for it.

> **tip**
>
> Once you find a savvy reviewer, you might want to see what else that reviewer liked. To read other reviews by a particular reviewer, click the See All Reviews By... link at the top right of any review.

The easiest way to hunt for that information is to browse the Guides by category. You can, as well, search for particular Guides, by using the search box at the top of the Reviews & Guides page and selecting Guides from the pull-down list. When you browse, of course, you typically get a variety of subcategories to choose from; just keep clicking through until you find the types of Guides you're looking for.

When you narrow your search down to a list of specific Guides, as shown in Figure 4.4, you'll see a list of "tags" under the summary of each Guide. These are, at least in theory, the most important keywords that relate to that particular Guide. When you search the Guides, you're actually searching these tags, which are applied by the writers of each Guide.

When it comes down to reading the individual Guides, what you get will differ wildly from one Guide to another. Some are embarrassingly short, others quite comprehensive in their scope. Some include helpful pictures; most, like the Guide in Figure 4.5, are solely text-based.

tip

You can sort a list of Guides in a number of different ways. The default sort is by Most Helpful, as determined by user voting (via the Yes and No buttons at the bottom of each Guide). You can also sort by Least Helpful (but why would you want to?), Most Recent, and Oldest.

When you find a Guide you particularly like, don't forget to click the Yes button at the bottom of the page, to indicate that it was helpful for you. If you find a Guide exceptionally unexceptional, click the No button to warn other users.

FIGURE 4.4

Browsing the Guides in a given category.

FIGURE 4.5

A typical Guide.

Writing Your Own Reviews and Guides

eBay's Reviews and Guides are not only for reading; you can also write your own Reviews and Guides for other users to read. Anyone can write a Review or Guide—and the more you write, the higher your Reviews & Guides ranking becomes. (High-ranking Review and Guide writers get an icon beside their user ID.)

Writing a Product Review

Writing a product review is easy. You don't have to bother supplying product details, such as model number or dimensions or whatever; all you have to supply is your opinion. Just follow these steps:

tip

Writing your own Reviews and Guides is a great way for you to enhance your reputation on eBay without having to conduct hundreds of auctions to build your feedback. It's also a great way to share your opinions (via Reviews) and knowledge about particular subjects (via Guides).

1. Go to the main Reviews & Guides page (reviews.ebay.com).

2. Use the search box at the top of the page to search for the particular product you want to review.

3. When the list of matching products appears, click on the link for that product's review page.

4. When the product review page appears, click the Write a Review or Be the First to Review It link.

5. When the Write a Review page appears, as shown in Figure 4.6, enter a title for your review. The title can be up to 55 characters in length.

FIGURE 4.6

Writing your own product review.

FIGURE 4.6

Writing your own product review.

6. Give the product a rating, from 1 to 5 (5 being excellent; 1 being poor).

7. Type your full review into the Review box. The review can be up to 3,500 characters long.

8. When you're done with your review, click the Submit Review button.

That's it; your review will now be listed among the other reviews for that particular product.

Creating a Guide

The process for writing a Guide is similar to writing a Review, although here it really helps if you're an expert or otherwise uniquely experienced with the topic at hand—that is, if you know enough to write a useful Guide. Follow these steps:

1. Go to the main Reviews & Guides page (reviews.ebay.com).

2. Click the Write a Guide link.

3. When the Write a Guide page appears, as shown in Figure 4.7, enter a title for your Guide. The title can be up to 55 characters in length.

tip

Use the formatting controls at the top of the Guide box to make your Guide more readable and visually appealing. You can also use these controls to add pictures and links to your Guide. Click the Preview button at the bottom of the page to see how your formatted Guide looks.

FIGURE 4.7

Creating a new Guide.

Reviews & Guides

Write a Guide

Share your thoughts and ideas with people all over the world on almost any topic. Give advice on everything from how to buy a digital camera to how to plan a wedding. Find out more about creating a guide.

Guide title

55 characters remaining.

Guide

Text: Normal   **B** *I*   Add: Picture | Link

Important guide tips

Things to consider

- Write a short introduction explaining the purpose of your guide.
- Your first 200 characters will appear when people search for your topic.
- Insert pictures or links to almost any eBay page.

Things to avoid

- Copying and pasting from other documents.
- Inappropriate comments and profanity.
- Links outside of eBay.
- Personal information such as your email, phone number, etc.

eBay reserves the right to remove any guide that doesn't comply with our policy.

4. Type the text for your Guide into the Guide box. Remember that the first 200 characters of your Guide will be all that appears when people search for Guides by topic.

5. Enter up to five "tags" that other members can use as keywords to search for your Guide.

6. When you're done with your Guide, click the Save and Continue button.

THE ABSOLUTE MINIMUM

Here are the key points to remember from this chapter:

- eBay helps you research specific products by offering reviews written by other users.

- eBay's Guides provide overview information and how-tos for general categories and activities.

- You can rate any given Guide or Review for usefulness (Yes, it's useful or No, it's not); these ratings contribute to a reviewer's overall ranking.

- Any eBay user can write a Review or Guide; the more you write, the higher your Reviews & Guides ranking.

- Access all of eBay's Reviews and Guides at reviews.ebay.com.

5

MANAGING YOUR EBAY ACTIVITY WITH MY EBAY

If you're active at all on eBay, it's likely you'll have more than one auction to keep track of at any one time—and that's the case whether you're buying or selling. So just how do you keep track of all this auction activity?

The best way to monitor all the auctions you're participating in is to use eBay's self-professed "best-kept secret": My eBay. My eBay is a page—actually, a set of pages—that you can personalize to track your bidding and selling activity in your own way. I highly recommend that you avail yourself of this useful feature.

Accessing and Using My eBay

You access My eBay from any eBay page by clicking the My eBay link on the Navigation Bar. This opens My eBay in the My Summary view, which (as we'll discuss in a moment) presents a general overview of all your current auction activity. My eBay actually offers several different pages, which you access by clicking the appropriate links contained in the navigation panel along the left side of the page. We'll look at each of these pages individually.

My Summary View

The My Summary view, shown in Figure 5.1, is the default view when you access My eBay. It consists of several distinct sections:

- **Buying Reminders**, which prompts you about actions you need to take regarding those items you've recently purchased.
- **Selling Reminders**, which prompts you about actions you need to take regarding those items you've recently sold.
- **My Messages**, which contains important messages from eBay or from other sellers and buyers.
- **Items I'm Watching**, which lists those auction items you've placed on your watch list.
- **Buying Totals**, which summarizes those items you're bidding on and those you've won.
- **Items I'm Bidding On**, which lists all items you're currently bidding on.
- **Item's I've Made Best Offers On**, which lists those items you've made a best offer on, for those auctions that utilize this feature.
- **Items I've Won**, which lists recent auctions in which you were the high bidder.
- **Items I Didn't Win**, which lists recent auctions in which you were outbid.
- **Selling Totals**, which summarizes those items you currently have for sale or have recently sold.
- **Items I'm Selling**, which lists all items you currently have for sale.
- **Items I've Sold**, which lists all items you've recently sold.
- **General eBay Announcements**, which includes links to the most recent eBay system news.

> **tip**
>
> One other nice thing about the My Summary view is that you can customize it to display as much—or as little—information as you wish. Just click the Customize Summary link near the top of the page to remove sections you don't often use.

FIGURE 5.1

The My eBay My Summary page.

I use My Summary as my "home page" for all my eBay activities. It presents a great visual overview of all your important eBay activity, and lets you link directly to individual activities.

All Buying Page

You use the All Buying view, shown in Figure 5.2, to keep track of all items you're either bidding on or watching—or have won or lost. The page contains the following sections:

- Buying Reminders
- Items I'm Watching
- Buying Totals
- Items I'm Bidding On
- Items I've Made Best Offers On
- Items I've Won
- Items I Didn't Win

The Items I've Won list is worth an extra glance. Not only does it list those auctions in which you're the winning bidder, but it also includes an Action column that lets you know what you need to do next for each item—leave feedback, view payment status, and so on. Click the link in the Action column to perform that action.

Also interesting is the Items I'm Bidding On list, which presents all your current bidding activity—even those auctions in which you've been outbid. All auctions you're currently winning are in green; all auctions you're currently losing are in red. And, at the bottom of the page, you'll find a set of links to various buying-related services on the eBay site.

All Buying
View by Seller Select Seller

Get Official eBay News. Visit the Announcement Board!

Buying Reminders (Last 31 days)

☆ I need to leave feedback for 1 item.

Back to top

Items I'm Watching (No items) Customize Display

You are not watching any items.
To watch an item, click the "Watch this item" link on any item page.

Back to top

Buying Totals

| Bidding: | Bidding on: 0 | Winning: 0 | Winning cost: $0.00 |
| Won: | Quantity: 1 | Amount: $21.99 | (Last 7 days) |

Back to top

Items I'm Bidding On (No items) Customize Display

You are not bidding on any items.
Items that you've previously bid on and that ended may display in the "Items I've Won" or "Items I Didn't Win" views.

All Selling Page

You use the All Selling Page, shown in Figure 5.3, to keep track of all the items you're currently selling or have recently sold. The page contains several lists of use to sellers:

- Selling Reminders
- Scheduled Items
- Selling Totals
- Items I'm Selling
- Items I've Sold
- Unsold Items

One of the things I like about the Items I'm Selling section is the column for # of Watchers. This lists how many potential bidders have placed your item on their watch lists; it's a good indication of total demand, and a predictor of last-minute sniping.

Like the Items I've Won list on the All Buying page, the Items I've Sold list is especially useful. The Action column lists the next action you need to take for every one of your closed auctions; click the link to perform the appropriate action.

note

If you're using eBay's Selling Manager feature (discussed in Chapter 21, "Managing Your Sales with eBay Selling Manager"), the My eBay All Selling View page is replaced by a Selling Manager view.

FIGURE 5.3
The My eBay All
Selling page.

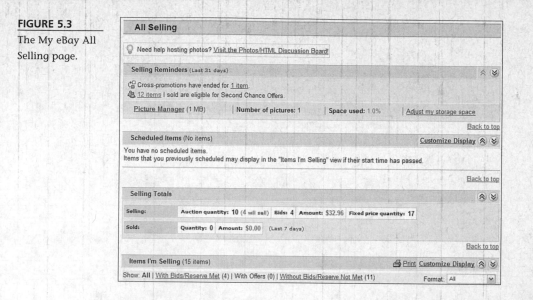

Also useful is the Items I'm Selling list, which lets you see, in a single glance, the status of everything you're currently selling on eBay. All items that currently have a bid higher than your minimum or reserve price are listed in green; all items that haven't yet reached the minimum bid level are listed in red. And, at the bottom of the page, you'll find a set of links to various selling-related services on the eBay site.

My Messages Page

The My Messages page, shown in Figure 5.4, lists all recent messages and announcements from eBay. Click a message title to read the complete message.

Next to each message is an icon that indicates the status of the message. Table 5.1 details each of the status icons.

Table 5.1   Message Status Icons

Icon	Status
	Unread
	Read
	Responded to
	Forwarded
	Flagged

FIGURE 5.4

The My eBay My Messages page.

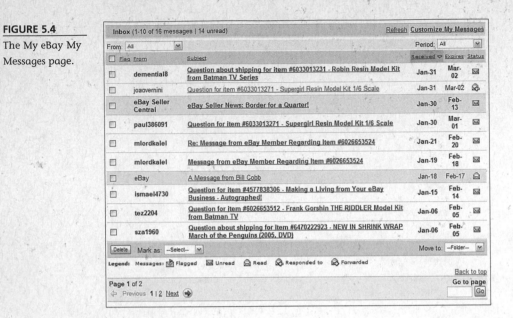

All Favorites Page

The All Favorites page, shown in Figure 5.5, is where you can access your most-used categories, searches, and sellers. There are three lists on this page:

- My Favorite Searches
- My Favorite Sellers
- My Favorite Categories

You can add items to your favorites by clicking the Add links to the right of each list—Add New Search, Add New Seller or Store, and Add New Category. From there, follow the onscreen instructions to add the items you want to appear on the All Favorites page in the future.

My Account Page

The My Account page, shown in Figure 5.6, is where you can manage your eBay seller's account and leave feedback about specific transactions.

The My Account Summary list, at the top of the page, displays your last eBay invoice total, any payments and credits made since your last

tip

The My Account page is particularly useful because it contains direct links to some of eBay's normally well-hidden customer service features, including fees and credits, payment terms, and credit card setup. It's easier to click these services here than to hunt them down on eBay's Site Map page.

invoice, and any fees accessed since your last invoice. There's also a section that lets you pay your eBay fees via PayPal.

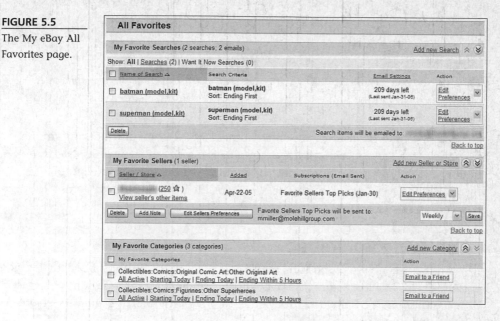

Managing and Personalizing My eBay

Each of the My eBay views can be personalized according to your personal tastes. Let's take a quick look at these common view management features.

Sorting and Filtering

The information in any My eBay list (what eBay calls an *information table*) can be sorted by any individual column. Just click the column header to sort by that column.

You can also filter the listings presented in most tables to cut down on information overload. At the top of each information table is a series of Show links; click a link to filter the information accordingly. For example, in the Items I've Won table (in the All Buying view), you can choose to show All items, or just those items Awaiting Payment or Awaiting Feedback.

Hiding or Displaying Columns

If you don't need to see all possible information for specific listings, My eBay lets you customize which columns are displayed for each individual information table. Just click the Customize Display link above the information table, and then select which columns you want to see.

Changing How Many Listings to Display

For most My eBay information tables, you can select how many days' worth of listings you want to display; you can display up to 60 days' worth of items if you want. Just pull down the Period list at the top of a given information table and make a new selection.

> **❝ Mike Sez ❞**
>
> My eBay is such a useful tool that I make it my primary gateway to the entire eBay site. I never use eBay's home page—I use My eBay instead. It's the very first bookmark in my web browser!

Leaving Notes to Yourself

Every now then you might have an auction that requires additional action on your part, or somehow needs further annotation. Fortunately, My eBay lets you add electronic "sticky notes" to any auction listing. Just check the option box next to a particular listing and then click the Add Note button; add your comments into the resulting text box.

Printing Key Information

The information presented in My eBay looks great onscreen but can be a little much if you need a hard copy. Fortunately, My eBay lets you print a simplified, printer-friendly version of any information table. All you have to do is click the Print link next to any section of any view page. For example, to print a list of auctions you've won, go to the All Buying view and click the Print link at the top of the Items I've Won section.

THE ABSOLUTE MINIMUM

Here are the key points to remember from this chapter:

- My eBay lets you track all your eBay activities and information in one place.

- My eBay includes separate pages for tracking items you're bidding on or watching, items you're selling, your favorite searches and categories, and your eBay account.

- You can customize My eBay for your own personal preferences—including how you like your lists sorted, and how many days' worth of items you want to display.

6

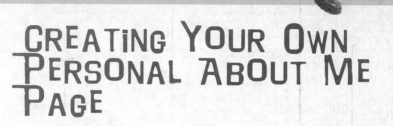

CREATING YOUR OWN PERSONAL ABOUT ME PAGE

If you buy or sell a lot of items on eBay, wouldn't it be nice to have a web page you could show to other users? You know, a page that would tell all those buyers and sellers you deal with all about yourself—and the items you have for sale?

Well, eBay lets you create such a page. It's called *About Me*.

Introducing the About Me Page

eBay's About Me page is a personal web page just for you. It's a great way to personalize the eBay experience, tell a little about yourself, and inspire bidder trust. It's also easy to do—no HTML coding necessary. (My personal About Me page is shown in Figure 6.1.)

FIGURE 6.1

About *Me*, your author!

Michael Miller: Best-Selling Author and eBay Professional

About Michael Miller

Michael Miller is a writer, musician, and consultant, operating under the moniker of The Molehill Group. He has been an eBay member since Saturday, Aug 22, 1998.

Among the more than sixty books he has authored over the past fifteen years are the best-selling **Absolute Beginner's Guide to eBay** and **Absolute Beginner's Guide to Launching an eBay Business**. He also wrote the award-winning **The Complete Idiot's Guide to Online Auctions**, now out of print. His bibliography includes numerous books about computer, business, and music topics.

His latest book is **Tricks of the eBay Masters**, which consists of 600 tips and tricks submitted by hundreds of other eBay users. The book is now available at bookstores everywhere.

Listings

Current Items for Sale

Item	Start	End	Price	Title	High Bidder/Status
4563065874	Jul-17-05	Feb-12-06 18:34:24	$14.99	BOOK: Microsoft Windows XP for Home Users - Autographed	Available
4606980320	Jan-22-06	Feb-21-06 08:38:54	$19.99	BOOK: How Home Theater and HDTV Work NEW AUTOGRAPHED	Available
4606981448	Jan-22-06	Feb-21-06 08:43:10	$17.99	BOOK: Tricks of the eBay Masters NEW AUTOGRAPHED	Available
4606982175	Jan-22-06	Feb-21-06 08:45:47	$14.99	The Complete Idiot's Guide to Playing Drums AUTOGRAPHED	Available
4606982761	Jan-22-06	Feb-21-06 08:47:53	$17.99	Making a Living from Your eBay Business AUTOGRAPHED	Available
6033013008	Jan-29-06	Feb-05-06 11:35:46	$19.99	BATRINA Batgirl Unzipped Resin Model Kit from Batman	No Bids Yet

You can view any user's About Me page by clicking the Me icon next to his or her user name on any item listing page. (If no icon is displayed, that user doesn't have an About Me page.) You can also search for other users' About Me pages by clicking the Advanced Search link at the top of eBay's home page and using the Find a Member search option.

Creating Your Own About Me Page

As I said, you don't have to be a web programmer to create your own About Me page. All you have to do is click a few options and fill in some blanks, and you're ready to go.

Follow these steps:

1. On any eBay page, click the Site Map link (above the Navigation Bar).
2. When the Site Map page appears, go to the Connect section and click About Me.
3. When the main About Me page appears, click the Click Here button.

4. When the next page appears, as shown in Figure 6.2, click the Create Your Page button.

FIGURE 6.2

Your About Me page starts here!

5. When the Choose Your Editing Options page appears, check the Use Our Easy Step-by-Step Process option, then click the Continue button.

6. When the Enter Page Content page appears, as shown in Figure 6.3, start by entering a title into the Page Title box.

FIGURE 6.3

Enter all the information you want to include on your About Me page.

7. On the same page, you can now enter two paragraphs of information, using the supplied formatting controls or (by clicking the Enter Your Own HTML link) with HTML codes.

8. Still on the same page, enter a URL to link to any picture you want to include on your page, as well as an optional title for the picture.

9. In the Show Your eBay Activity section, choose how many feedback comments and current auction listings you want to display.

10. If you want to include any links to external web pages, enter them in the Add Links section.

11. When you're done entering all this information on the Enter Page Content page, click the Continue button.

12. When the Preview and Submit page appears, as shown in Figure 6.4, choose a layout for your page, then click the Submit button.

note

If you're an HTML wizard and want to code your own About Me page, select the Enter Your Own HTML Code option instead.

FIGURE 6.4

Choose a layout for your About Me page.

> **About Me: Preview and Submit**
>
> 1. Choose Page Creation Option   2. Enter Page Content   3 **Preview and Submit**
>
> Select a page layout from the three shown here (Layout A is shown below).
>
> ○ **Layout "A"**   ○ **Layout "B"**   ○ **Layout "C"**
>
> Once you've chosen a layout that you like, click the **Submit** button below.
>
> **Note:** If you don't have JavaScript enabled on your computer, you'll still be able to choose any of these layouts. However, you won't be able to preview your selection below.
>
> [<Back]   [Submit>]
>
> **Preview - Here's what your page will look like**
>
> **About Me: rudolfolasperi2005 (3)**   LAYOUT A
>
> # This is a page about me!

You'll now see a confirmation page, which includes a link to your new About Me page. Click this link to view your new page.

tip

You can edit your About Me page at any time by repeating the preceding steps.

Publicizing Your eBay Auctions with About Me

The great thing about the About Me page is that it's a page with an unchanging URL that always lists your current auctions. When you want to direct other users to your eBay auctions, it's easier to direct them to your About Me page than it is to enter the individual URLs for all your item listing pages.

The address for your About Me page is shown in the address box of your Web browser. The address is typically in the form of members.ebay.com/ aboutme/*userid*/; just replace *userid* with your own user ID and you should have the URL. (My eBay ID is trapperjohn2000, so my About Me address is members.ebay.com/aboutme/ trapperjohn2000/.)

You can then insert this URL into your personal Web page, your email signature, or any other item you can think of. It's a great way to publicize your ongoing eBay activity!

> ❝ **Mike Sez** ❞
>
> The About Me page is also a good way for other eBay users to get to know you—especially those who are bidding in your auctions, or hosting auctions in which you're bidding. Be sure to include text that positions you as a reputable eBay citizen—and not some goofball flake who's likely to cause trouble.

THE ABSOLUTE MINIMUM

Here are the key points to remember from this chapter:

- The About Me page is your personal page on the eBay site—you can create it in less than five minutes, no HTML coding necessary.

- Your About Me page can include descriptive text, a photo, links to your favorite sites, a list of your current auctions, and a list of your most recent feedback comments.

- You can use your About Me page to publicize your eBay activities outside of the eBay site.

PART III

BUYING MERCHANDISE ON EBAY

7

SEARCHING FOR ITEMS TO BUY

Let's get right down to it: eBay is the largest online shopping site on the Web, no questions asked. It's big. It's bigger than big. It's, like, really incredibly massively big. Think of the biggest thing you've ever seen, and eBay is bigger than that.

If you want to browse through the largest selection of merchandise for sale on the Internet, this is definitely the place to go.

However, eBay's size (it's big, remember?) sometimes makes it difficult to find that *one* item you're looking for. So how do you find that one special item among the 36 million or so items that are listed for sale on eBay on any given day?

Browsing or Searching—Which One Is for You?

There are two main ways to locate items to bid on and buy on eBay. You can leisurely browse through eBay's thousands of categories and subcategories, or you can perform a targeted search for specific items.

Table 7.1 shows you what's good and what's bad about both browsing and searching.

Table 7.1 Browsing Versus Searching—Strengths and Weaknesses

Question	Browsing	Searching
How easy is it to do?	Easy—just click through the categories and subcategories	Not as easy—you have to enter specific keywords in a query
How quickly can you find a specific item?	Slow—all that clicking takes time	Fast—you get immediate results for your query
How many items will you find?	A lot—which may be too many	Not quite as many—which may be just enough
Will you find the specific item you're looking for?	Not always—sometimes items aren't categorized properly	Yes—assuming the seller puts the right keywords in the listing title
Can you isolate items geographically?	Yes—you can narrow your results by region	Yes—you can narrow your results by region
Can you find other bidders and sellers?	No—there's no way to browse through the millions of other eBay users	Yes—eBay lets you search by user name

The bottom line: If you're not sure what you're looking for, or if you're looking for all types of items within a general category, you should browse. If you're looking for a specific item or type of item, you should search.

Browsing: The Easy (?) Way to Find Things

eBay has an ever-increasing number of categories, listing all sorts of items—antiques, books, coins, collectibles, comics, computers, dolls, electronics, figures, gemstones, glass, jewelry, magazines, music, photography, pottery, sports

> **" Mike Sez "**
>
> Many eBay categories are so large they're practically unbrowsable. (Do you really want to click through a hundred pages of listings to find the item you want?) I definitely recommend searching over browsing—you'll find what you're looking for a *lot* faster!

memorabilia, stamps, toys, and many, many more. To view all the items within a specific category or subcategory, you need to browse through eBay's category listings.

eBay's main categories are listed on its home page. You can also access a complete list of eBay's categories and subcategories by clicking the Buy link on the eBay Navigation Bar; this takes you to eBay's Buy hub, shown in Figure 7.1. The Buy hub lists all of eBay's major product categories, along with the major subcategories for each category.

FIGURE 7.1

eBay's Buy hub.

You see, to make browsing easier, eBay's major categories are divided into a hierarchy of subcategories. For example, if you click the Antiques link on the Buy hub page, you'll see a formidable list of subcategories within the Antiques major category—Antiquities, Architectural & Garden, Asian Antiques, and a dozen more. In fact, many of eBay's subcategories have their own subcategories—which makes them sub-subcategories, I guess!

So when you access a main category page, like the one in Figure 7.2, you see a list of all available subcategories. Click a subcategory link, and you'll see either a list of additional subcategories or a list of available items.

When you finally get to the list of items within a category or subcategory, the page looks similar to the one in Figure 7.3. At the top of the page are three tabs; these tabs display All Items for sale, Auctions only, or Buy It Now items only. The first listings on the page are the Featured items (sellers pay extra for this placement); below that (or on the next page, sometimes) is the complete list of items for sale, with items ending soonest listed first.

FIGURE 7.3

eBay item listings.

Some listings have pictures or icons either before or after the title. If it's a picture, great; that means the listing has an accompanying photograph. Same thing if you see a green Picture icon. A Gift icon indicates that the seller offers various gift services, such as gift wrap. The New icon indicates that the item has been listed within the past 24 hours. The Buy It Now icon (in the middle Bids column) indicates that the seller has chosen the Buy It Now option for this item. And the PayPal icon is displayed when the seller accepts payment via PayPal.

Table 7.2 shows the various icons you might encounter.

Table 7.2   Listing Icons

Feature	Icon
Picture	
Gallery	
Gift	
New Listing	
Buy It Now	=Buy It Now
PayPal	

Searching: The Powerful Way to Find Things

You could browse through the merchandise categories listed on eBay's home page, as I just described, but given the huge number of categories, this might take forever and a day—and, besides, you're never quite sure whether all sellers have picked the right categories for their merchandise. (Does a Batman statue belong in the Collectibles: Comics: Figurines category or the Toys & Hobbies: Action Figures: Batman category?) In most cases, a better solution is to use eBay's built-in search engine.

Using eBay's Basic Search Function

eBay's home page has a simple search box, shown in Figure 7.4, which works fine for simple searches. Just enter one or more keywords that describe what you're looking for, click the Search button, and view your results. It's pretty easy.

FIGURE 7.4

Simple searching from eBay's home page.

Using the Find It Now Page

More sophisticated searches can be had when you click the Advanced Search link below the home page Search box. This takes you to the Find Items page, shown in Figure 7.5. From here you can:

■ Search by keyword, same as you can from the simple Search box

■ Restrict your search to a specific category

■ Search by both title and description

■ Search completed listings only

■ Sort your results by time, price, distance, or payment method

■ Personalize how you want your search results displayed

FIGURE 7.5

More sophisti-
cated searching
from the Find
Items page.

You can also click the links at the left side of the page to perform different types of searches. You can search by seller, by buyer, or by item number. You can also search for items in eBay Stores, or search for specific Stores. In addition, you can search for other eBay members, or search for a Trading Assistant in your area. Just click the link to perform a specific search.

Using the Expanded Find It Now Page

The Find Items page isn't the last word in eBay searches. When you click the Advanced Search link on the Find Items page (not to be confused with the similar link on eBay's home page), the Find Items page expands to include more options, as shown in Figure 7.6. In addition to the options present on the normal Find It Now page, this page offers the following advanced search functions:

■ Choose to search for all the words in a query, any of the words in a query, an exact phrase, or an exact match for the query

FIGURE 7.6

Even more search
options on the
Advanced Search
page.

Search: Find Items

Learn more about saving favorite searches.
Customize search options

Search
Items
· Find Items
· By eBay Motors Categories
· Items by Seller
· Items by Bidder
· By Item Number
Stores
· Items in Stores
· Find Stores
Members
· Find a Member
· Find Contact Information
· Find a Trading Assistant

Enter keyword or item number

In this category
All Categories

Search

See general search tips and advanced search commands.

☐ Search title **and** description ☐ Completed listings only
All of these words

Exclude these words

Exclude words from your search

Items Priced
Min: US $ ☐ Max: US $ ☐

From Sellers
⊙ From any Sellers
○ From specific sellers (enter sellers' user IDs)
Include
Search up to 10 sellers, separate names by a comma or a space.
○ From My Favorite Sellers
Search sellers from My Favorite Sellers list

Location
⊙ Preferred Locations on eBay.com

- Exclude specific words from the results of a search
- Narrow your search to items within a specific price range
- Include or exclude items from specific sellers, or from your Favorite Sellers
- Narrow your search to items located in or available to specific countries outside the U.S.
- Limit your results to items located a specified distance from where you live
- Limit your results to items listed in a specific currency
- Search for items offered in multiple quantities or lots
- Narrow your search to items offered with the Buy It Now option
- Limit your results to items that can be paid for via PayPal
- Show only those items that have a Get It Fast option (that is, sellers that offer expedited shipping)
- Show only those items that display a Gift icon
- Display only those items from sellers who donate part of their proceeds to charity, via eBay's Giving Works program

note

eBay's Get It Fast program helps you find items that you can pay for and receive quickly. An item with the Get It Fast option will ship within one business day of your cleared payment. Pay via PayPal to further expedite your purchase.

■ Show only those items (in the Real Estate category) that have ad format listings, as opposed to traditional auction listings

■ Limit your search to items ending within a specified time period

■ Display only those items that have a specified number of bids

Whew—that's a lot of options! The bottom line is that you can use the expanded Find It Now page to conduct very targeted searches, using just about any criteria you can think of. Given the huge number of items listed on eBay on any given day, this ability to generate more targeted results is welcome.

Fine-Tuning Your Search Results

When you click the Search button (any Search button, that is), eBay searches its current auction listings and generates a list of auctions that match your search query. In addition to the matching listings on the right side of the page, the left side of the search results page displays a list of matching categories, as well as the Search Options section shown in Figure 7.7. You can use these options to narrow your results to show only those auctions that match some or all of the following criteria:

FIGURE 7.7

Narrowing down
your search
results with
Search Options.

Search Options

Location:
☐ Worldwide
☐ Items within 200
miles of 46032

Show only:
☐ Items listed with PayPal
☐ Buy It Now items
☐ Get It Fast items
☐ Completed listings
☐ Gift items
☐ Items listed as lots
☐ Listings
  Ending within
  1 hour
☐ Items priced
  to

Show Items

Customize options displayed above.

■ Items listed for shipment in the U.S. only, in North America, or worldwide

■ Items located a specified distance from your location

■ Items listed with the PayPal payment option

■ Buy It Now items

■ Get It Fast items

■ Completed listings

- Gift items
- Items listed as lots (multiple quantities)
- Listings ending within a specified time period
- Items selling within a specified price range

Select the options you want then click the Show Items button. eBay now filters the search results to match the new criteria you selected.

Complex Searches—for Simpler Results

Whichever search page you choose to use, you can generate better results by using special commands and operators in your search queries. Table 7.3 lists the commands you can use when searching on eBay.

Table 7.3   eBay Search Commands

To Do This	Use This Command	Example
Search for part of a word	*word**	bat*
Search for either word	*(word1,word2)*	(batman,robin) (NOTE: Do not include spaces after the comma.)
Search for an exact phrase	*"word1 word2 word3"*	"batman pez dispenser"
Must exclude a word	*-word*	batman-pez
Must exclude two or more words	*-(word1,word2)*	-(batman,robin)

Note that eBay automatically assumes that you want to search for items that match all the words in your query. This is the equivalent of inserting a Boolean AND between all the words in your query; a query for batman robin essentially looks for items that match "batman" AND "robin."

Saving Your Searches—and Receiving Notification of New Matching Items

You've taken the time to create a complex search. You figure you'll want to repeat that search at some point in the future, to keep looking for the items you want. You don't want to reenter the query every time you perform the search.

What do you do?

caution

If you're an experienced searcher, you're probably used to using Boolean operators (AND, OR, NOT, and so on) to fine-tune your query. Well, forget your ANDs and NOTs; eBay doesn't permit the use of Boolean operators in its search function. In fact, if you enter Boolean operators in your query, eBay will treat them as keywords—and search for them!

When it comes to repeating your searches, eBay makes it easy. All Items Matching pages (which display your search results) include an Add to Favorite Searches link, at the top right of the page. Click this link, and eBay displays the Add to My Favorite Searches page, shown in Figure 7.8.

FIGURE 7.8
Save common searches for use later.

Add to My Favorite Searches

Search Criteria
Items matching 'goodyear blimp'
Sort: Ending First

Save Options
◉ Create a new search
○ Replace an existing search:

> superman (model,kit)
> batman (model,kit)

Search Name
goodyear blimp
30 characters maximum

☑ Email me daily whenever there are new items for the following period: 6 months ▾
Email notifications are a convenient way to see new listings you're interested in. Learn more

💡 **Note**: Your current search criteria may result in an email sent to you every day. You may want to refine this search by adding more specific keywords.

Save Search Cancel

From here, you can opt to save this search as a new search or use it to replace an existing saved search; give the search a name; and have eBay email you whenever new items are listed for sale that match your search criteria. Click the Save Search button to save the search, which will now be listed on the All Favorites tab of your My eBay page, as shown in Figure 7.9.

The last option available on the Add to My Favorite Searches page bears special mention. This option instructs eBay to automatically notify you when new items that match your saved search come up for auction. Just check this option and select a time period to keep watching (from 7 day to 12 months); eBay will send you an email (one a day) when new items that match your search criteria come up for auction. The email contains links for each new item in your search; click a link to open your web browser and display the matching item.

> ❝ **Mike Sez** ❞
>
> eBay's email notification service is a great tool for active eBay bidders or for anyone searching for that elusive item. I love having eBay tell me when it has something for me, rather than having to log on and do a manual search every day. I highly recommend this service!

Want It Now? Then Ask for It!

If you can't find exactly what you want on the eBay site, all hope is not lost. eBay offers a feature called Want It Now, which lets you post the online equivalent of an "item wanted" ad; sellers who have what you want can then contact you to make a deal.

Here's how it works:

1. Go to eBay's home page and click the Want It Now link (in the Specialty Sites section). Alternately, just go directly to pages.ebay.com/wantitnow/.

2. When the Want It Now page appears, as shown in Figure 7.10, click the Post to Want It Now button.

FIGURE 7.10
eBay's Want It
Now page.

3. eBay now displays the Create a Post page, shown in Figure 7.11. Enter a short title for your query into the I Am Searching For box.

4. Enter a description of what you're looking for into the Describe It in More Detail box.

5. Select a category for the item from the pull-down menu.

FIGURE 7.11

Creating a Want
It Now request.

> **Want It Now: Create a Post**   Help
>
> Tell millions of sellers what you're looking for and get responses emailed to you. It's **free**. Learn more about Want It Now.
>
> **I am searching for**
>
> Tip: Be specific. Think of words sellers might use to search for your post.
> 55 characters left.
>
> **Describe it in more detail**
>
> Tip: Be as detailed as possible; specify brand, condition, color, size, price
> range, etc. See examples.
> 500 characters left.
>
> **Category**
> Select a category...
> Choose the best category to help sellers find your item.
> If you prefer, you may specify a category number instead.
>
> **Picture (optional)**
> Browse...
> Preview picture
>
> **Important posting tips**
> • If you're very specific in your Want It Now post, you'll be about twice as likely to find what you want. See examples.
> • Don't include any contact information in your post (phone number, etc.). eBay will automatically email you if a seller responds.
> • Don't list items you are selling. Want It Now is only for buyers seeking eBay items.
> • View Want It Now policies.

6. If you want to show a picture of what you're looking for, click the Browse button to select and upload a digital photo from your computer's hard drive.

7. Click the Post to Want It Now button.

Your request now appears in eBay's Want It Now database, where it can be searched by interested sellers. Your request stays live for 60 days, or until you find something to buy.

Sellers can either browse or search the Want It Now listings from the main Want It Now page. If they have an item that fits your request, they click the Respond button in the listing. This automatically sends you an email with a link to the seller's item listing. Click the View This Item button to view the item listing; you can then decide to bid on or buy the item—or not. It's a great way to locate otherwise hard-to-find items.

THE ABSOLUTE MINIMUM

Here are the key points to remember from this chapter:

- Browse through eBay's categories and subcategories when you're not sure of the exact item you're looking for.

- Use eBay's search pages to track down specific items for sale.

- Use wildcards and other search operators to fine-tune your item search.

- Click the Add to Favorite Searches link to save your search criteria for future use—and to set up automatic email notification of matching items.

- If you can't find what you're looking for, use eBay's Want It Now feature to post a request for a particular item.

8

BIDDING IN ONLINE AUCTIONS

There are two ways to buy items on eBay—via the traditional online auction format, or at a fixed price. Not all items offered by eBay sellers have a fixed-price option; the auction format is still the most popular way to sell and buy items on eBay.

To many new users, however, the concept of bidding in an online auction is exotic and perhaps a little intimidating. It needn't be. Every day, millions of people just like you place bids in eBay auctions; anyone can do it, and it's really quite easy.

So how does bidding work? In a nutshell, it's as simple as telling eBay how much you'd be willing to pay for an item—and then finding out whether anyone else is willing to pay more than you. If you've made the highest bid, you win the auction and you buy the item.

It's important to remember that it doesn't cost you anything to bid. You only have to pay if you win—and even then, you don't have to pay any fees to eBay. (All eBay fees are charged to the seller.) You'll have to pay the seller the amount of your winning bid, plus any necessary shipping and handling costs to get the item to you.

Sounds easy enough, doesn't it?

Understanding the Bidding Process

It's important that you know all about the item you want to buy before you place your bid. It's also important that you know how eBay's bidding process works—or you could end up paying too much, or (even worse) not enough to win the auction!

Deciding How Much to Bid

Determining how much to bid on an item on eBay is no more complex than determining how much you'd pay for an item at a flea market or garage sale. You should bid an amount no higher and no lower than what the item is worth to you—and what you can afford. It doesn't matter what the current bid level is; you should make your bid in the amount of what you're willing to pay.

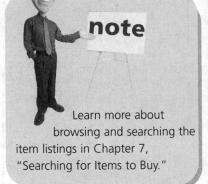

note

Learn more about browsing and searching the item listings in Chapter 7, "Searching for Items to Buy."

However, that doesn't mean you'll actually have to pay the full amount that you're willing to pay. Thanks to eBay's automated bidding software (discussed in the next section, "Understanding Proxy Bidding"), the price you pay will only be as high as necessary to beat out the next-highest bidder. If you bid $40 but the next highest bidder bid only $20, you'll win the auction with a $20.50 bid—just high enough to beat the $20 bidder.

And you should make that $40 bid even if, at the time, the current bid is only $1. Now, you might think that if the bidding is at the $1 level, you should bid no more than $2 or so. This isn't the case, again thanks to eBay's automated bidding software. If the item is worth $40 to you, bid the $40—and let eBay's proxy software handle the mechanics of the bidding process.

How, then, do you determine that an item is worth $40—or $4 or $400? The key thing is to never bid blind; always make sure you know the true value of an item before you offer a bid.

This means that you need to do a little research before you make a bid. If you're bidding on a piece of new merchandise, check the price in a catalog, at your local retailer, or with an online retailer. And you can use eBay's search function to search for other similar items, and see what they sold for. (Remember to search *completed* auctions, so you can see the final selling price.) You don't want to pay more than the going price, as determined by similar eBay auctions.

Understanding Proxy Bidding

The automated bidding software used by eBay is called *proxy* software. Actually, it works like an automated robot, making all your bids for you, based on the maximum amount you're willing to pay. When you're bidding, eBay's proxy software can save you time and help ensure that you get the items you want without overspending your budget.

On eBay, proxy software operates automatically as an agent that is authorized to act in your place— but with some predefined bidding parameters. You define the maximum amount you are willing to bid, and then the proxy software takes over and does your bidding for you.

The proxy software bids as little as possible to out-bid new competition, up to the maximum bid you specified. If it needs to up your bid $1, it does. If it needs to up your bid $5, it does—until it hits your bid ceiling, when it stops and bows out of the bidding.

The proxy software bids in the official bid incre-ments used by eBay. For example, if the next bid is $0.50 higher than the current bid, the proxy software ups your bid $0.50. In no instance does the software place a bid higher than the next bid increment. (It's pretty smart software!)

> **" Mike Sez "**
>
> If you remember nothing else from this book, remember this: Always enter the highest amount that you're willing to pay for an item, no matter what the current bid level. If you think an item is worth $40, enter $40 as your maximum bid—and don't worry if the cur-rent bid is half that amount. You also shouldn't get upset if the bidding goes higher than your specified maximum; have the dis-cipline to bid only as high as you initially thought the item was worth. If you're bidding on a col-lectible, invest in an up-to-date price guide (or reference one online). Whatever you're bidding on, search eBay for completed auctions on similar items, and determine a reasonable price range. Make it a point to shop around, and make your bid accordingly.

Of course, because all bidders are using eBay's proxy software, what happens when you have two users bidding against each other? Simple—you get a proxy bidding war! In this instance, each proxy automatically ups its bid in response to the last bid by the other proxy, which rapidly (seemingly instantaneously) increases the bid price until one of the proxies reaches its maximum bid level.

Let's say one proxy has been programmed with a maximum bid of $25, and another with a maximum bid of $26. Even though the current bid level might be $10, the bids rapidly increase from $10 to $11 to $12 and on to $26, at which point the first proxy drops out and the second proxy holds the high bid.

Bid Increments

To better understand proxy bidding, it helps to know eBay's bid increments. The bid increment is automatically calculated by eBay based on the current price of the item—the higher the price, the higher the bid increment, as shown in Table 8.1.

Table 8.1   eBay Bid Increments

Current Price	Bid Increment
$0.01–$0.99	$0.05
$1.00–$4.99	$0.25
$5.00–$24.99	$0.50
$25.00–$99.99	$1.00
$100.00–$249.99	$2.50
$250.00–$499.99	$5.00
$500.00–$999.99	$10.00
$1,000.00–$2,499.99	$25.00
$2,500.00–$4,999.99	$50.00
$5,000.00 and up	$100.00

For example, if the current bid on an item is $2.00, the bid increment is $0.25—which makes the next bid $2.25. If the current bid on an item is $30.00, the bid increment is $1.00—which makes the next bid $31.00. You see how it works.

Proxy Bidding, by Example

Let's walk through a detailed example of proxy bidding. The process is totally automated, and goes something like this:

1. You see an item that has a current bid of $100, and you tell eBay that you're willing to pay $115 for it. The $115 becomes your maximum bid.

2. The bid increment on this item is $2.50, so eBay's bidding software—your proxy—bids $102.50 in your name. This becomes the current high bid.

3. Another bidder sees this item, and bids the next bid increment (as specified on the item listing page), $105.

4. Your proxy sees the new bid, and ups its bid automatically to $107.50.

5. A third bidder sees the item, and enters a maximum bid of $150. In accordance with the current bid increment, his proxy enters a bid of $110.

6. Your proxy responds with a bid of $112.50.

7. The third bidder's proxy responds with a bid of $117.50, which is higher than your maximum bid of $115.

8. Your proxy drops out of the bidding, and eBay notifies you (by email) that your bid has been surpassed. (If the auction were to end right then, the third bidder would win the auction with a bid of $115. Even though he specified a $150 maximum bid, the bidding never got that high.)

9. At this point, you can place a new maximum bid for the item, or you can throw in the towel and let the new bidder have the item.

Proxy Bidding Advice

The nice thing about proxy bidding is that you can engage in a fierce bidding war—and never get your hands dirty! The proxy software does all the dirty work for you, and just notifies you of the results.

When you're placing your bid, realize that just because you set a maximum bid price doesn't mean you'll have to actually pay that price. The proxy software works in your favor to keep your final price as low as possible; don't assume that just because you specified a price, the bidding will always rise to that level.

> **note**
>
> When you view the bid history for an item, only actual bids—not automatically generated proxy bids—are displayed.

Also feel comfortable that the proxy software will never exceed your maximum bid price. It just won't happen; the software is smart enough to know your limits. And by bidding your maximum right away, you guarantee that you won't get carried away and pay too much at the end of a heated competition. Remember, if you lose an auction because the bidding goes higher than your maximum, you didn't want to pay that much for the merchandise anyway. Get comfortable with that—and be glad the proxy software helped you stay within your limits.

Of course, some bidders don't like proxy bidding. It is true that if two or more people are bidding for the same item, the bids can automatically (and quickly) rocket up until they max out. For this reason, some bidders prefer to bid the bare minimum on every single one of their bids—effectively defeating the purpose of the proxy software. Of course, if you choose to operate this way, you have to be a lot more hands-on with your bidding, essentially checking back on all your bids as frequently as necessary to ensure that you always end up on top.

How to Read an Item Listing

Before we do any actual bidding, however, let's take a look at a typical eBay item listing—and see what you can discover about the item and its seller.

Every eBay listing page includes several distinct sections, each of which is equally important—which means that you need to take your time and read through the *entire* item listing before you place your bid. Don't skim; read carefully and pay attention to the details. If the seller mentions a known fault with the merchandise (in the Description section) but you gloss over it, that's your mistake; you have no right to complain when you receive the item after the auction, fault and all. It's your responsibility to read—and agree to—all the information in the listing.

Let's look at each of these sections in detail.

Title, Number, and Your Information

The very top of the item listing, shown in Figure 8.1, displays the listing title (on the left) and the item number (on the right). The item number is important; you use this number to reference the auction in all correspondence, and when paying by PayPal or other payment services.

FIGURE 8.1

The title and number of the current auction— along with details of your bid.

⬅ Back to list of items	Listed in category: Toys & Hobbies > Models, Kits > Super Hero
Dick Tracy Model Kit Polar Lights Aurora Reproduction	Item number: 6042174519
You are signed in	

Just below the title is a section that displays your personal information regarding the current auction. If you haven't yet bid, this section is fairly empty; it will tell you if you're signed in, or if you're tracking this item in My eBay.

If you've placed a bid, this section will expand to display the status of your bid—whether you're the high bidder or you've been outbid. If you're the *seller* of an item, this section will display the current bid price.

Auction Details

The Auction Details section is next, as shown on the left side of Figure 8.2. This section tells you about the status of the current auction. In particular, you will see the current bid price, the time left in the auction, the number of bids placed (history), the ID of the current high bidder, shipping costs (if stated by the seller), and the location of the item. You'll also see links to add this item to your My eBay Watch list (Watch This Item) or to email the listing page to a friend.

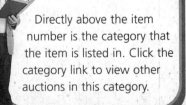

tip

Directly above the item number is the category that the item is listed in. Click the category link to view other auctions in this category.

FIGURE 8.2

The Auction
Details and Seller
Information
sections.

At the bottom of the Auction Details section is a section for listing and payment
details—starting time, starting bid, duration, and payment methods. By default, this
section is hidden; click the Show link to display these details.

Seller Information

On the right side of the Auction Details section
(also shown in Figure 8.2) is the Meet the Seller
section, which displays important seller information. Most important is the seller's eBay ID and
current feedback rating. There are also a handful of useful seller-related links, including these:

- *Read feedback comments*—to learn more
  about the seller's eBay history

- *Ask seller a question*—to send a question
  via email to the seller

- *Add to Favorite Sellers*—to track all future
  auctions by this seller

- *View seller's other items*—to see what else
  the seller currently has for auction

- *View seller's Store* (if the seller has an eBay
  Store)

At the bottom of the Meet the Seller section is
the Buy Safely section. This section includes
another link to the seller's feedback comments,
indicates whether the item is eligible for PayPal's
Buyer Protection program, and displays the
seller's returns policy (if offered).

tip

If you want to add a note
about this auction to your
Microsoft Outlook calendar,
scroll down to the very bottom of the page, to the
"What else can you do?"
heading, and click the Add
to Calendar link.

tip

To see who else has bid on
this item, you can click the
history link.

Description

The Description section, shown in Figure 8.3, offers a description of the item for sale, as written by the seller. Because the main item description is written completely by the seller, the amount of detail varies from auction to auction. Some sellers provide a wealth of detail; some write terse one-line descriptions. If the seller doesn't include enough detail in the description, you can always email for more information—or decide that if this wasn't important enough for the seller to spend more time on, it's not important enough for you to bid on, either.

> **" Mike Sez "**
>
> If I find an item I'm interested in, I like to take a look at that seller's other items. I've often found other items worth buying from a particular seller. (And some sellers will combine items for lower shipping costs if you buy more than one item.)

FIGURE 8.3

A typical eBay item description.

Description

This is a new, unbuilt solid resin model kit of the Dean Cain Superman and Teri Hatcher Lois Lane from the 1990s *Lois and Clark* television show. The model shows Superman holding Lois, who is wearing a negligee, and is called **Super Lovers**. The kit comes in 4 parts: Superman, Lois, Superman's cape, and the big S-shield base. The kit is in 1/6th scale and stands about 12" tall when complete. (The last picture shows what the kit might look like when built and painted; obviously, it comes unbuilt and unpainted.) The Superman figure in particular is a great likeness of actor Dean Cain. This is a great find for the serious kit builder or collector.

Depending on the type of item, the Description section might also include some stock details about the item, provided by eBay; for example, a listing for a DVD (like the one in Figure 8.4) might include main actors, director, rating, region code, display format (widescreen or full screen), and so on, along with the DVD cover art. Additional information, such as plot synopsis, critics' reviews, and (for CDs) track listings, might also be provided under the main item description.

Description

Jules And Jim

Item Specifics - DVDs

Format:	DVD	Rating:	NR
Leading Role:	Henri Serre, Jeanne Moreau, Oskar Werner	Release Date:	Mar 29, 2005
Director:	François Truffaut	UPC:	037429184226
Region Code:	Region 1: US, CA	Display Format:	Widescreen
Genre:	Foreign	Condition:	New
Sub-Genre:	--		

Stock Photo

Portions of this page Copyright 1981 - 2006 Muze Inc. **muze** All rights reserved.

Additional information

Often accompanying the text description are one or more pictures of the item. Some of these pictures might appear a tad small; if you see a Supersize Picture link under a thumbnail picture, click the picture to view it at a larger size.

Shipping, Payment Details, and Return Policy

The Shipping, Payment Details, and Return Policy section, shown in Figure 8.5, lists the shipping/handling charge for the item, if the seller has stated a flat fee. In some auctions, this section will include a Shipping Calculator; enter your ZIP code to calculate your specific shipping charge.

Also listed here are details on whether the seller offers shipping insurance, where the seller will ship to (U.S. only or internationally), and the seller's payment instructions and return policy.

> **"Mike Sez"**
>
> Some item listings include a counter at the bottom of the Description section. Watch the counter over a several-day period to judge the interest in this item. A large counter number (in the hundreds) indicates a lot of interest, and a lot of potential last-minute bidders. A small counter number (in the single digits or the teens) indicates less interest—which means you may be able to win this item without bidding too high.

Shipping, payment details and return policy

Shipping Cost	Services Available	Service Transit Time*	Available to
US $2.50	US Postal Service Media Mail™	Estimated delivery 2-9 days	United States only

*Sellers are not responsible for service transit time. Transit times are provided by the carrier, exclude weekends and holidays, and may vary with package origin and destination, particularly during peak periods.

Will ship to United States.

Pay only $1.00 shipping **for each additional item from this seller's other listings!**
Learn about shipping discounts

Shipping insurance
Not offered

Payment Methods Accepted

Next up is another short section, shown in Figure 8.6, listing the payment methods accepted by the seller. Most sellers accept personal check and money orders; many accept credit cards via the PayPal service.

FIGURE 8.6

The Payment
Methods Accepted
section.

Payment methods accepted

This seller, trapperjohn2000, **prefers PayPal**.

PayPal
VISA AMEX DISCOVER eCHECK

- Personal check
- Money order/Cashiers check

Learn about payment methods.

eBay recommended services
PayPal is the safe way to pay online. Your financial information is never
shared with sellers. Plus, you get free PayPal Buyer Protection on qualified
listings.

Ready to Bid?

eBay put the main bidding section, shown in Figure 8.7, at the very bottom of the
page. All you have to do is enter your bid into the Your Maximum Bid box, and
then click the Place Bid button.

FIGURE 8.7

Use the Ready to
Bid? section to
place your bid.

Ready to bid?   help
Jules And Jim Criterion Collection (2005, DVD)

Item title: Jules And Jim Criterion Collection (2005, DVD)

Current bid: US $4.99

Your maximum bid: US $ [   ] (Enter US $5.24 **or more**)

[Place Bid >]   You will confirm in the next step.

eBay automatically bids on your behalf **up to** your maximum bid.
Learn about bidding.

Before You Bid

Although anyone is free to browse on eBay, to place a bid you have to be a registered user. If you haven't registered yet, now's the time. (For information on registering, see Chapter 2, "Joining Up and Getting
Started.")

Before you place your bid, be sure to read all the
details of the item you're interested in. In particular, look at the following:

- Is the item you're bidding on new or used?
  Does the item come with any sort of warranty, or does the seller offer a returns
  plicy? What's your recourse if you're dissatisfied with the item?

- What condition is the item in? Is it an
  original, or a reproduction? Is there any
  way to verify that condition—through
  photos of the item, perhaps?

- Check out the seller's feedback rating—is it
  positive? (Never deal with a user with a negative total feedback number.) You
  might even want to click the Read Feedback Comments link in the Seller

" Mike Sez "

If you have any ques-
tions about a particu-
lar item, ask 'em! Click the Ask
Seller a Question link in the Seller
Information section to send the
seller an email, and ask whatever
questions you want. If the seller
doesn't respond, pass this auction
by. And if something about the
listing sounds too good to be
true, it probably is!

Information section to view his or her feedback profile; this is where you can read the individual comments about this person left by other users.

- What methods of payment will the seller accept? Are you comfortable using one of these payment options?

- How much shipping and handling is the seller charging? Are these fees in line with what you think actual shipping will cost? If you or the seller lives outside the U.S., will the seller ship internationally?

In other words, take your time and become knowledgeable about and comfortable with both the item and the seller before you place your bid. If you find anything—anything at all—that makes you uncomfortable, don't bid.

All that said, let's look at a final checklist for buyers; check off each item before you make your bid.

Checklist: Before You Bid

- ☐ Make sure you're an official registered eBay member.
- ☐ Read the item description—thoroughly.
- ☐ Note the payment methods that the seller will accept.
- ☐ Note how the seller intends to ship the item, and the shipping/handling price being charged.
- ☐ Check the seller's feedback rating—and click the feedback rating to browse through comments from other eBay users.
- ☐ Note the current bid level, and the next bid price.
- ☐ Research the value of the item. (That means searching eBay for pricing on completed auctions of similar items, as well as doing your own online and offline research.)

continues

note

The seller's feedback rating reflects the number of successful auctions the seller has conducted. The higher the rating, the more reliable the seller. (Learn more about feedback in Chapter 3, "Understanding and Using Feedback.")

"Mike Sez"

It's okay for a seller's shipping/handling fee to be a little higher than actual shipping costs, as charged by the shipping service; the seller has to pay for packing materials, labels, and so forth. But if the charge runs more than 10%–20% higher than the actual shipping costs (up to a few dollars or so on larger, more expensive items), the seller is viewing shipping/handling as a profit center, at your expense.

☐ Determine the maximum amount you're willing to pay for the item.

☐ Subtract the estimated shipping/handling price from the price you're willing to pay; this becomes your maximum bid price.

☐ Email the seller if you have any questions about anything.

☐ Decide whether you really want to bid; every bid you make should be a serious, binding bid.

Just Do It—Placing a Bid

You've waited long enough. Now it's time to finally place your bid!

Here's what you do:

1. Scroll down to the Ready to Bid? section of the listing page, and enter your maximum bid amount.

2. If you're bidding in a Dutch auction (in which the quantity is more than one), enter the number of items you want to bid on. (More on Dutch auctions in a moment.)

3. Click the Place Bid button.

4. When the Submit Your Bid page appears, enter your user information (if prompted), confirm your bid, and then click the Submit button.

5. Your bid is officially entered and the item listing page is redisplayed. At the top of the page, in the blue shaded box, is your bidder status; this is where you learn whether you're the current high bidder or whether you've already been outbid.

Remember, eBay's proxy bidding system will automatically place your bids for you, up to but not exceeding your specified maximum bid amount. If the minimum bid is currently $10, and you entered a maximum bid of $20, eBay enters your bid as $10. Your bid will get raised automatically if and when other bidders enter higher bids.

Bidding in Other Types of Auctions

The preceding section covered the typical eBay auction, one without a lot of bells and whistles. eBay offers a lot of different auction options, however, and the bidding procedure is slightly different depending on the type of auction being held.

Dutch Auctions

A Dutch auction is an auction in which the seller has more than one of an item for sale. An example might be a seller with a half-dozen T-shirts (all identical), or a gross of inkjet cartridges. Although most sellers on Dutch auctions are small businesses that want to move multiple quantities of an item, you'll also find some individuals with several like items to sell.

In a Dutch auction, the seller specifies both the minimum bid and the number of items available in the auction, as shown in Figure 8.8. As in a normal auction, bidders bid at or above that minimum for the item—although, in a Dutch auction, bidders can specify a specific quantity that they're interested in purchasing.

FIGURE 8.8

An example of a Dutch auction—note the quantity available.

1980 S Lincoln Proof - Nice Coins Dutch Auction	Item number: 8390642461

You are signed in

	Starting bid:	US $0.99 Place Bid >	**Meet the seller**
	End time:	**1 hour 15 mins** (Mar-09-06 11:54:58 PST)	Seller: _____ (2648 ⭐) Power Seller
			Feedback: 99.9% Positive
	Shipping costs:	Check item description and payment instructions or contact seller for details	Member: since Nov-25-98 in United States
			■ Read feedback comments
			■ Ask seller a question
			■ Add to Favorite Sellers
	Ships to:	United States	■ View seller's other items: Store	List
	Item location:	St Johns River United States	■ Visit seller's Store:
	Quantity:	10 available	
	History:	Bidders list	**Buy safely**
View larger picture			1. **Check the seller's reputation**
	You can also:	**Watch this item**	Score: 2648	99.9% Positive
		Email to a friend	Read feedback comments
			2. **Learn how you are protected**
			Read our safe buying tips

Listing and payment details: **Show**

When you're bidding in a Dutch auction, you not only have to place your bid, but also have to indicate how many of the item you'd like to buy. You enter the desired amount in the Quantity box in the Ready to Bid? section of the listing page. (This box—shown in Figure 8.9—appears only in Dutch auctions, not in regular auctions.)

FIGURE 8.9

Enter the quantity you want for a Dutch auction item.

Ready to bid?		help
1980 S Lincoln Proof - Nice Coins Dutch Auction		
Item title:	1980 S Lincoln Proof - Nice Coins Dutch Auction	
Starting bid:	US $0.99	
Quantity:	10 available	
Your maximum bid:	US $ [ ] (Enter US $0.99 or more)	
Your quantity:	x 1	
	Place Bid > You will confirm in the next step.	

Unlike a regular eBay auction, Multiple Item Auctions can have many winners. Learn about Multiple Item Auctions.

Determining who "wins" a Dutch auction is a little different from determining who wins a normal auction. In a Dutch auction, the highest bidders purchase the items, but all buyers pay only the amount that matches the lowest successful bid.

Dutch Auctions, by Example

Let's work through an example. Say a seller has 10 identical copies of a particular *Lord of the Rings* T-shirt. The seller indicates the number of items available (10) and the minimum bid (let's say $5). Potential buyers enter their bids, which must be equal to or higher than the minimum bid of $5; each buyer also indicates the quantity (from 1 to 10) that he or she is interested in purchasing.

If 11 people bid $5 each (for one shirt apiece), the first 10 bidders will win the auction, each paying $5 for their items, and the last bidder will be out of luck. But if the 11th person had placed a higher bid—$6, let's say—then that 11th bidder would be listed as the #1 bidder, and the last $5 bidder (chronologically) would be knocked from the list. All 10 winning bidders, however—including the person who bid $6— would have to pay only $5 for the item.

Highest bidders, lowest bids. Get it?

In a Dutch auction, the minimum price ends up being raised only if enough bidders place bids above the minimum bid. In our example, if 9 bidders bid over the minimum, but the 10th bidder bid $5, all bidders would still pay $5. But if the lowest bid was $6 (and the other bidders bid from $6 to $10), all 10 bidders would pay $6 (the lowest current bid). So posting a higher bid increases a buyer's chances of winning an item at a Dutch auction, but it also increases the risk of raising the price for everybody.

When a potential buyer bids on multiple copies of the item, those toward the end of the list may not get the quantity they desire. Still using our T-shirt example, if the top bidder wants three shirts, the remaining shirts are distributed among the next seven bidders—leaving the last or lowest two bidders out in the cold.

Tips on Bidding in Dutch Auctions

Dutch auctions actually benefit the buyer more than any other type of auction by letting higher bidders pay the lowest bid price. Should you bid on a Dutch auction? Why not? If someone is selling something you want, by all means, bid!

note

Remember, the higher bidders get first dibs on multiple quantities. So if the lowest bidder wants multiple quantities of the item on the block, he or she may find that there aren't enough to go around. If only a partial quantity is available, the bidder can officially walk away from his or her bid.

How much should you bid? Ah, there's the issue. I actually like bidding on Dutch auctions later in the game so that I can get a handle on how many other bidders I'm competing with. The number of bidders versus the quantity of items available determines my strategy:

- If the seller has a large quantity of items and a small number of bidders, bid the minimum. In this scenario, everybody wins because there's more than enough merchandise to go around.

- If the seller has a small quantity of items and a large number of bidders, you probably should bid higher than the minimum. In fact, in this scenario, treat it like a normal auction and bid the highest amount you're willing to pay. The worst thing that could happen is you lose the auction; the second worst is that you're a winning bidder and you have to pay your maximum bid; the best scenario is that you're a winning bidder but get to pay a lower amount (because of a lower bid entered by another winning bidder).

Reserve Price Auctions

In a *reserve price* auction, the seller has reserved the option to set a second price (the *reserve price*) that is higher than the opening bid. At the end of an auction, if the high bid does not meet or exceed the seller's reserve price, the auction is unsuccessful and the seller does *not* sell the item to the high bidder. Sellers sometimes use a reserve price on high-end items if they want to make sure that the market does not undervalue what they are selling.

In other words, the reserve price is the lowest price at which a seller is willing to sell an item (unrelated to the opening bid price). The seller specifies the reserve price when the item is initially listed (naturally, the reserve price should be above the minimum bid price). The reserve price is known only to the seller (and to eBay) and is seldom disclosed to bidders.

A reserve price auction begins just like any other auction, at the minimum bid price. The only difference is the reserve price indication in the listing's auction details, as shown in Figure 8.10. You place your bid as you would in a normal auction, and the auction proceeds pretty much as normal.

If your maximum bid is equal to or greater than the reserve price, the item's current price is raised to the reserve price, and the reserve price has officially been met. If, through the course of the auction, the reserve price is *not* met, the auction ends with the item unsold.

note

The reserve price option is not available for Dutch auctions. In a Dutch auction, the minimum price is the minimum price, period.

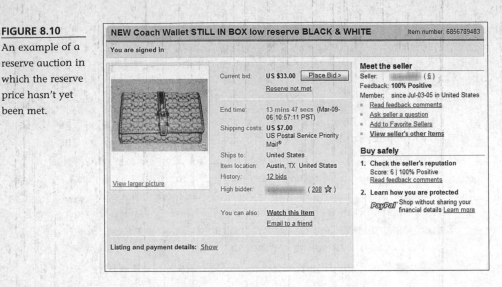

Reserve Price Auctions, by Example

Let's look at a brief example of a reserve price auction. Suppose a seller has a leather jacket to sell that she feels is worth $50—but she wants to set a lower initial bid, to get the bidding going early. So the seller sets $25 as the initial bid, and $50 as the reserve price.

The first bidder on this item sees the $25 initial bid (the reserve price isn't displayed, of course) and bids $25. The bidder is notified that he has the current high bid, but that the reserve price has not been met. If the auction were to end right now, the item would *not* be sold—the seller is obligated to sell only if the reserve price is met.

The bidding continues, and the bid price increases until it hits $50. At that point, the most recent bidder is notified both that he is the high bidder and that the reserve price has been met. If the auction ends now—or at any point afterward—the seller *is* obligated to sell, because the reserve price ($50) has been met.

So, in this example, any bids under $50 don't win the auction; any bids $50 and over can be winning bids.

Tips for Bidding in Reserve Price Auctions

If you want to bid in a reserve price auction, what should your strategy be? It depends on how badly you want the item.

If you really, really, really want the item, you should place your first bid and see whether you hit the reserve price. If you didn't, place a new, higher bid, and see whether it hits the reserve price. If you still didn't, repeat until your bid is high enough to meet or exceed the reserve price and guarantee a win.

For many bidders, however, this is simply a strategy to ensure writing a large check. In most cases, play a reserve price auction as you would a normal auction, and let the high bid be the high bid. If you have the high bid and the reserve price isn't met, it's no skin off your nose; it simply means that the seller set an unreasonable reserve price. You always have the option of contacting the seller post-auction to see whether he or she is willing to sell at the current bid price, even though the reserve hasn't been met, using eBay's Second Chance Offer feature. The seller isn't obligated to do so, of course, but some might be willing to let the merchandise go to forgo starting a whole new auction (and paying another listing fee)—or they may be willing to negotiate a selling price somewhere in between your bid and the reserve. You never know until you ask!

What to Do After You've Bid

Whichever type of auction we're dealing with, let's assume that you've found an item you want and you've placed a bid. What happens next?

The answer to this question is a four-letter word: *wait*. And, as Tom Petty says, the waiting is the hardest part.

Immediately after you place a high bid, eBay automatically sends you an email notifying you of your bid status. You'll also receive an email once a day from eBay, notifying you of your status in any and all auctions in which you're the highest bidder. In addition, if you get outbid on an item, eBay sends you an immediate email informing you of such.

Otherwise, feel free to check in on all of your auctions in progress, just to see how things are proceeding. Remember what they say—a watched kettle never boils. Constantly tracking your auctions won't make the time go any faster.

Keeping Track of Your Bids

The easiest way to keep track of your bids is with the All Buying view on your My eBay page. Just click the My eBay link in the eBay Navigation Bar to view all the items on which you're currently bidding. (Just don't obsess about it!)

Increasing Your Bid Amount

As you get further along in a particularly active auction, you might realize that your maximum bid isn't going to hold, and you want to ensure a large enough bid to

win a long, hard-fought auction. How can you increase your bid—
even though you're currently the high bidder?

To increase your current bid, all you have to do is
return to the item listing page and place a new
bid, making sure that your new maximum bid is
higher than your old maximum bid. (You can't
decrease your maximum bid!) When you enter
this new bid, it replaces your previous bid.

Pretty easy, isn't it?

Oh, No! You've Been Outbid!

It happens. Your auction is progressing, and then
you get that dreaded email from eBay informing
you that you've been outbid.

What do you do?

First, you have to decide whether you want to
continue to play in this auction. If you decided
up front that an item was only worth, let's say,
$10, and the bidding has progressed to $15, you
might want to let this one go.

> **caution**
>
> Know that increasing
> your maximum bid while
> you're the current high
> bidder can inadvertently
> increase your existing bid.
> That's because eBay's proxy bidding
> software will increase the bid to the
> next bid increment even if the new
> bid is placed by the current high
> bidder. This might only affect your
> bid by a few pennies (or dollars,
> depending on how far away you are
> from the next bid increment), but
> it's something to be aware of.

On the other hand, if you hedged your bet with a low bid early on, you might want
to jump back into the fray with a higher bid. If so, return to the item's listing page
and make a new bid. Maybe your new bid will be higher than the current high bidder's maximum bid.

Or maybe not. You don't know until you try!

Retracting a Bad Bid

Everybody makes mistakes. What happens if you
place a bid in an auction that you shouldn't
have placed?

Fortunately—but reluctantly—eBay lets you
retract bids under certain circumstances.

When does eBay allow you to retract your bid?
Well, if the seller has substantially changed the
description of the item after you bid, you're free to
change your mind, too. You can also retract your bid if you made a "clear error" in
the amount of your bid. What's a "clear error?" Well, bidding $100 when you meant
to bid $10 is clearly an error; other circumstances are left up to your judgment.

> **"Mike Sez"**
>
> When the bidding
> exceeds the top level
> you've set for yourself, just walk
> away. Absolutely, positively, do
> *not* let yourself get caught up in a
> bidding frenzy—and end up pay-
> ing more than the item is worth
> to you!

The thing is, you can always retract a bid (because you can always claim a "clear error"), but you won't win any friends doing so. In fact, if you retract too many bids, eBay will come after you and possibly kick you off the site. So retract a bid if you have to, but don't make a habit of it.

How do you retract a bid? It's actually fairly easy; just follow these steps:

1. Go to eBay's Site Map page and click the Bid Retractions link, in the Buying Resources section. (Alternately, you can go directly to offer.ebay.com/ws/eBayISAPI.dll?RetractBidShow.)

2. When the Bid Retractions page appears, enter the item number of the auction and then choose an explanation for your retraction from the pull-down list.

3. Click the Retract Bid button; your bid is now deleted from the auction in process.

> **" Mike Sez "**
>
> It's common courtesy—and common sense—to email the seller before you retract a bid, explaining the circumstances and begging forgiveness.

Bidding in the Final Moments

It's during the last hour of most auctions that the bidding really heats up. If you wait for an email to inform you when you've been outbid during an auction's final minutes, you might not have enough time to log onto eBay and make a new bid. For that reason, many bidders will log on to eBay (and onto the individual auction about to end) and manually monitor the auction's closing minutes. Just remember to hit the Refresh or Reload button on your browser frequently, to keep the item listing page up-to-date with the latest bids!

Five Common Bidding Mistakes

You'll learn some tips on how to be a better bidder in Chapter 13, "Secrets of Successful Bidders." But let's take a moment and examine some of the things you can do *wrong*—actions that can either keep you from winning or cause you to pay too much.

> **note**
>
> The reason for all this last-minute bidding activity is the use of a technique called *sniping*. Learn more about how to snipe in Chapter 12, "Sniping to Win."

Mistake #1: Bidding Too Early

When you're interested in a particular item, it's tempting to place your bid as soon as you read the item description. The problem with this is that as soon as that bid is entered, you've announced your intentions to other bidders—who might then react by placing even higher bids. So, right away, you've started a bidding war—which you could lose.

There's really no benefit to bidding early in a long auction. So what if you place your bid on day one of a seven-day auction? The only bid that really counts is the one that's in as the auction closes. Besides, when you bid early, the bidding price goes up faster. It's better to hold off and place a later bid, one that other bidders won't have as much time to respond to. Bid early, and you're likely to either lose to a higher bidder or unnecessarily drive the price higher; bid later, and you're more likely to win—with a lower bid.

Mistake #2: Bidding Too Low

If you really, really, really want to win a particular auction, there's no point in being cheap. You think you can get by with a low-ball bid, so that's what you offer. The problem is, if the item is really worth a higher price, someone else will bid that amount—and you'll lose the auction.

It's especially tempting to bid low when the seller sets an unrealistically low starting price. Don't get suckered in by a low price early in the auction. If you think an item is really worth a particular price, bid that full amount. Remember, eBay's bidding software automatically sets the current bid level for you, so you'll never pay more than you have to—and if there's not much bidding, you might actually end up paying a lower amount. But if you want to win, you have to bid high enough to beat all other bidders. Don't be cheap!

Mistake #3: Bidding Too High

On the other hand, don't be a dummy and bid an unrealistically high amount for something that isn't worth that much. You'd be shocked at how many items sell for *more* than their fair value on eBay; a lot of buyers just don't know what things are worth when they place their bids, and end up overpaying. Do your homework ahead of time, and find out what that item is really worth. Then place an appropriate bid—and don't bid more than that. If you get outbid, tough; the item wasn't worth that much, anyway!

Mistake #4: Getting Caught Up in a Bidding Frenzy

One reason that many items sell for too high a price is that it's easy to get caught up in a bidding frenzy. If an item is popular and several bidders are interested, you'll see the current bid price keep going up and up and up as each bidder tries to stay in the game. I know the feeling; when bidding starts to heat up, you don't want to lose. So you keep placing higher bids, trying to stay a few dollars ahead of the other bidders—and end up bidding up the price way too high.

The solution to this problem is simple—don't lose your head in the heat of the moment! Set a maximum amount you'll pay for the item, and do not—repeat, *do not*—bid any higher than that amount, no matter how hot and heavy the bidding. It's okay to lose one every now and then!

Mistake #5: Not Reading the Fine Print

You've found an item you want. The bid price is reasonable. You think you can win the auction, and get a pretty good deal, besides.

But when the auction ends, you get an email from the seller telling you that the final price is several dollars higher than what you expected. That's because the seller added a shipping and handling fee to the selling price. Now, you should expect to pay shipping/handling; that's your responsibility as the buyer, and you should factor that into your total cost of the auction. But many inexperienced bidders get surprised by this charge and end up with an unsatisfactory auction experience.

So make sure you know what the shipping and handling fee is before you place your bid. If the seller doesn't include this fee in the item listing, email him with your ZIP code and ask him to estimate the fees to your location. And always be on the lookout for higher-than-normal shipping/handling fees, or other unexpected charges. Although it's common for sellers to include a "handling charge" on top of actual shipping charges (to pay for boxes, packing material, and so on), you don't want to pay *too much* over the actual costs. Jacking up the handling charges is one way unscrupulous sellers make a little extra money on each transaction, and you don't want to play along. Bottom line? Be sure to read the fine print before you bid—especially where it concerns shipping and handling charges.

You Won! Now What?

You've somehow waited patiently (or not) throughout the entire progress. As the clock ticked down to zero, no other viable competitors entered the arena, and your high bid stood. You won!

Now things *really* start to happen. You'll receive an email from eBay notifying you that you've won the auction. You'll also receive an email from the item's seller, telling you how much you need to pay, and where to send the payment. Then you'll need to reply to the seller, make your payment, and wait for the item to arrive. It's all pretty much common sense stuff, and fairly easy, as you'll learn in Chapter 10, "Paying for Your Purchase—and Waiting for It to Arrive."

THE ABSOLUTE MINIMUM

Here are the key points to remember from this chapter:

- Before you place a bid, you have to be a registered eBay user—and you should check out the feedback rating and comments of the item's seller.

- You place your bid in the Ready to Bid? section of the item listing page; then you enter your user ID, password, and the maximum bid you're willing to make.

- eBay's proxy bidding software manages your bidding, raising your bid as necessary up to but not exceeding your specified maximum bid amount.

- If, at any point during the auction, you get outbid, you have two options: Place another (higher) bid, or walk away free and clear.

- When you win an auction, you'll be notified by eBay; you should then contact the seller to arrange payment and shipping terms.

9

BUYING FIXED-PRICE ITEMS

eBay was conceived as an online auction site, and is still known for its auction-format listings. But there's more to eBay than auctions; you can also buy merchandise on eBay without all that bidding and waiting.

If you want your merchandise *now*, you need to check out eBay's various fixed-priced item listings. Whether it's an auction with a Buy It Now option or an item for sale (not auction) in an eBay Store, there's a lot of merchandise available, no bidding required!

Get It Quick with Buy It Now

Tired of waiting around for the end of an auction—only to find out you didn't have the winning bid? Well, there's a way to buy some items you see for auction without going through the bidding process. All you have to do is look for those auctions that have a Buy It Now (BIN) option.

Understanding Buy It Now

Buy It Now is an option that some (but not all) sellers add to their auctions. Figure 9.1 shows an auction with the Buy It Now option, as identified by the Buy It Now price and button at the top of the listing.

With Buy It Now, the item is sold (and the auction ended) if the very first bidder places a bid for a specified price. This effectively lets you purchase the item at a fixed price, bypassing the entire auction process; you don't have to wait for the auction to end to see if you've won or not.

eBay also offers true fixed-price listings—that is, item listings with no bidding allowed, just a flat fixed price. These listings work pretty much like Buy It Now auctions, except that your only option is to buy at the stated price; there's no option to place a bid lower than the BIN price.

> **note**
>
> Some users refer to auctions with the Buy It Now option as "fixed-price" auctions—even though they're slightly different from eBay's *real* fixed-priced listings.

FIGURE 9.1

A Buy It Now auction.

Purchasing with the Buy It Now Option

Buying an item with Buy It Now is really simple. Just follow these steps:

1. Click the Buy It Now button.

2. When the Review and Commit to Buy page appears, as shown in Figure 9.2, click the Commit to Buy button.

3. When the Buy It Now Confirmation page appears, as shown in Figure 9.3, click the Pay Now button to arrange payment.

FIGURE 9.2

Committing to buy an item via Buy It Now.

Review and Commit to Buy

Hello trapperjohn2000! (Not you?)

Item title: SUPERMAN: KINGDOM COME SYMBOL XL T SHIRT: GRAPHITTI
Buy It Now price: US $22.00

Shipping and handling: See item page or contact seller for details.
Payment methods: PayPal, Personal check, Money order/Cashiers check, Other - See Payment Instructions.

By clicking on the button below, you commit to buy this item from the seller.

[Commit to Buy]

You are agreeing to a contract -- You will enter into a legally binding contract to purchase the item from the seller. You are responsible for reading the full item listing, including the seller's instructions and accepted payment methods. Seller assumes all responsibility for listing this item.

FIGURE 9.3

Arranging payment for a Buy It Now purchase.

Buy It Now Confirmation   Item number: 6601345734

Email to a friend | Printer Version

✔ **You bought this item**

[Pay Now >]   or continue shopping with this seller

Click **Pay Now** to confirm shipping, get total price, and arrange payment through: PayPal; personal check; money order; other.

You'll immediately be notified that you've won the auction and the auction will be officially closed.

Bidding a Lower Price in a Buy It Now Auction

Of course, you don't have to pay the Buy It Now price. Instead, you can place a bid at a lower price and hope that you win the auction, which then proceeds normally. (The Buy It Now option disappears when the first bid is made—or, in a reserve price auction, when the reserve price is met.) But if you want the item *now*—and you're willing to pay the asking price—you can use the Buy It Now option to make an immediate purchase.

" Mike Sez "

You should use Buy It Now only if you really, really, really want the item; if you think the Buy It Now price is reasonable; if you fear that the final price will be higher than the Buy It Now price; or if you don't want to wait for the auction to run its course to complete your purchase.

Buy It Easier with eBay Express

As I write these words (in March 2006), eBay is in the process of readying another, easier way to purchase items at a fixed price. This new part of the eBay marketplace is called eBay Express (express.ebay.com), and it promises a streamlined shopping and checkout experience for fixed-priced items.

What eBay Express does is consolidate non-auction listings from both the main eBay site and eBay Stores. That is, you can use eBay Express to find all the fixed-priced items offered by eBay sellers, without having to search the site, browse the Stores, or wait for an auction process to end.

All items offered via eBay Express can be paid for via credit card, typically using PayPal. Even better, you can purchase multiple items from multiple sellers, and have all your purchases consolidated into a single shopping cart and checkout system. Buy multiple items, make a single payment—not a bad deal.

eBay also promises that items offered via eBay Express will come from its very best sellers. For an item to be included in eBay Express, the seller must have at least a 98% positive feedback rating, have a PayPal Premier or Business account, and include a photograph of the item for sale. For buyers, shopping at eBay Express should be just like shopping at Amazon.com or other similar online storefronts.

Do Your Shopping at eBay Stores

In addition to those fixed-price items offered as part of the traditional eBay auction listings, you can also find fixed-price items for sale in eBay Stores. An eBay Store is an online storefront where eBay merchants can sell their goods without putting them up for auction—and keep them for sale indefinitely, without the typical auction expiration.

You can browse through thousands of different eBay merchants at the eBay Stores page (stores.ebay.com), shown in Figure 9.4. eBay Stores merchants are organized by the same categories as the eBay auction site—Antiques, Art, Books, and so on. You can also search for a specific store or a store selling a certain type of item, or view an alphabetical list of all stores.

tip

You can also access eBay Stores from the regular eBay site. Just click the eBay Stores link in the Specialty Sites box on eBay's main page.

Browsing and Buying in an eBay Store

As you can see in Figure 9.5, the typical eBay Store offers fixed-price merchandise
that isn't available for auction on eBay, as well as any auction items the merchant
currently has listed. When you access a particular eBay Store, you have access to this
entire collection of merchandise; if you tried searching on eBay proper, you wouldn't
find the non-auction items the retailer might have for sale.

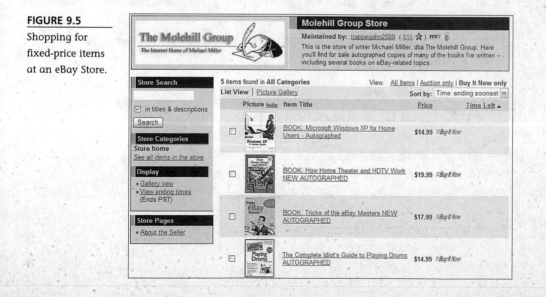

Buying an item from an eBay Store is a little like buying from any other online merchant, and a little like winning an item in an eBay auction. On the one hand, you're buying from an actual merchant at a fixed price, and you can always pay by credit card (typically via PayPal). On the other hand, you have all the niceties you have on eBay, including the ability to check the merchant's feedback rating.

After you locate an item you want, you're taken to the "virtual storefront" of the eBay Store that is selling the item. When you're in a specific store, you can purchase the item you were looking at or shop for additional items. Your checkout is handled from within the store.

Searching eBay Stores

When you perform a standard eBay product search, results from eBay Stores appear at the end of the search results. If you want to limit the search results only to merchandise offered via eBay Stores, you have to perform a special search.

Follow these steps:

1. Click the Advanced Search link at the top of the eBay home page.

2. When the Find Items page appears, click the Items in Stores link in the left-hand column.

3. When the Search: Items in Stores page appears, enter one or more keywords in the Enter Keyword or Item Number box.

4. Define other search parameters, as necessary.

5. Click the Search button to start the search. eBay displays your results on a separate Items Matching page.

tip

You can also search eBay Stores from the eBay Stores page; use the Search for Items in Stores section at the top of the page.

Just Like Amazon: Half.com

eBay Stores and eBay Express aren't the only places you can find fixed-price merchandise in the eBay universe. eBay also runs a site called Half.com, which offers new and used merchandise for sale from a variety of merchants.

As you can see in Figure 9.6, the Half.com home page (half.ebay.com) looks a little like Amazon.com's home page. That's by design; Half.com was originally conceived as an Amazon competitor. Today, Half.com offers merchandise from both large and small retailers, and from individuals, too. The site specializes in CDs, DVDs, video games, books, and textbooks.

FIGURE 9.6

eBay's Half.com site.

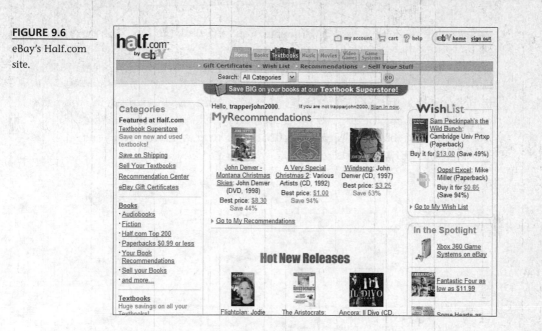

When you search for a specific item on the Half.com, the site returns a list of all the sellers who have that item for sale, like the one in Figure 9.7. The list is sorted into new and used items, with the used items further sorted by condition—like new, very good, good, acceptable, and so on. This is a great way to compare prices between sellers; click the More Info link next to a specific seller link to learn more, or click the Buy button to make your purchase.

FIGURE 9.7

Searching for items for sale on Half.com.

When you make a purchase at Half.com, you're buying directly from the individual seller, just as you do in an eBay auction. The big difference, of course, is that it's not an auction; you're buying an item (new or used) at a fixed price. The other difference is that you don't pay the seller separately; all your Half.com purchases end up in the same shopping cart, just like at Amazon.com. As you can see in Figure 9.8, you check out once for all your purchases, and make just one payment (to Half.com). Half.com then pays the individual sellers, who ship you your merchandise separately. It's fairly painless.

FIGURE 9.8

Items from multiple sellers end up in the same Half.com shopping cart.

THE ABSOLUTE MINIMUM

Here are the key points to remember from this chapter:

- Many sellers offer a Buy It Now option in their auctions; this lets you purchase the item immediately, without waiting for the auction to end.

- eBay Express consolidates fixed-price listings from eBay auctions and eBay Stores with a single shopping cart and checkout.

- eBay Stores offer fixed-price merchandise not otherwise available via eBay auctions.

- eBay's Half.com also offers fixed-priced merchandise for sale from both individuals and merchants—all from one common shopping cart and checkout.

10

PAYING FOR YOUR PURCHASE-AND WAITING FOR IT TO ARRIVE

You've somehow waited patiently (or not) throughout the entire auction process. As the clock ticked down to zero, no other viable competitors entered the arena, and your high bid stood. You won!

If you lose an auction, there's nothing more to do; your work is done, unfortunately. But when you're an auction winner, you have a bit of work to do—not the least of which is paying for the item you won! Read on to learn more about what happens after you've won and auction, and how to arrange payment.

To prepare you for what comes next after you've won an eBay auction, you should work through the tasks in this post-auction checklist.

Checklist: After You've Won

☐ Receive eBay's end-of-auction email

☐ Use eBay's Pay Now feature

or

Wait for the seller to contact you and respond to the seller's email

or

Use the Request Total link on the closed listing page to request the total amount due to the seller

☐ Choose a shipping method, if a choice is offered

☐ Decide whether you want insurance

☐ Choose a payment method

☐ Send payment

☐ Receive the item

☐ Examine the item

☐ Email the seller that you've received the item

☐ Leave feedback for the seller

Making Contact with the Seller

The first thing that happens after an auction ends is that eBay sends you an email notifying you that you've won the aforementioned auction. Depending on what kinds of payments the seller specified, you may be able to pay directly from this email message.

In some instances, you might also receive an email message or invoice directly from the seller. The seller's email should tell you how much you need to pay (your high bid amount plus shipping and handling) and where to send the payment.

If you don't hear from the seller within 24 hours, you might want to take the initiative and send your own email. (This is especially important if the shipping/handling charges were not specified ahead of time, and you need to know the total charges so you can send the proper payment.) Click the seller's name on the listing page to generate an email message, introduce yourself, and gently inquire about shipping and handling costs and where you should send your payment.

Calculating the Final Price

In most cases, the price you pay will include your high bid and a reasonable amount of shipping and handling fees. Don't be surprised if the shipping/handling actually runs a little more than what you might know the actual shipping to be; remember, the seller has to cover the costs of packaging supplies and the labor involved to pack and ship the item. If shipping/handling runs a few bucks more than actual shipping, don't sweat it.

You should also consider whether you need shipping insurance on this item. In most cases buyers don't opt for insurance, but if you're buying a high-priced, rare, or very fragile item, you might want to protect yourself against damage in shipment. (That's if the seller offers insurance, of course; not all sellers do.)

Many sellers offer several shipping options (insurance versus no insurance, UPS versus FedEx versus USPS Priority Mail, and so on), at different costs to you. Others ship only one way. If given the choice, pick the best compromise between cost and speed. If not given the choice, you have to go with what the seller offers.

> ## " Mike Sez "
>
> Insurance might not make sense for lower-priced items. For example, the U.S. Postal Service charges $1.35 for the first $50 worth of insurance, which isn't necessarily a bargain for lower-priced items. However, if your item is higher-priced—or might be easily damaged—it might be worth it to insure the package.

If you have special shipping concerns (for example, FedEx doesn't deliver to your address), you should raise them *before* you bid on an item. If you can't work out something else, don't bid in this auction.

Paying for Your Item

How can you pay for your auction item? As you recall from Chapter 8, "Bidding in Online Auctions," most sellers specify which payment methods they accept in their auction listings. Once you've won an auction, you can choose which of these methods of payment you want to use.

> ## tip
>
> Always check which methods of payment are accepted by a seller before you place a bid.

Paying by Credit Card—via PayPal

Paying via credit card is the preferred method for most buyers. Assuming that you pay your credit card bill in full when it arrives, there are no fees involved. Unlike with money orders or cashier's checks, you don't have to leave home to arrange payment. You also have an excellent paper trail for your payment; you know almost immediately if the seller has received payment. And, unlike personal checks, credit cards ensure faster shipment; as soon as you authorize payment, the buyer receives his funds and can ship the item to you.

Unfortunately, most private individuals don't have the capability to accept credit card payment—and most sellers on eBay happen to be individuals. Many small businesses sell items on eBay, however, and most of these firms *do* accept payment by credit card.

There is, however, a way for an individual seller to accept credit card payments: by using PayPal. PayPal is an online payment service (owned by eBay) that serves as the middleman for these transactions; you pay PayPal via credit card, and PayPal handles all the credit card paperwork and sends a check to the seller (or deposits funds in the seller's checking account).

From your standpoint as a buyer, using PayPal is transparent—you don't even have to pay any additional fees (outside of your normal credit card fees, of course). You make your payment via credit card the same way you would as if you were shopping at any large online merchant. So if you see a PayPal logo in the item listing (like the one in Figure 10.1), you're in luck; that means you can use your credit card to pay, if you win.

> **tip**
>
> If you need an item in a hurry—around the holidays, for example—choosing a seller who accepts credit cards can be the key to a successful transaction. (If in doubt, email the seller while the auction is still in progress and ask!)

FIGURE 10.1

Look for the PayPal logo at the bottom of an auction listing.

If the seller accepts PayPal payments, your end-of-auction notification will look like the one in Figure 10.2. This same Pay Now button also appears in the closed auction listing page on eBay, as shown in Figure 10.3. You can pay from either the end-of-auction email or the auction listing page—or, if you're already registered with PayPal, you can pay directly from the PayPal website.

FIGURE 10.2

Pay directly from eBay's end-of-auction notification email...

FIGURE 10.3

...or pay from the closed auction listing page.

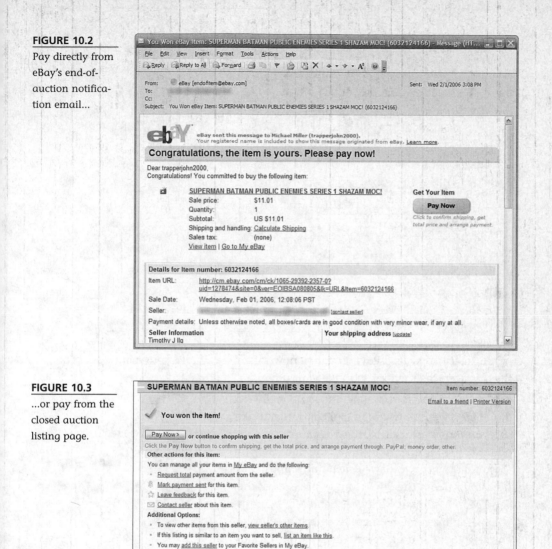

When you click the Pay Now button, you're transferred to a Review Your Purchase page, like the one shown in Figure 10.4. Make sure that all the transaction details are correct, and then scroll to the bottom of the page, select a payment method, and click the Continue button.

FIGURE 10.4

Choose how you
want to pay.

> **Review Your Purchase From** — — — — — — — — — — — Help
>
> You are paying for **1 item** totaling US **$17.41** from — — — — — —
> To continue payment for — — — — — — , click the **Continue** button at the bottom of the page.
>
> **Review shipping address**
>
> Seller should ship to: **Michael Miller**
>   — — — — — — — —
>   Carmel, IN 46032
>   United States
>   Change shipping address
>
> **Review payment details**
>
> 💡 Want to save time?   [Pay All Your PayPal Sellers At Once >]
>
> Seller: — — — — — — — — — (1698 ⭐) 🏆 Power Seller
>
> | Item Title | Qty. | Price | Subtotal |
> |---|---|---|---|
> | SUPERMAN BATMAN PUBLIC ENEMIES SERIES 1 SHAZAM MOCI (6032124166) | 1 | US $11.01 | US $11.01 |
>
> **Payment Instructions**
> Unless otherwise noted, all boxes/cards are in
> good condition with very minor wear, if any at all.
>
> Shipping and handling via US Postal Service Priority Mail: US $6.40
> Shipping insurance: (not offered)   --
> Seller discounts (-) or charges (+):   Add
> **Seller Total:**   US $17.41
> recalculate
>
> ☐ I will enter an eBay gift certificate or coupon on PayPal.
> Questions about the total? Request total from seller

If you select to pay via PayPal, you're now taken to a PayPal payment page. Follow the onscreen instructions to make your payment.

You can also pay for an eBay auction directly from the PayPal website (www.paypal.com). Just make sure you know the seller's eBay ID or email address, the number and title of the auction, and the total amount you owe (including shipping and handling). From the PayPal main page, click the Send Money tab to display the Send Money page. Follow the instructions there to enter the seller's email address and necessary auction information.

Of course, PayPal isn't just for credit card payments. You can make PayPal payments from your debit card, via a checking account withdrawal, or via withdrawal of standing funds in your PayPal account. Just choose the payment method you prefer, when prompted.

> **note**
>
> If you're not yet a PayPal member, you might be prompted to create a Personal account before you can initiate a payment. Personal membership is free.

Other Payment Methods

If the seller doesn't accept PayPal payments, or if you want to pay via another method, you should check one of the non-PayPal payment methods at the bottom of the Review Your Purchase page. When you click the Continue button, you see the

Email Seller page shown in Figure 10.5. Make sure that all the information here is correct, and then click the Email Information to Seller button.

FIGURE 10.5

Sending your payment information to the seller.

Pay via Money Order / Cashier's Check: Email Seller   Help

1. Email Information to Seller   2. Send Payment

Please review the payment details below, then click the **Email Information to Seller** button after confirm. You will receive a copy of this email.

Your email to the seller

Dear

I will be sending payment of **US $17.41** via **money order / cashier's check** shortly.

Please ship to the following address:	I will send my money order / cashier's check to the following address:
Michael Miller	
Carmel, IN 46032	Hopewell Junction, NY 12533
United States	United States
Edit Address	

I am paying for:

Item #	Item Title	Qty.	Price	Subtotal
6032124166	SUPERMAN BATMAN PUBLIC ENEMIES SERIES 1 SHAZAM MOC!	1	US $11.01	US $11.01

Subtotal:	US $11.01
Shipping and handling via US Postal Service Priority Mail:	US $6.40
Shipping insurance (not offered):	--
Seller discounts (-) or charges (+):	US $0.00

If you're paying by personal check, now is the time to write the check and put it in the mail. If you're paying by cashier's check or money order, head to the bank or post office, cut a payment, and then put it in the mail. Remember to include your name and shipping address, along with the item number and description, with your payment. (Or just include a printout of the Send Information to the Seller email that eBay sent to you.)

Paying by Check

Even though most buyers today pay via credit card (thanks to PayPal), payment by personal check remains popular. It's pretty easy for you as a buyer to pull out your checkbook, write a check, and put it in the mail.

That said, not all sellers today accept personal checks. In addition, paying by check will probably slow down your item's shipment. That's because savvy sellers will hold items paid for by a personal check for one to two weeks, until the check clears your bank. Other sellers will look at

tip

One of the nice things about paying via PayPal is the site's Buyer Protection plan. Qualified auction purchases are eligible for up to $1,000 coverage, so if you get stiffed by a negligent seller or receive something significantly different from what you ordered, you're protected. Look for the PayPal Buyer Protection icon in the auction listing's Seller Information box to make sure you're buying from a qualified seller.

a buyer's feedback rating, and if it's strong, they'll go ahead and ship the merchandise when they receive the check. But don't expect a seller to ship immediately if you pay by personal check, especially if he hasn't dealt with you before or you're a relatively new eBay user. And don't be surprised if a seller doesn't accept personal checks; always check the seller's preferred payment methods before you place your bid.

Paying by Money Order or Cashier's Check

Some sellers state that they prefer cashier's checks or money orders, and try to discourage payment by personal check. This is understandable; to the seller, cashier's checks and money orders are just like cash, but a personal check isn't good until it clears the bank.

To you, the buyer, there are two potential downsides to paying via money order or cashier's check. First, it's a hassle; you have to go to the bank or post office or credit union, wait in line, fill out a form, and then arrange funding. Depending on your local conditions, that could be a time-consuming process.

Second, depending on where you get your money orders, there may be a fee involved. The U.S. Postal Service, for example, charges $0.90 to cut a money order. Your bank may charge less (or more—or, in rare instances, nothing), but it's one more fee to add to what you're paying for the auction item. If you won a relatively low-priced item, the charge might not be worth it.

tip

One of the best places to purchase a money order is your local Wal-Mart, which charges less than $0.50.

Paying by Cash

Nothing could be simpler than paying by cash. Cram some greenbacks and a few coins into an envelope, stick a stamp on it, and you're done.

Right?

Wrong.

Paying by cash is definitely the least recommended method of payment. In fact, eBay discourages payment via cash, and for good reason.

First, it's hard to hide cash in an envelope. Even if you wrap the bills in several sheets of paper and use a double envelope, there's something about a wad of cash that draws attention.

Second, cash is easy to steal. Some disreputable types might see a cash-laden envelope sitting in a mailbox and make a grab for it. Easy to do.

Third, there's nothing to track. If the seller says he never received your payment, there's nothing to trace to prove otherwise. (That's why cash is the preferred method of payment for illegal drug dealers—it's virtually untraceable.)

So, unless the auction item is priced absurdly low (so low you don't care if the money gets ripped off), you should probably avoid paying by cash.

Using Escrow

A final payment option, used primarily in higher-priced auctions, is the use of an escrow service. This is a company that acts as a neutral third party between the buyer (you) and the seller, holding your money until you receive the seller's merchandise. If you don't get the goods (or the goods are unacceptable), you get your money back; the seller gets paid only when you're happy.

Here's how a typical escrow transaction works:

1. At the end of an auction, you and the seller contact each other and agree to use an escrow service. The escrow service's fees can be split between the two parties or (more typically) can be paid by you, the buyer. Fees differ widely from service to service.

2. You send payment (by check, money order, cashier's check, or credit card) to the escrow service.

3. After your payment is approved, the escrow service instructs the seller to ship the item.

eBay recommends using escrow for all auctions above $500 for which the seller doesn't accept credit card or PayPal payments.

4. You receive the item, verify its acceptability, and notify the escrow service that all is fine.

5. The escrow service pays the seller.

Although you can use any third-party escrow service, eBay recommends Escrow.com (www.escrow.com). Go there for further information and instructions.

Evaluating Different Methods of Payments

Now you know how you *can* pay; you still want to know how you *should* pay.

Which Method Is Fastest?

When it comes to speed, paying by credit card (typically via PayPal) wins hands down. The seller receives his funds a few seconds after you click the Send button on the payment page, which means that shipment can occur almost immediately.

Paying by personal check is definitely the slowest method. Not only do you have to wait for the postal service to deliver your check to the seller, but you also have to wait for the seller to wait—for your check to clear your bank. All this waiting means that the seller probably won't be able to ship your item for at least two weeks after the end of the auction, and maybe longer.

Coming somewhere in the middle are money orders and cashier's checks. You still have to depend on snail-mail delivery of your payment, but when the seller receives it, he can ship your item immediately. Depending on the speed of the mail, figure anywhere from two days to a week before your item is shipped.

Which Method Is Safest?

Of course, how you pay for an item can increase or decrease your protection during a transaction; some methods of payment are safer for you than others.

The least safe method of payment for a buyer is cash; there's nothing to track, and it's very easy for someone to steal an envelope full of cash. Also considered less safe (although considerably safer than sending cash) are cashier's checks and money orders; like cash, they provide no money trail to trace if you want to track down the seller. Paying by check gives you a minor trail to trace, but when the check is cashed, it's still pretty much a done deal.

A much safer way to pay is by credit card. When you pay by credit card, you can always go to the credit card company and dispute your charges if the item you bought never arrived or was misrepresented. The same safety measures typically apply to credit card payments made through PayPal and other bill pay services— although you should check with the bill pay service, just to be sure.

For the ultimate protection when buying an expensive item in a person-to-person option, use an escrow service. Because the escrow service acts as a neutral third party between you and the seller, if you don't receive what you won—or are otherwise dissatisfied with the item—you get your money back, guaranteed.

Which Method Should You Use?

Use Table 10.1 to determine how you want to pay, based on several key conditions.

> **" Mike Sez "**
>
> If you have the choice (and have a credit card), my personal recommendation is to pay by plastic. You'll have a paper trail if anything goes south, as well as protection from your credit card company (above a certain amount). If payment by plastic isn't available, I pay by check if I'm not in a hurry, or by money order if I am.

Table 10.1   When to Use Which Payment Method

Situation	Payment Method
Very low-priced item (<$5 total), trusted seller, no time to write a check or get to the bank, no desire to use credit card	Cash
Low-priced item, no hurry for shipment	Check
Low-priced item, need fast shipment, trusted seller, don't want to use credit card	Money order/cashier's check
Higher-priced item or need fast shipment	Credit card/PayPal
High-priced item, desire protection in case item doesn't meet expectations, don't mind paying additional fees	Escrow

Waiting for Your Doorbell to Ring...

After you've sent your payment, you have to wait for the item to arrive. If the wait is too long, you should contact the seller and confirm that the item was actually shipped out on a particular date; if an item appears to be lost in shipment, the two of you can work together to track down the shipment with the shipping service. Just be sure to allow adequate time for your payment to clear and for the item to actually ship from the seller to you. (This might range from a few days for a credit card payment to a few weeks if you pay via personal check.)

This is also the stage of the process where some unlucky buyers discover that they're dealing with deadbeat sellers—frauds who take your money but never ship your item. If you find yourself in this situation, there are options available to you; turn to Chapter 11, "Protecting Yourself from Shady Sellers," to learn more.

Receiving the Goods

In most transactions, fortunately, the item you purchase arrives promptly. Now you should unpack the item and inspect it for any damage. If the item is something that can be tried out, you should make sure that it actually works. If all is fine, email the seller to say that you received the merchandise and that you're happy. If all isn't fine, email the seller and let him or her know that you have a problem.

If you have a problem—or if you didn't receive the merchandise at all after a reasonable amount of time—you should first try to work out a compromise with the seller. Most sellers will bend over backward to make you happy; some won't.

> **tip**
>
> When your item arrives, check it out immediately. Don't wait a month before determining that there's something wrong; find out now whether the item is in good shape and delivers what was promised.

If you can't work out anything with the seller, turn to eBay for assistance. See Chapter 11 for instructions on what to do when a deal goes bad.

Finishing Things Up and Leaving Feedback

You've made your bid, won the auction, paid the seller, and received the merchandise. Now you're done—right?

Wrong.

The very last thing you need to do is leave feedback about the seller. Whether it was a good transaction or a bad one, you need to let your fellow eBay members know how things turned out.

To leave feedback, go to the listing page for the item you just bought, click the Leave Feedback to Seller link, and then fill in the resulting form. You can leave positive, negative, or neutral feedback, as well as a one-line comment about the transaction. Make sure you really want to leave the comments you've written, and then click the Leave Comment button. Your feedback will be registered and added to the seller's other feedback comments.

See Chapter 3, "Understanding and Using Feedback," for more advice about the type of feedback to leave in different situations.

THE ABSOLUTE MINIMUM

Here are the key points to remember from this chapter:

- When an auction is over, eBay notifies both you and the seller via email.
- If you're paying by credit card, you can initiate payment directly from the end-of-auction email.
- Paying by credit card (via PayPal) is the fastest and safest option for most buyers.
- Paying by cashier's check or money order is also a good option, although not as fast as paying via credit card.
- Paying by personal check is safer than cashier's check or money order and provides a nice paper trail—but it can slow down shipment of your item by one to two weeks.
- After you receive the merchandise, let the seller know that you're satisfied (or not) and leave feedback on the eBay site.

11

PROTECTING YOURSELF FROM SHADY SELLERS

When you're bidding for and buying items on eBay, you're pretty much in "buyer beware" territory. You agree to buy an item, almost sight unseen, from someone whom you know practically nothing about. You send that person a check or arrange payment via credit card, and then hope and pray that you get something shipped back in return—and that the thing that's shipped is the thing you thought you were buying, in good condition. If you don't like what you got—or if you received nothing at all—the seller has your money. And what recourse do you have?

Remember, when you buy something through an eBay auction, when it comes down to making the financial transaction, you're dealing with an individual—*not* eBay. And as you'll soon learn, every person you deal with behaves differently and expects different behavior of you. In the course of your eBay dealings, it's not unlikely that you might run into a shady seller who never sends you the item you purchased—or tries to pass off a lower-quality item for what was described in the item listing. What can you do to protect yourself against other users who aren't as honest as you are?

Fortunately, you can do several things to protect yourself on eBay—and, in general, shopping at eBay is no more dangerous than shopping at a local garage sale. This chapter details some of the standard guidelines and procedures you can follow to ensure that your eBay buying and selling experience is not only successful, but profitable and enjoyable as well.

Protecting Yourself Before You Buy

The first line of defense against frauds and cheats is to intelligently choose the people you deal with. On eBay, the best way to do this is via the Feedback system.

You should always check a seller's feedback rating before you bid. If it's overwhelmingly positive, you can feel safer than if the seller has a lot of negative feedback. For even better protection, click the seller's name in the item listing to view his Member Profile, where you can read individual feedback comments. Be smart and avoid those sellers who have a history of delivering less than what was promised—which you can tell by reading what other members had to say about him.

You can also use the Member Profile page to view the user's ID history (shifty users sometimes change IDs frequently) and other items for sale. You can even email the seller to ask for more information; just click the Contact Member button. If the seller won't work with you—or if the information doesn't check out—then don't deal with him!

note

To learn more about feedback and the Member Profile page, see Chapter 3, "Understanding and Using Feedback."

Protecting Yourself After the Auction

What do you do if you follow all this advice and still end up receiving unacceptable merchandise—or no merchandise at all?

First, know that eBay doesn't accept any responsibility for any transactions conducted on its site. It's not the buyer or the seller, only a relatively disinterested third party.

However, that doesn't mean you shouldn't contact eBay if you're the recipient of a sour deal—you should, and eBay encourages you to do so. At the very least, eBay will start tracking the seller's other activities and perhaps kick the seller off the site if a pattern of fraudulent activity can be shown. Best-case scenario, eBay will actually refund some of the money you've lost.

Getting Help from eBay

eBay offers a Purchase Protection Program that protects you up to $200 (with a $25 deductible) for any auction transaction gone bad. This Purchase Protection Program is the final step in a long process with an equally long name—the Item Not Received or Significantly Not as Described Process. (Whew!)

Understanding the Process

The Item Not Received or Significantly Not Described Process (let's just call it The Process) outlines specific steps you need to follow if you don't receive an item you've purchased, or if the item isn't what you thought you were buying. You can initiate The Process between ten and sixty days after the end of an auction, and it goes like this:

1. **Contact the seller**. If, after a reasonable waiting period, you haven't received an item (or think the seller pulled a "bait and switch" on you), try to work it out with the seller first. Email the seller directly (and politely) and see how he responds.

2. **Open a dispute**. If the seller doesn't respond to your satisfaction, you can open a Item Not Received or Significantly Described dispute. You can do this by going to your My eBay page and click the Dispute Console link at the bottom left. When the Dispute Console page appears, as shown in Figure 11.1, click the Items Not Received or Not As Described link. When the next page appears, click the Report an Item Not Received or Not As Described link. When the

" Mike Sez "

eBay regards its Feedback system as the best protection against fraudulent transactions. I certainly recommend that, whether a transaction went swell or went south, you leave feedback about your partner in every transaction. I know that I check the feedback rating of every seller I choose to deal with; it really is a good way to judge the quality of the other party in your eBay transactions.

tip

In addition, you should leave formal negative feedback about any bad sellers you encounter; it's your duty to warn other buyers before they get suckered, too.

note

Learn more about The Process at pages.ebay.com/ help/tp/inr-snad-process.html.

Report an Item Not Received page appears, enter the item number and click Continue. Follow the onscreen instructions from there.

3. **eBay contacts the seller**. eBay will now send an automated email to the seller, encouraging him to contact you and work out the problem. More often than not, this prompting will cause the seller to resolve the issue.

4. **The seller responds**. The seller should then respond to eBay's email, either by noting how the issue was resolved, or by requesting further communication.

5. **You communicate with the seller**. If the seller hasn't already shipped the item, eBay now encourages the two of you to talk some more. (Via eBay's online posting system, of course.) This is yet another opportunity to work out the problem.

6a. **Close the dispute**. If the issue is resolved to your satisfaction, you should now close the dispute. Or…

6b. **File a claim**. If 30 days have passed since the end of the auction and you haven't been able to work out your dispute, you're now eligible to file a claim under eBay's Purchase Protection Program. Just return to the Dispute Console, click the link for the open dispute, and follow the onscreen instructions from there. Note, however, that if you paid via PayPal,

note

If you paid for your purchase via PayPal, eBay directs you to PayPal's Buyer Protection Plan (discussed later in this chapter) to handle the complaint. In other words, PayPal's protection comes first, then eBay's—unless you didn't pay via PayPal, in which case eBay's plan is the only one that counts. (Whew!)

eBay directs you to PayPal's Buyer Protection Plan (discussed later in this chapter) to handle the claim.

Understanding eBay's Purchase Protection Program

eBay's Standard Purchase Protection Program is available to all buyers with non-negative feedback. Here are some of the details you need to know:

caution

Be reasonable before you file a dispute. For example, if you paid by personal check, the buyer will hold the check for up to two weeks before he ships the item—so you can't expect to receive the item in ten days. Also factor in weekends and holidays before you determine that you're not going to receive an item.

- You're insured (for up to $200) on items with a final value over $25. If the item is priced under $25, you're on your own.

- There's a $25 deductible on each claim. If you submit a claim for a $35 item, you'll get $10 back ($35 minus the $25 deductible). If you submit a claim for $200, you'll get $175 back.

- You'll be reimbursed only for the final bid price, not for any other fees—such as shipping, handling, or escrow fees.

- To qualify, both your feedback rating and the seller's feedback rating have to be zero or above.

- All items that meet eBay's user agreement are covered; items that violate the user agreement aren't covered.

- You can get reimbursed if you send money to a seller and you don't receive the item. You can also get reimbursed if you receive the item, but it's significantly different than described in the auction listing. However, you won't be reimbursed if something happens to the item in transit; if the shipping company loses or damages the item, that's the company's problem to fix.

- You have to wait until 30 days after the auction to begin the complaint process—and have to file within 60 days of the auction end.

- You can file a maximum of three claims in a six-month period.

Filing a Claim

How do you get your money back if you've been burned? Here are the basic steps to take:

1. Go through the Item Not Received or Significantly Not Described Process, as previously described.

2. Somewhere between 30 and 60 days after the end of the auction, close your dispute (via the Dispute Console) and select "I feel I have no other option but to escalate this to a claim."

3. If your transaction is eligible for coverage, you'll be presented with a link to the Standard Purchase Protection claim form; click this link. (You can also access this form by clicking the Dispute Console link on your My eBay page.)

4. Fill out the Standard Purchase Protection Claim form, then click the Submit button to file your claim.

5. Within 14 days of submitting your claim, an eBay claims administrator will contact you via email. If you're asked to provide proof of payment, you'll need to send eBay a copy of a receipt, money order, personal, check, and so on. If you paid by credit card, eBay will require proof of denial of reimbursement through your credit card company. You can mail or fax this information to eBay.

6. If you're filing a claim for an item "significantly not as described," the eBay claims administrator may ask you to provide a letter of authenticity or appraisal from an independent authenticator.

7. Sometime in the next 45 days you will be contacted by the eBay claims administrator. If your claim is approved, you'll be sent a check for the disputed amount (less the $25 deductible).

I hope you'll never have to use eBay's Purchase Protection Program. But if you are the unfortunate recipient of an unscrupulous seller, it's good to know that eBay is looking out for you.

Using PayPal's Buyer Protection Plan

If you paid for your purchase via PayPal, you may be eligible for another level of purchase protection, thanks to PayPal's Buyer Protection plan. Under this plan, PayPal will reimburse you for up to $1,000 if you don't receive an item you paid for, or if the item is significantly not as described.

The PayPal Buyer Protection plan isn't offered for all sellers; only those sellers that meet the following requirements can participate:

- Feedback rating of at least 50
- Feedback percentage of at least 98% positive
- Seller has a verified Premier or Business PayPal account, in good standing

To make sure you're buying from a protected seller, look for the Free PayPal Buyer Protection message in the Buy Safely portion of the Meet the Seller section of an auction listing, as shown in Figure 11.2.

FIGURE 11.2

This seller is protected via the PayPal Buyer Protection plan.

Meet the seller

Seller: trapperjohn2000 (833 ⭐) m🅿

Feedback: **100% Positive**

Member: since Aug-22-98 in United States

▪ Read feedback comments

▪ Ask seller a question

▪ Add to Favorite Sellers

▪ View seller's other items: Store | List

▪ Visit seller's Store:
   🏪 Molehill Group Store

Buy safely

1. **Check the seller's reputation**
   Score: 833 | 100% Positive
   Read feedback comments

2. **Learn how you are protected**
   Free PayPal Buyer
   PayPal Protection.
   See eligibility

You must file a claim within 45 days of the date of payment. In addition, you can only file one claim per auction listing, and a total of three claims each calendar year.

Resolving Conflicts

Sometimes a problem auction doesn't have a clear-cut good guy and bad guy. If you ever find yourself in an extreme finger-pointing situation, it might be time to engage in online dispute resolution.

To negotiate these sticky types of disputes, eBay offers mediation services through SquareTrade (www.squaretrade.com). This site settles disputes through a possible two-part process. You start out with what SquareTrade calls Online Dispute Resolution; this free service uses an automated negotiation tool to try to get you and the seller to neutral ground. Communication is via email; the process helps to cool down both parties and let you work out a solution between the two of you.

If the two of you can't work it out in this manner, you have the option of engaging a SquareTrade mediator to examine the case and come to an impartial decision. This will cost you $20, and both parties agree to abide with the results. If the SquareTrade mediator says you're owed a refund, the seller has to pay you. If the representative says there's no basis for your claim, you have to stop complaining. (At least to the other person.)

Beyond eBay

Beyond eBay, you can contact other agencies if you've been disadvantaged in a deal. For example, if mail fraud is involved (which it is if any part of the transaction—either payment or shipping—was handled through the mail), you can file a complaint with your local U.S. Post Office or state attorney general's office. If you've had a large amount of money ripped off or if your credit card number was stolen, you should also contact your local police department.

You can also register a complaint with the National Fraud Information Center (www.fraud.org), which is a project of the National Consumers League. This site will transmit the information you provide to the appropriate law enforcement agencies.

Finally, you can file a complaint about any fraudulent auction transaction with the Federal Trade Commission (FTC). Although the FTC doesn't resolve individual consumer problems, it can and will act if it sees a pattern of possible law violations. You can contact the FTC online (www.ftc.gov/ftc/consumer.htm) or via phone (877-FTC-HELP).

Reporting Inappropriate Behavior

There is a long list of activities that buyers and sellers can engage in that eBay expressly prohibits. Most of these offenses—detailed in the list that follows—involve blatantly manipulating auction results, whether by the seller or by an overly interested bidder. If eBay catches a user doing any of these, that user will be either temporarily suspended (kind of a first warning) or permanently banned from the service.

What activities are we talking about? Here's a short list:

- **Shill bidding**, which involves bidding on your own item in a deliberate attempt to artificially drive up its price. A shill bid can involve the use of secondary eBay registrations, user aliases, family members, friends, or associates to pump up the price; other bidders then have to top a higher price to stay in the game.

- **Bid shielding**, which is the practice of using shill bidding (but not a shill associated with the seller) to artificially increase the price of an item temporarily, in an attempt to protect the low bid level of a third bidder. Essentially, the artificially high bid scares off other bidders, and then the shill retracts the super-high bid at the last moment, leaving the bidding wide open for the initial, lower bidder.

- **Bid siphoning**, which happens when a third party (unrelated to the seller or bidder) emails bidders in a currently open auction, offering a similar or identical item at a price below the current bid level. This siphons off potential sales away from the registered seller and makes an end-run around eBay's fee system.

- **Bid discovery**, which happens when the bidder places a very high bid on the item (well over the current high bidder's assumed maximum bid level) and then retracts the bid. This returns the high bid to the former high bidder, but at that bidder's maximum bid level—which wasn't previously public.

- **Unwanted bidding**, which happens when a buyer is warned away from an auction (because of poor feedback, past experience, or other reasons) yet persists on placing a bid. If the seller reports you to eBay for this offense, you can be indefinitely suspended from the service.

- **Repeatedly backing out of transactions**. Backing out of one or two transactions won't win you any friends, but it also won't get you kicked off eBay. However, if you back out of a lot of transactions—as either a buyer or a seller—eBay will toss you off. It's chronic incomplete transactions that eBay notices.

- **Auction interference**, which happens when a bidder sends threatening emails to other bidders to warn them away from a seller or an item. You're not allowed to interfere with in-process auctions—and you're *definitely* not allowed to threaten other users! eBay will bump you if they find out.

- **Transaction interception**, which is out-and-out fraud. You represent yourself as another eBay seller, intercepting the ended auctions of that seller (generally with forged email messages) and convincing buyers to send you payment for the items. Getting caught at this one will cause you more trouble than just a simple eBay expulsion.

- **Spamming**, which occurs when you send bulk email (spam) to masses of other users. If eBay finds out, it'll kick you off, simple as that.

Of course, you have to be caught before you can be punished. The main way eBay finds out about these activities is from other users—the real victims of these offensive behaviors.

If you suspect any of these bidding offenses in any specific auction (even if you yourself are not participating in the auction), you should notify eBay at pages.ebay.com/help/tp/programs-investigations.html. Be sure to include all relevant information and copies of all email correspondence with the suspected offender.

Tips for Protecting Yourself on eBay

When all is said and done, eBay is a fairly safe environment to conduct person-to-person transactions. The vast majority of eBay users are honest individuals, and you'll no doubt enjoy hundreds of good transactions before you hit your first bad one.

That said, here are some tips on how to better protect yourself when you're dealing on eBay:

- Remember that you're dealing with human beings. Be nice, be polite, and, above all, *communicate!* Send emails confirming receipt of payment or shipment of merchandise. Say "please" and "thank you." And don't send short, snippy emails in the heat of the moment. Be tolerant and friendly, and you'll be a better eBay citizen.

- Realize that, in most cases, you're dealing with individuals, not businesses. Keep that in mind if things don't go quite as smoothly as they would if you ordered from Amazon.com or L.L.Bean. Most folks don't have automated shipping systems installed in their living rooms!

- Know that experienced eBay users take the feedback system very seriously—if not obsessively. Positive feedback is expected for every successful transaction, and negative feedback should be used in only the most dire of circumstances. When in doubt, just don't leave any feedback at all.

- If you have questions about an item for sale, or about any part of the transaction, ask! Email the seller if you're not sure about payment or shipping terms. Good communication eliminates surprises and misinterpretations; don't assume anything.

- When the item you purchased arrives, inspect it thoroughly and confirm that it's as described. If you feel you were misled, contact the seller immediately, explain the situation, and see what you can work out. (You'd be surprised how many sellers will go out of their way to make their customers happy.)

- If the merchandise doesn't arrive in a timely fashion, contact the seller immediately. If the item appears to be lost in transit, track down the letter/package via the shipping service. If the item never arrives, it's the seller's responsibility to file an insurance claim with the carrier (if the item was insured), and you should receive a refund from the seller.

THE ABSOLUTE MINIMUM

Here are the key points to remember from this chapter:

- Buying an item on eBay is generally about as safe as buying something from a local garage sale—with the caveat of "buyer beware."

- To protect against unscrupulous sellers, eBay offers its Standard Purchase Protection Program, which includes $200 worth of insurance per transaction for aggrieved buyers.

- If you pay via PayPal, you may be eligible for up to $1,000 in protection from the PayPal Buyer Protection plan.

- You're better protected if you pay by credit card or use an escrow service.

- If you do get ripped off, contact eBay, your local authorities, and the FTC.

12

SNIPING TO WIN

If you have any experience with eBay auctions, you've seen the following phenomenon. On day one of the auction, there are a few initial bids. On day two, the number of new bids trails off. On days three through six, few if any bids are placed. Then, on the seventh and last day of the auction, all hell breaks loose—with the heaviest bidding taking place in the auction's final minutes.

What's happening here? It's simple: Interested bidders are employing a technique called *sniping*, and saving their best bids for last.

What Sniping Is—and How It Works

Sniping is a technique used to win auctions by not bidding at all over the course of the auction, but then swooping in at the very last minute with an insurmountable bid. The thinking behind this strategy is simple. By not disclosing your interest, you don't contribute to bidding up the price during the course of the auction. By bidding at the last minute, you don't leave enough time for other bidders to respond to your bid. The successful sniper makes one bid only—and makes it count.

Sniping happens on eBay because the end time of each auction is rigidly enforced. If you know that an auction ends at 12:01:30, you can time your snipe to hit at 12:01:29, leaving no time for any other bidders to trump your bid. Some other auction sites, such as Yahoo! Auctions, have flexible end times; if there is bidding within the last five minutes of an auction, the auction is automatically extended by another five minutes, giving extra time for other bidders to respond to a snipe.

Sniping: Pros and Cons

eBay management doesn't have an official position on sniping, although it has the company's tacit approval. Many experienced eBay users not only participate in sniping, but also regard it as a kind of game. (Sellers like sniping, of course, as long as it helps to drive up the prices of their items.) It's the community of less-experienced users—or those used to more traditional auctions—that is less likely to embrace sniping as a practice.

Most bidders who despise sniping say that it takes all the fun out of the auction process. Experienced snipers say that sniping itself is fun, that it can be kind of a game to see just how late you can bid and still make it count before the auction closes.

Whether you like it or not, sniping works. After all, if you place a high enough bid at the last second, there's no time for anyone to respond with a higher bid. The last high bidder always wins, and a sniper stands a very good chance of being the last high bidder.

Can a sniper lose an auction? Yes, under these scenarios:

- First, there might be another sniper in the queue who places a higher snipe than your maximum bid. A last-second bid of $35 will beat out a last-second bid of $30 any day.

- Second, your snipe might be too early, allowing time for the previous high bidder to receive an outbid notice and respond with a higher bid.

- Third, your snipe might not be high enough to beat out an existing high bid. (That's why I told you earlier to always bid the maximum amount you want to pay—it can ward off some cheap snipers.) If the current bid is $25 but the high bid (not known to you) is $35, you'd be beat if you "only" bid $30.

If you've ever been outbid on an item at the very last moment, you know that sniping can win auctions. Even if you hate sniping, the only way to beat a sniper is to snipe yourself.

Successful Sniping, Step-by-Step

Successful sniping requires large amounts of patience and split-second timing—but will reward you with a higher number of winning bids. Just follow these steps:

1. Identify the item you want to buy—and then *don't bid!* Resist the temptation to place a bid when you first notice an item. Make a note of the auction (and its closing time), or even put the item on your watch list; but don't let anyone else know your intentions.

2. Five minutes before the close of the auction, make sure you're logged on to the Internet, and access the auction in question.

3. Open a second browser window to the auction in question.

4. Display the Windows clock on your desktop, and configure it to display both minutes and seconds. (Or just grab a watch with a second hand or a stopwatch.)

5. In your first browser window, enter your maximum bid and click the Submit button to display the confirmation screen. *Don't confirm the bid yet!* Wait for the confirmation screen.

6. In your second browser window, click the Refresh or Reload button to update the official auction time. Keep doing this until the time remaining until close is 60 seconds.

7. Now, using either the Windows clock or your watch or stopwatch, count down 50 seconds, until there are only 10 seconds left in the auction. (You might want to confirm the synchronization midway through your countdown by refreshing your second browser window again.)

"Mike Sez"

It's a good idea to synch your Windows clock with eBay's official time. To view the current eBay time, go to cgi3.ebay.com/aw-cgi/eBayISAPI.dll?TimeShow.

8. When exactly 10 seconds are left in the auction, click the Confirm Bid button in your first browser window to send your bid.

9. Wait 10 seconds, and then click the Refresh or Reload button in your second browser window. The auction should now be closed, and (if your sniping was successful) you should be listed as the winning bidder.

Why bid 10 seconds before close? It takes about this long to transmit the bid from your computer to the online auction site and for the bid to be registered. If you bid any earlier than this, you leave time for the auction to send an outbid notice to the previous high bidder—and you don't want that person to know that until it's too late to do anything about it.

Using Automated Sniping Services and Software

If you can't personally be present to snipe at the end of an auction, check out an automated sniping program or web-based sniping service. These programs and services let you enter the item number of the auction and your maximum bid beforehand, and then go online at precisely the right time to place a last-minute snipe—even if you're not at home or you're otherwise occupied.

The best of these auto-snipe tools are listed in Table 12.1.

Table 12.1 Automated Sniping Programs and Websites

Tool	Type	Pricing	Website
Auction Sentry	Software	$14.95 ($24.95 for Deluxe edition)	www.auction-sentry.com
AuctionSniper	Web service	1% of final price ($0.25 min/$9.95 max)	www.auctionsniper.com
AuctionStealer	Web service	$8.99–$11.99/ month	www.auctionstealer.com
AuctionTamer	Software	$24.95/year	www.auctiontamer.com
BidNapper	Web service	$9.95/month	www.bidnapper.com
BidRobot	Web service	$5.00–$99.00/ month, depending on number of snipes and amount won	www.bidrobot.com
BidSlammer	Web service	$0.10/losing bid or 1% of final price ($0.25 min/$5.00 max)	www.bidslammer.com
Cricket Power Sniper	Software	$24.99	www.cricketsniper.com
eSnipe	Web service	1% of final price ($0.25 min/ $10.00 max)	www.esnipe.com
HammerSnipe	Web service	Free	www.hammertap.com/ HammerSnipe.html
Merlin Auction Magic	Software	$14.95	www.merlinsoftware.com
Vrane Sniper	Web service	Free	www.vrane.com

The Absolute Minimum

Here are the key points to remember from this chapter:

- Sniping is the art of saving your bid until the very final seconds of an auction.

- Sniping works because it doesn't tip your hand early (and thus drive up the bid price) and it doesn't allow time for competing bidders to respond to your bid.

- The best way to snipe is to open two windows on your desktop, one watching the current bid results and the other primed for your last-second bid.

- To snipe when you're away from home or asleep, use an automated sniping service or program.

13

SECRETS OF SUCCESSFUL BIDDERS

You want to be a player. You want to bid with the best of them. When you bid, you want to win. When you win, you don't want to overpay.

This is the chapter you've been waiting for. Read on to discover the secrets and strategies that will help you be a successful eBay bidder!

Secrets for Finding What You Want

We'll start out with some secrets to help you find items on which to bid. eBay's top buyers are quite adept at finding exactly what they want—and for a reasonable price!

Secret #1: Search; Don't Browse

If you know what you're looking for, don't go through the time-consuming hassle of clicking and loading and clicking and loading to access a particular item category. Using an auction's search function will find what you want a lot quicker.

Secret #2: Search Smart

Searching for an item on eBay is easy; finding what you really want is hard. You're more likely to find what you're looking for if you can use the auction site's advanced search capabilities to fine-tune your query. Some specific search tips can help you perform more effective—and efficient—searches:

- **Narrow your search.** Some of the more popular categories on eBay will list thousands of items. If you do a search on `nba`, for example, you'll be overwhelmed by the results; narrow your search within these large categories (to `nba jerseys` or `nba tickets`) to better describe the specific item you're looking for.

- **Make your queries precise—but not too precise.** When you're deciding which keywords to use, pick words that are precise, but not overly restrictive. If you must use a very general word, modify it with a more specific word—or you're apt to generate a huge number of results that have little relevance to the specific information you're searching for. As an example, `model` is a pretty general keyword; `Star Wars Death Star model` is a much more precise query. On the other hand, if you search for an `old Star Wars Death Star model partially assembled without instructions not painted`, you probably won't return any matching results. If you get few if any results, take some of the parameters out of your query to broaden your search.

- **Use wildcards.** If you're not sure of spelling, use a wildcard to replace the letters in question. Also, wildcards help you find variations on a keyword. For example, if you want Superman, Supergirl, and Superdog, enter `super*` to find all "super" words.

- **Vary your vocabulary—and your spelling.** Don't assume that everyone spells a given word the same way—or knows how to spell it properly. Also, don't forget about synonyms. What you call pink, someone else might call mauve. What's big to you might be large to someone else. Think of all the ways the item you're looking for can be described, and include as many of the words as possible in your query.

- **Fine-tune your results.** Did eBay's search engine return an overwhelming number of matching items? If so, you need to fine-tune your search to be more specific. Look at the results generated from your initial search. Think about the good matches and the bad matches and why they ended up in the results list. Then, enter a new query that uses additional or different keywords and modifiers. Your goal is to make the next list of results a higher quality than the last.

- **Different day, different results.** Remember that new items are constantly added to any given auction site, and closed auctions are constantly removed from the listings. If you didn't find anything that matched your query today, try again tomorrow; you'll probably find a different list of items for sale. (Another good reason to save your favorite searches and use eBay's email notification service.)

Secret #3: Search for Misspellings

Here's a good way to take advantage of other users' mistakes. Some eBay sellers aren't great spellers—or are just prone to typing errors. This means you'll find some items listed for auction under misspelled titles. It's not hard to find the occasional Dell personal *commuter*, Apple *ipud*, or jewel *neklace*.

The problem for these sellers—and the opportunity for you—is that when you're searching for an item (correctly), listings with misspellings won't appear in the search results. If potential bidders can't find the listings, they can't bid on them, either—leaving these misspelled listings with few if any bidders. If you can locate these misspelled listings, you can often snap up a real deal without competition from other bidders.

The key, of course, is figuring out how an item might be misspelled. Let's say you're looking for a bargain on a camcorder. Instead of searching just for camcorder, you might also search for cam-corder, camcoarder, camcarder, and camcroder. Give it a try—you'll be surprised what you find.

And if you don't want to think up all the possible misspellings yourself, you can use the Fat Fingers website (www.fatfingers.com) to do it automatically. Enter a query into the Fat Fingers search box, and it will search eBay for that phrase and phrases that contain similar misspelled words. It really works!

Secret #4: Search for Last-Minute Bargains

When you search the eBay listings, be sure to display the results with auctions ending today listed first. Scan the list for soon-to-end items with no bids or few bids, and pick off some bargains that have slipped others' attention.

Secret #5: Check the Seller's Other Current Auctions

You'd be surprised how many times a seller has more than one item you're interested in. Click the View Seller's Other Auctions link to see everything else the seller has for auction—and bid accordingly!

Secrets for Winning the Auction—At a Reasonable Price

Once you've found what you want, the next trick is to make sure you end up as the winning bidder—without overpaying. Here are some secrets that will enhance your chances of being the high bidder, without bidding too high.

Secret #6: Do Your Research

Don't bid blind; make sure you know the true value of an item before you offer a bid. Look around at auctions of similar items; what prices are they going for? And don't neglect researching outside of eBay; sometimes, you can find what you're looking for at a discount store or in a catalog or at another online site—where you'll probably get a real warranty and a better return policy. Shop around, and don't assume that the price you see at an auction is always the best deal available.

Be informed, and you won't bid too high—or too low.

Secret #7: There's More Where That Came From

In 99.9% of eBay's auctions, that "one of a kind" item really isn't one of a kind. In fact, some sellers (especially merchant sellers) will have multiple quantities of an item, which they release to auction in dribs and drabs over time. In addition, some collectibles are bought and sold and bought and sold by multiple buyers and sellers over time, continually changing hands via new auctions. If you don't get this particular item, there's a good chance you'll get to bid on something similar soon.

Along the same lines, you should never—I repeat, *never*—bid on the very first item you see. In almost all instances there are several other items on eBay similar to the first item you saw. Look at the entire list of items before you choose which one to bid on. Seldom is the first item you see the one you really want or the best deal.

Secret #8: Don't Show Your Hand

This is the first of the two key components to the sniping strategy: Don't place an early bid on an item. That just signals your interest and attracts other bidders—which results in a higher price.

Secret #9: Wait Until the Last Seconds to Bid

The second component of the sniping strategy is the snipe itself—the literal last-second bid. Wait until there are only 10–15 seconds left in an auction, and then place your best bid. By bidding so late in the process, you don't give competing bidders any time to respond. If your bid was high enough, you'll win without fear of being outbid in response.

Secret #10: Watch, Don't Bid

When it comes to not bidding (for sniping purposes), one of the key tools is eBay's Watch This Item feature. You can place any auction item on your watch list and keep tabs on the bidding while you wait to snipe. Just click the Watch This Item link on the item listing page, and then watch the items on your My eBay page.

Secret #11: Watch the Finish

Don't forget the downside to sniping—that you can be sniped, too. Don't get outbid at the last minute. Because most auction activity occurs at the very end of the auction, track the last hour of your most important auctions, and be prepared to react quickly to last-second snipers.

Secret #12: Get in Sync

When you're sniping, precision counts. Make sure that you're in sync with eBay's official clock (cgi3.ebay.com/aw-cgi/eBayISAPI.dll?TimeShow). If you're a few seconds slow, you could lose a sniping contest!

Secret #13: Look for Off-Peak Auctions

You already know that the final minute of the auction is the best time to place your bid. But are there specific times of the day that offer better bargains for bidders?

The answer, of course, is yes. Believe it or not, some sellers schedule their auctions to end in the wee hours of the morning—when there aren't a lot of bidders awake to make last-minute snipes. Look for auctions ending between midnight and 5:00 a.m. Pacific time if you want some competition-free sniping.

Secret #14: Bid in the Off Season

Although there is some category-specific seasonality, the best overall time of the year to pick up eBay bargains is during the summer months. Summer is the slowest period on eBay, which means there are fewer people bidding—and lower prices for you.

Secret #15: Put Your Best Foot Forward

When you do bid, don't weasel around. Make your bid the maximum amount the item is worth to you, and be done with it.

Secret #16: Don't Let the Proxy Bid Things Up

If two or more people are bidding on the same item, eBay's proxy bidding software can automatically (and quickly) rocket up the price until the bidder with the lower maximum bid maxes out. It's kind of an automated bidding frenzy conducted by two mindless robots.

Some bidders refuse to participate in proxy bidding. If the price is to increase, they want to do it manually. If you want to hold total control over the entire bidding process, how do you defeat the automatic bidding software? Simple: Make sure that your maximum bid is the same price as the next incremental bid and no higher. It might take a bit more work—and it's not the way I like to do things, personally—but it does put you in total control of the bidding process.

Secret #17: Know When to Say No

Be disciplined. Set a maximum price you're willing to pay for an item, and *don't exceed it!* It's okay to lose an auction.

Don't automatically rebid just because you've been outbid. It's too easy to get caught up in the excitement of a fast-paced auction. Learn how to keep your cool; know when to say no.

Secret #18: Check the Seller's Past Auctions

While you're checking up on a seller, use eBay's search function to display all the seller's completed auctions. See whether the seller has sold multiples of this particular item in the past. There's no need to get into a bidding war if the same item will come up for auction again next week.

Secret #19: Bid in Odd Numbers

When you bid, don't bid an even amount. Instead, bid a few pennies more than an even buck; for example, if you want to bid $10, bid $10.03 instead. That way, your bid will beat any bids at the same approximate amount—$10.03 beats $10 any day—without your having to place a new bid at the next whole bid increment.

> " **Mike Sez** "
>
> The "odd number bid" tip is one of the best tips in this book. I can't tell you how many auctions I've won by just pennies!

Secrets for Safer Bidding

Many would-be buyers are reticent about the whole online auction process. To that end, here is some practical advice to make bidding on eBay as safe as possible.

Secret #20: Check the Feedback

Check out the seller's feedback rating. Make sure that the seller of the item you want has a good feedback rating—and avoid any sellers who don't. You should also click the seller's numerical feedback rating to display actual comments from other users who have dealt with this user before. The best way to avoid bad sellers is to find out that they're bad sellers beforehand.

Secret #21: Ask Questions

If you're unclear about any aspect of an item you're interested in, ask the seller questions via email. In addition to answering your specific questions, some sellers have additional information or pictures they can send you one-on-one. There's no excuse for ignorance; if you're not sure, ask!

Secret #22: If It Sounds Too Good to Be True, It Probably Is

A rare copy of *Action Comics* #1 for only $25? A brand-new laptop computer for only $100? There has to be a catch. That *Action Comics* is probably a facsimile reprint, and the brand-new laptop PC is actually a remanufactured unit missing some key parts. Be suspicious of improbable or impossible deals; always ask questions that confirm or reject your suspicions.

Secret #23: Use a Middleman for Expensive Items

If you buy a high-priced item through a person-to-person auction, consider using an escrow service. Although you'll pay for the service (in the neighborhood of 5%, typically paid by you, the buyer), it's a good safety net in case the seller doesn't ship or the item isn't what was described. In addition, you can use escrow services to accept credit card payments when the seller doesn't or can't accept credit cards directly.

Secret #24: When You Win It, Inspect It

When you receive the item you paid for, open it up and inspect it—*immediately!* Don't wait a month before you look at it and then expect the seller to rectify a situation that was long considered closed. Okay the item, and then send the seller an email saying you got it and it's okay. If you sit on it too long, it's yours— no matter what.

Secret #25: If You Get Ripped Off, Tell eBay About It

If you have a problem with a seller, first try working it out between the two of you. If things don't get resolved, contact eBay with your grievance; you can use eBay's Purchase Protection Program to register your complaint and (hopefully) get reimbursed for your loss. (And don't forget to leave negative feedback on the snake who did you wrong!)

Secrets That Any Bidder Can Use

We'll end this chapter with some tips that should prove useful to any eBay bidder. Read on!

Secret #26: Use the eBay Toolbar

eBay offers a neat little add-on for your Web browser that makes it easy to track auctions you've bid on, or that are on your watch list. When you install the eBay Toolbar, it appears as part of your Web browser, under all your normal toolbars. (Figure 13.1 shows the eBay Toolbar as it appears in Internet Explorer.)

FIGURE 13.1

Track your auctions in your Web browser with the eBay Toolbar.

The eBay Toolbar also includes some other useful features, including the capability to search auction listings from the toolbar, go directly to your My eBay page, and view the top picks in selected categories. The eBay Toolbar is free, and available for downloading at pages.ebay.com/ebay_toolbar/.

Secret #27: Use My eBay to Track Your Auctions

Don't let your auction activity get away from you. If you're a regular eBay user, the best way to track all your auction activity on a single page is by using My eBay. My eBay can also track your favorite auction categories, as well as your account status—and let you access the pages you use most often, without having to click through useless parts

> **note**
>
> Learn more about My eBay in Chapter 5, "Managing Your eBay Activity with My eBay."

of the site. Personalize My eBay the way you like and then bookmark it; it's a great home page for the heavy auction trader.

Secret #28: Read the Fine Print

What methods of payment can you use? What about shipping? Any other details that might impact your decision to bid? Read the entire item listing before you place your bid—so you aren't surprised by the fine print in any auction.

Secret #29: Don't Forget Shipping Costs...

When you're placing your bid, remember that you'll actually have to pay more than you bid; you have to pay shipping and handling to put the item in your hands. If S&H costs aren't detailed in the item listing, figure them out yourself, or email the seller to get a reasonable estimate. That ultra-cheap $2 item looks pretty expensive if you have to add $5 shipping and handling to the base price.

Secret #30: ...But Don't Overpay for Shipping

Not only should you not get taken by surprise by shipping costs, but you also shouldn't be taken advantage of by unrealistic shipping and handling charges. Get a ballpark feel for shipping on a specific item from the seller's location to where you live. Expect a little overage on the seller's part (she has to buy packing materials, labels, and such), but not too much. If you know that shipping should be in the $2 range, accept a $3 charge—but question a $5 charge.

Secret #31: Pay Quickly

Don't delay—*pay!* Look, the seller needs the money, and the sooner you pay, the sooner you'll get what you paid for. (And the fastest way to pay, of course, is with your credit card, via PayPal.)

Secret #32: Don't Be a Deadbeat

Don't bid unless you really intend to buy. Nobody likes a deadbeat—and if you do it often enough, you'll get kicked off the auction site, permanently.

Secret #33: Pay by Credit Card

Now that most auctions are credit card enabled (via PayPal), use that option. Paying via credit card is relatively safe and leaves a good paper trail—and ensures that your item will be shipped quickly.

Secret #34: Money Orders Cost Money

The seller says that money orders or cashier's checks speed shipment. Depending on your bank, it might cost a few dollars to cut a money order or cashier's check. Be sure to factor these costs into your total expenditure—and question whether you really want to pay to cut a money order for a $5 item.

Secret #35: Provide All the Information Necessary

When you send your payment, be sure to include your name, shipping address, email address, and item name and description. Even better, enclose a copy of the item's Checkout or listing page, with additional information written on it. (I can't tell you how many envelopes I've opened with only a check or money order inside; you gotta tell 'em who the payment is from and what it's for!)

Secret #36: If It's Pricy, Insure It

If you bought a rare or high-priced item, ask the seller to insure the item for shipping. Pay the extra cost; it's worth it in peace of mind alone.

Secret #37: Document Everything

In case something goes south, it helps to have good records of all aspects of your transaction. Print copies of the confirmation email, plus all email between you and the seller. Be sure to write down the seller's user ID, email address, and physical address. If the transaction is ever disputed, you'll have all the backup you need to plead your case.

Secret #38: Keep a Log

Not only should you document all the correspondence for an individual auction, but you also should keep a log of all the auctions you've won. If you do a lot of bidding, it's all too easy to lose track of which items you've paid for and which you've received. You don't want to let weeks (or months!) go by before you notice that you haven't received an item you paid for!

Secret #39: Communicate!

Don't assume anything; communicate what you think you know. If you have questions during an auction, ask them. When the auction is over, email the seller. When the seller emails you, email him or her back to confirm. Email the seller when you send payment and again to confirm receipt of the item. The more everyone knows, the fewer surprises there are.

Also, remember that not everyone reads his email daily, so don't expect an immediate response. Still, if you don't receive a response, send another email. If you're at all concerned at any point, get the seller's phone number or physical address from the auction site and call or write her. A good phone conversation can clear up a wealth of misunderstandings.

> **tip**
>
> Want even more advice? Then check out my companion book, *Tricks of the eBay Masters, 2nd Edition* (Que, 2006). It's filled with 600 tricks and tips that any eBay buyer can use!

Secret #40: Be Nice

You're dealing with another human being, someone who has feelings that can be hurt. A little bit of common courtesy goes a long way. Say please and thank you, be understanding and tolerant, and treat your trading partner in the same way you'd like to be treated. Follow the golden rule; do unto other auction traders as you would have them do unto you.

THE ABSOLUTE MINIMUM

Here are the key points to remember from this chapter:

- Sniping—a literal last-second bid—is the most successful tool for winning eBay auctions.
- Keep track of items you haven't yet bid for by using the Watch This Item and My eBay features.
- When you place your bid, make it the highest amount you're willing to pay—and then walk away if the bidding goes higher.
- The best time of year to pick up good deals is during the summer.
- You can sometimes win an auction by bidding in an odd amount—$20.03 instead of $20.00, for example.
- The faster you pay, the faster you'll receive the item you won!

PART IV

SELLING MERCHANDISE ON EBAY

14

BEFORE YOU SELL: DO YOUR HOMEWORK!

Selling your first item on eBay can be a real rush—and a genuinely stressful experience. What's the right price to set? What category should it go into? What do I do if it doesn't sell—or if it does? As you gain more experience selling, you still run into a lot of these same issues. Pricing is always a guessing game, as is category placement. But as you sell more and more items on eBay, you run into a new issue: Where do you get more stuff to sell?

Now, to anyone with a garage full of junk, that might not seem like a real issue. You want more stuff to sell? Just go out to the garage and grab something! For those of you who want to make some big bucks, however, you need to find a constant flow of merchandise to put up for auction. The more you have to sell, the more money you can make.

Researching the Market

Before you determine what you want to sell on eBay, it pays to do your homework. I'm talking research here—research about what's selling, what's not, and for what price. There's a lot of research you can do for free—or you can pay for a professionally prepared analysis.

Search eBay's Completed Auctions

One of the best ways to research the market is to simply search eBay's completed auctions. (This research has the added benefit of being free.) You want to search the completed auctions for items similar to what you're thinking of selling. Examining the final results can tell you not only how popular an item is (how many bids it received—if any), but also the true worth of the item, as evidenced by the final high bid. Just make sure you click the Completed Listings box on the search page, of course.

As you compare the completed auctions, make sure that you're comparing apples to apples. You'll see wildly differing final prices for new items versus used ones, items in different conditions, items bundled with other items or accessories, items of different size or color, and items of different ages. You can't compare the value of a new item with a used one; try to find items of the same approximate age and condition when doing your comparison.

Once you've whittled your comparison list down to those auctions that are truly similar, you will immediately start to notice patterns. Some auctions end with no bids; most will have many bids. Study those successful auctions to determine what made them successful. Was it the headline, the item, the description, the price, and so on? Once you learn this technique you can study various products and get a good grasp of what's going on. Everything successful on eBay is hiding in plain sight, for all to see.

> **caution**
>
> Don't waste your time searching auctions still in progress. Because so much bidding takes place in the last hour of the auction (that's sniping, remember?), a mid-auction price is likely to bear no relation to the final price—which you can find by searching completed auctions.

Use eBay's Hot Categories Report

When you want to find out the best types of merchandise to sell, it helps to know which product categories are hot. Fortunately, eBay makes this relatively easy, with its monthly Hot Categories Report. As you can see in Figure 14.1, this list details the hottest product categories on the eBay site—which are the best categories in which to sell.

FIGURE 14.1

Find out what's hot with eBay's Hot Categories Report.

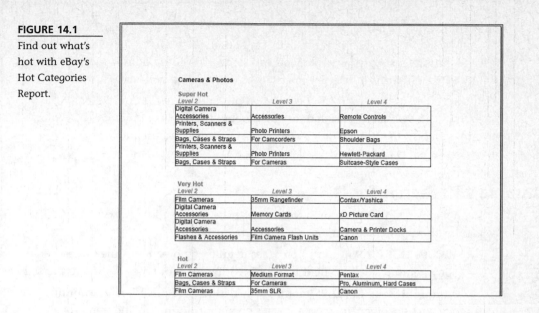

Cameras & Photos

Super Hot

Level 2	Level 3	Level 4
Digital Camera Accessories	Accessories	Remote Controls
Printers, Scanners & Supplies	Photo Printers	Epson
Bags, Cases & Straps	For Camcorders	Shoulder Bags
Printers, Scanners & Supplies	Photo Printers	Hewlett-Packard
Bags, Cases & Straps	For Cameras	Suitcase-Style Cases

Very Hot

Level 2	Level 3	Level 4
Film Cameras	35mm Rangefinder	Contax/Yashica
Digital Camera Accessories	Memory Cards	xD Picture Card
Digital Camera Accessories	Accessories	Camera & Printer Docks
Flashes & Accessories	Film Camera Flash Units	Canon

Hot

Level 2	Level 3	Level 4
Film Cameras	Medium Format	Pentax
Bags, Cases & Straps	For Cameras	Pro, Aluminum, Hard Cases
Film Cameras	35mm SLR	Canon

To access the Hot Categories Report, click the Sell link on the eBay Navigation Bar to open the Sell hub, then click the The Hot List link. Remember, the report is updated every 30 days—so check it monthly!

Search eBay's Marketplace Research Database

The Hot Categories report isn't eBay's only research tool. eBay pulls together other essential sales statistics in its Marketplace Research database, which you can search (for a fee). What sort of information are we talking about? Here's a sample, for any given item:

- Average sold price
- Sold price range
- Start price range
- Average BIN (Buy It Now) price
- BIN price range
- Average shipping cost
- Last sold price
- Last sold date/time
- Number successfully sold
- Average bids per item

Then there are the charts, including trend charts for average sold price, number successfully sold, and average bids per item; and distribution charts for average start price and number successfully sold. You can search the entire database, or filter your results by date, specific sellers, specific stores, country, and so on.

eBay's Marketplace Research can be accessed at pages.ebay.com/marketplace_research/. Three different packages are available—the Fast Pass provides $2.99 for two days' access; the Basic plan costs $9.99 per month; and the more robust Pro plan (which offers more search options) costs $24.99 per month.

Use Ándale's Research Tools

You can supplement eBay's search tools with those from Ándale (www.andale.com), a popular third-party site. Ándale's key reports include

- **What's Hot** ($3.95/month) provides detailed reports about the hottest-selling eBay items; it's an excellent tool for identifying what types of products to sell.

- **Ándale Research** ($7.95/month) provides detailed pricing reports for any specific product or category on eBay; it's good for tracking pricing trends over time and determining what day of the week to list and what initial price to set.

- **Sales Analyzer** ($5.95/month) is designed to help you better understand your own eBay sales. It provides a detailed analysis of your total sales, sell-through rate, return on investment, and other key metrics.

Figure 14.2 shows the What's Hot report, which is similar to but more detailed than eBay's Hot Categories report. I find this and the Ándale Research reports worth the money, especially if you're a high-volume seller.

FIGURE 14.2

Mine the third-party data presented in Ándale's What's Hot report.

Finding Items to Sell

Most eBay users get started by selling items they find in their attics, garages, and basements. (Makes you think of eBay as a giant garage sale, doesn't it?) But what do you do when you've completely cleaned out the attic?

There are many places to find quantities of items to sell on eBay. We'll discuss a few of the more popular ones here—although it's likely you have a few ideas of your own. Just remember that you need to buy low and sell high—so be on the lookout for places where you can buy stuff *cheap*.

You should also be on the lookout for *trends*. Just because something's hot today doesn't mean it's going to be hot tomorrow. You wouldn't have wanted to be the proud owner of a garage-full of Pokemon cards just as the Poke-bubble burst, would you? So when you're hunting for merchandise you can auction on eBay, try to stay on top of the coming trends—and don't buy in at the tail end of an old trend.

Of course, it's difficult to stay on top of the trends in thousands of different categories, even using the various research tools we previously discussed. For that reason, many eBay power sellers specialize in a half-dozen or fewer types of merchandise. You can track the trends in a handful of categories (by watching the current auctions—and the current selling prices); you can't be as aware of the trends in a larger number of categories.

So specialize, stay on top of trends, and keep your eyes open!

Garage Sales and Yard Sales

If eBay is like a giant garage sale, you might as well start with the bona fide original source. Many eBay sellers scrounge around their local garage and yard sales, looking for any merchandise that they can sell for more money on eBay. It isn't difficult; you can pick up a lot of stuff for a quarter or a dollar, and sell it for 5 or 10 times that amount online. Just be sure to get to the sale early, or all the good bargains will be picked over already!

Flea Markets

Flea markets offer merchandise similar to what you find in garage sales. The bargains might be a little less easy to come by, however, but if you keep a sharp eye you can find some items particularly suited for eBay auction.

Estate Sales

Not to be insensitive, but dead people provide some of the best deals you can find. It's the equivalent of raiding somebody else's garage or attic for old stuff to sell. Check out the weekly estate sales and auctions in your area, be prepared to buy in quantity, and see what turns up.

Live Auctions

Any live auction in your area is worth checking out, at least once. Just don't let yourself get caught up in the bidding process—you want to be able to make a profit when you resell the merchandise on eBay!

Vintage and Used Retailers

Head down to the funky side of town and take a gander at what the various "vintage" and used-merchandise retailers have to offer. These are particularly good sources of collectibles, although you might have to haggle a little to get down to a decent price.

Thrift Stores

Think Goodwill and similar stores here. You can typically find some decent merchandise at low cost—and help out a nonprofit organization, to boot.

Discount and Dollar Stores

These "big lot" retailers are surprisingly good sources of eBay-ready merchandise. Most of these retailers carry overruns and closeouts at attractive prices. You can pick up merchandise here cheap, and then make it sound very attractive in your eBay listing ("brand new," "last year's model," "sealed in box," and so on).

Closeout Sales

You don't have to shop at a cheap retailer to find a good deal. Many mainline merchants offer terrific deals at the end of a season or when it's time to get in next year's merchandise. If you can get enough good stuff at a closeout price, you have a good starting inventory for your eBay sales.

Going Out of Business Sales

Even better, look for a merchant flying the white flag of surrender. When a retailer is going out of business and says "everything must go," that means that bargains are yours to be had—and don't be afraid to try to make a lower-priced deal.

Classified Ads

This isn't as good a source as some of the others, but if you watch the classifieds on a regular basis, you might stumble over some collectibles being sold for less than the going price online. Just buy a daily newspaper and keep your eyes peeled.

Friends and Family

You can sell stuff you find in your garage—what about your neighbor's garages? Think about cutting a deal as a "middleman" to sell your friends' and family's stuff on eBay, especially if they're ignorant of the process themselves. (And remember to keep a fair share of the profits for yourself; you're doing all the work, right?)

Liquidators and Wholesalers

There are several Web sites that specialize in selling liquidated merchandise, typically in bulk lots. These items might be closeouts, factory seconds, customers returns, or overstocked items—products the manufacturer made too many of and wants to get rid of. If you're interested in investing in some liquidated merchandise to sell, some good sites to check out include Liquidation.com (www.liquidation.com), Overstock.com (www.overstock.com), and TDW Closeouts (www.tdwcloseouts.com). All of these sites offer various goods from many manufacturers. (The Overstock.com site is shown in Figure 14.3.)

In addition, many wholesalers operate over the Web, providing you the opportunity to buy large lots of new merchandise. The best way to search for a distributor is to use the directory provided by Wholesale411 (www.wholesale411.com).

> **tip**
>
> If you're looking for particular types of items to sell, check out Ándale Suppliers (www.andale.com). This is a free service that tries to match merchandise suppliers with potential buyers—like you!

FIGURE 14.3

Find closeout merchandise to resell on eBay at Overstock.com

eBay!

This leads us to the final place to look for items to sell on eBay: eBay itself! Yes, it's possible to make money buying something on eBay and then turning around and selling it to someone else on eBay later. The key is timing. Remember, you have to buy low and sell high, which means getting in at the start of a trend. It's possible—although it takes a lot of hard work, and not a little skill.

tip

If you're interested in buying large quantities for resale, check out eBay's Wholesale Lots listings (pages.ebay.com/catindex/catwholesale.html).

Picking the Right Category

This one sounds simple. You have an item, you find the category that best describes the item, and you're done with it. To be fair, sometimes it is that simple. If you have *Singin' in the Rain* on DVD, you put it in the "DVDs & Movies: DVD" category, no questions asked.

What if you have a model of an American Airlines jet? Does it go in the "Collectibles: Transportation: Aviation: Airlines: American" category, or the "Toys & Hobbies: Model, Kits: Air" category?

Where you put your item should be dictated by where the highest number of potential bidders will look for it. Search the completed auction listings to get an idea of which items are in what categories, and for those categories that have a higher success rate. In the American jet model example, if there are more bidders traipsing through the Collectibles category, put it there; if there are more potential buyers who think of this as a model toy thing, put it in that category. (In reality, you'll probably find listings for this sort of item in both categories.) Think like your potential buyers, and put it where you would look for it if you were them.

If you really can't decide—if your item really does belong in more than one category—eBay lets you list your item in two categories. It costs twice the regular listing fee, but it potentially doubles your exposure. Just scroll down to the Second Category section on the Category page, and enter a second category. Your item listing will show up in both categories, just like that.

Setting the Right Price

How should you price your item? If you set your minimum price too high, you might scare off potential buyers. If you set your minimum price too low, you'll probably get more interested bidders, but you might end up selling your item for less than you want or than what it's worth.

So what's the right starting price?

Set It Low Enough to Be Attractive...

I like setting a price that's low enough to get some interested initial bidding going, but not so low that it won't get up to the price I think the item can really sell for. So how do you know what the final selling price will be? You don't. But you can get a good idea by searching eBay for completed auctions of similar items. eBay keeps most auctions on file for 30 days, so if anything similar has sold in that period of time, you can find it from eBay's advanced search page.

At the least, you want to be sure you're not setting the starting bid higher than the similar items' final selling price. If you do a search for completed auctions and find that *Star Wars* DVDs have been selling between $4 and $6, don't put a $10 starting price on the *Star Wars* DVD you want to sell. Ignore precedence and you won't get any bids. Instead, gauge the previous final selling prices and place your starting price at about a quarter of that level. (That would be a buck or so for our *Star Wars* example.)

Of course, you can always go the reserve price auction route—in which you get to set a low initial price and a high selling floor. In our *Star Wars* example, that might mean starting bidding at a penny (very attractive to potential bidders), but setting a reserve price of $4 or so. But when you run a reserve price auction, you run a very real risk of scaring away a lot of viable bidders. If you want to run that risk, fine; reserve auctions do let you get bidding started at a very attractive level, while protecting you if bids don't rise to the price you're looking for.

...But Don't Set It So Low That It's Not Believable

In some instances you need to worry about setting the starting price too *low*. If you set too low a minimum bid for your item, some potential bidders might think that something is wrong. (It's the old "if it's too good to be true, it probably is.") Although you might assume that bidding will take the price up into reasonable levels, too low a starting price can make your item look too cheap or otherwise flawed. If you start getting a lot of emails asking why you've set the price so low, you should have set a higher price.

Make Sure You Recover Your Costs...

Another factor in setting the starting price is what the item actually cost you. Now, if you're just selling some junk you found in the attic, this isn't a big concern. But if you're selling a large volume of items for profit, you don't want to sell too many items below what you paid for them. Many sellers like to set their starting price at their item cost—so if the item cost you $5, you set the minimum bid (or reserve price) at $5, and see what happens from there.

...But Not So High That You Pay Too High a Listing Fee

Of course (and there's always another "of course"), if you set a higher starting price, you'll pay a higher insertion fee. Here's where it helps to know the breaks—in eBay's fee schedule, that is. Table 14.1 shows the fee breaks as of February 2006.

Table 14.1   eBay's Insertion Fee Breaks

Price Point	Fee
$0–$0.99	$0.20
$1.00–$9.99	$0.35
$10.00–$24.99	$0.60
$25.00–$49.99	$1.20
$50.00–$199.99	$2.40
$200.00–$499.99	$3.60
$500.00 and up	$4.80

Let's think about what this means. At the very least, you want to come in just below the fee break. Which means that you want to list at $9.99 (which incurs a $0.35 fee) and not at $10.00 (which incurs a $0.60 fee). That extra penny could cost you $0.25!

It's in your best interest to minimize any and all fees you have to pay. If you're almost positive (based on completed auction activity) that your item will sell in the $20 range no matter what you price it at, price it as low as is reasonable.

Make Sure You Can Live with a Single Bid

What happens if you set the starting price at $5 and you get only one bid—at $5? Even if you thought the item was worth twice that, you can't back out now; you have to honor all bids in your auction, even if there's only one of them. You can't email the bidder and say, sorry, I really can't afford to sell it for this price. If you listed it, you agreed to sell it for any price at or above your minimum. It's a binding contract. So if the bidding is low, you'd better get comfortable with it—it's too late to change your mind now!

> **❝ Mike Sez ❞**
>
> As a rule of thumb, I set the initial item price at 10% to 25% of what I think the final selling price will be. When faced with a choice, I almost always opt for a lower, rather than a higher, starting price.

THE ABSOLUTE MINIMUM

Here are the key points to remember from this chapter:

- Before you decide what to sell—and for how much—you should research similar items in completed eBay auctions, or using one of the many research reports and tools provided by eBay and third-party sources.

- You can find items to sell on eBay just about anywhere, from garage sales to estate auctions to dollar stores. Just remember to buy low and sell high!

- When it comes time to pick the item category, think about where the most potential buyers would think to look for that item. If you can't decide between two categories, list the item in two categories—if you can absorb the double listing fees.

- Setting the starting price for an auction is more of an art than a science. In general, lower prices are best—if you can live with an item actually selling for the minimum price.

15

SELLING ITEMS VIA ONLINE AUCTION

You've poked around eBay some. Maybe you've bid on an item or two; maybe you've even been fortunate to be the high bidder in an auction for something you really wanted. Now you're looking at your collection of…well, whatever it is you collect, and you're thinking that maybe you ought to be getting some of that online auction action.

In other words, you're ready to put your first item up for bid on eBay.

Getting Ready to List

Before you list your first item, you need to get all your ducks in a row. That means determining what you're going to sell and for how much, as well as how you're going to describe and promote the item. If you try to list an item "cold," you'll find yourself stopping and starting as you move through the listing process; you'll be constantly running around trying to gather more information or make important listing decisions on-the-fly. Better to prepare for these decisions up front, as described in the following checklist.

Checklist: Before You List an Item for Auction

☐ Make sure that the item exists and is at hand, and has been cleaned up and spruced up as much as possible. (This includes putting the item in the original box, if you have it.)

☐ Note any flaws, damages, or missing parts.

☐ Determine what you think the final selling price will be, and then choose an appropriate minimum bid price.

☐ Take a picture or a scan of the item and prepare a JPG-format file for uploading.

☐ If you're selling a commonly sold item, such as a book, CD, or DVD, write down the item's UPC number or ISBN number—this is the product code typically found on the back or bottom of the packaging.

☐ Determine what listing options you might want to purchase—such as bold-facing the title or placing the item in the Gallery.

☐ Think up a catchy yet descriptive headline for the item.

☐ Write out a detailed description of the item.

☐ Determine what payment options you'll accept. (If you haven't yet signed up with PayPal, now is the time.)

☐ Determine how you want to ship the item.

☐ Weigh the item, and then try to determine the actual shipping costs. Use that information to set an up-front shipping and handling charge, if you want.

☐ If you haven't yet registered as an eBay user and entered your credit card information, do that now.

☐ Determine what day of the week—and what time of the day—you want your auction to end.

When all this is done, *then* you can create your listing!

Getting Started: Creating an Item Listing

Remember that before you can list an item for sale, you have to be a registered eBay user. It also helps to have your credit card on file so that you can pay the fees you will soon incur. (If you need to do either of these things, turn immediately to Chapter 2, "Joining Up and Getting Started.")

Assuming you're registered and filed, now what do you do? Well, listing an item for sale on eBay is pretty simple; all you have to do is work through the following series of steps.

Step 1: Get Ready to Sell

This is the easiest thing you'll do in the whole process. All you have to do is click the Sell link in the eBay Navigation Toolbar.

Step 2: Start Creating Your Listing

eBay now displays the Sell hub, shown in Figure 15.1. This is where you start creating your listing; click the Sell Your Item button to proceed.

note

The very first time you try to sell an item, this process is subtly different. First, if you haven't already created a Seller account, you'll be asked to do so. Second, the Sell hub might only show a Sell Your Item button; clicking this button will take you to a separate Choose Selling Format page.

FIGURE 15.1

eBay's Sell hub—where you start your new auction listing.

Step 3: Choose Your Category

The next page you see, shown in Figure 15.2, helps you select the best selling category for your item.

FIGURE 15.2

Select the category and subcategory for your item.

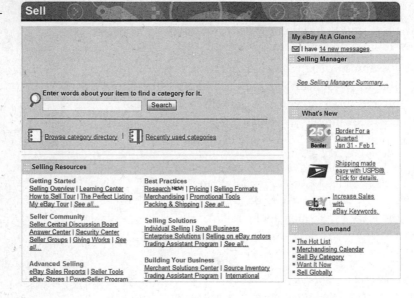

There are two ways to select a category. You can browse through all of eBay's available categories until you find the one you want, or you can let eBay suggest a category for you. We'll examine the first method first.

Browse Categories

To browse through all available categories, click the Browse Category Directory link. This displays an expanding hierarchical tree for all of eBay's major categories. Start by selecting a major category from the first category list, then select a subcategory from the next list, then a further subcategory from the next list, and so on. Continue selecting subcategories until there aren't any more subcategories to select.

tip

If you've previously listed a similar item, you can save a little time by skipping the choosing process. Just click the Recently Used Categories link and make a selection from those categories shown.

Search for Suggested Categories

A faster way to select a category is to search for it. All you have to do is enter a few descriptive keywords into the Enter Words About Your Item to Find a Category For It box, and then click the Search button. eBay now displays the Choose a Category page, as shown in Figure 15.3; select the best category from this list and click the Continue button.

Step 4: Find Your Product

Depending on the type of item you're selling, you may now see a Find Your Product window, which prompts you to enter identifying information about your item. This window is shown when you're selling certain types of commonly sold products, such as books, CDs, DVDs, video games, digital cameras, and the like.

When you enter the UPC bar code, ISBN number, model number or similar identifier for your item, eBay automatically creates your item listing with pre-filled item information. We'll discuss the pre-filled option in the "Selling Commonly Sold Items with Pre-Filled Item Information" section, later in this chapter. For now, let's assume you're listing the standard way—so, if you see the Find Your Product Window, click the Continue Without link to bypass the pre-filled information feature.

tip

Unless configured otherwise, eBay will now prompt you to select a second category for your listing. You probably don't want to do this, as listing in two categories doubles your listing fees. Just select the No Second Category option and click Continue to move on.

Step 5: Describe Your Item

The next page you see is the Describe Your Item page, shown in Figure 15.4. You use this page to enter the bulk of the information about the item you're selling.

Title and Subtitle

You start out by entering a title for your item; you can enter up to 55 characters. You can also enter a subtitle for your item (in the Subtitle box), although this will cost you an extra $0.50.

> **note**
>
> The Item Title field must contain standard numbers and text, and cannot contain any HTML code.

FIGURE 15.4
Provide a title and optional subtitle for your item.

Sell: Describe Your Item

Tell buyers about what you're selling.
- To get help: Click the name of the field or option you have a question about.
- To customize: Click a ⊕ button.

Comments   Customize   Help

Item details ⑦ ⊕ Add options

Category
- Toys & Hobbies > Models, Kits > Character Figures
Change category

Store category   Second store category
Other   -

Title
dick tracy model kit

Subtitle (fee varies)

Pictures

If you have a picture of your item and want eBay to host the picture for you, click the Add Pictures button in the Pictures section of the Describe Your item page. This displays the Add Pictures window, shown in Figure 15.5.

You can include one picture with your listing for free; additional pictures cost $0.15 apiece. To add a picture, click the appropriate Add Pictures button. When prompted, browse your hard disk for the picture you want, and then click Open to add the picture to the Add Pictures window.

> **note**
>
> The first time you use eBay Picture Services, you'll be prompted to download the necessary software. This takes but a minute, and you need it to upload your photos.

FIGURE 15.5

Adding pictures to your item listing.

The Add Pictures window offers some basic picture editing functions, which is useful if your photos aren't quite perfect. Once a picture is selected, you can rotate it; crop it; click the Auto Fix button to do a quick and automatic touchup; or click the Advanced Edit button to adjust brightness and contrast.

This is also where you select which picture options you want. The Standard option is free and gives you a 400 x 400 pixel picture at the bottom of your listing. The Supersize Pictures option costs $0.75, but lets you include a larger picture (up to 800 x 800 pixels) with a smaller click-to-enlarge thumbnail. The Picture Show option (free) lets you display multiple photos in a slideshow player. And the Picture Pack option provides a combination of Gallery, Supersize, and Picture Show features for up to six pictures, for a single $1.00 price.

tip

Listings with pictures are more successful than those without; turn to Chapter 18, "Using Pictures in Your Listings," to learn more about creating and inserting pictures for your item listings.

When you're done selecting your pictures, click the Upload Pictures button. This will upload your selected photos from your hard disk to the eBay server, and return you to the Describe Your Item page.

Item Specifics

Some categories prompt you to enter specific information in addition to your general description, via an Item Specifics section like the one shown in Figure 15.6. For example, if you're selling a DVD, you can enter the item's genre, subgenre, condition, display format (full screen or widescreen), rating, and region code. If you're selling a digital camera, you're asked for the camera's type, brand, resolution, condition, and other features. Entering these details is optional, but it provides useful information for potential buyers.

tip

If you want to host your pictures on another web server (instead of via eBay Picture Services), click the Host My Own Picture link in the Add Pictures window. This displays a new page where you can enter the picture file's web address. Or, if you've added pictures via HTML code in your item description, select the option The Description Already Contains a Picture URL for My Item. See Chapter 18 for more details on choosing a server to host the pictures for your auction listings.

FIGURE 15.6
Enter item specifics.

Description

Next up is the Item Description box, shown in Figure 15.7. This is where you enter a description—of any length—of the item you're selling. Provide as much information as you feel appropriate, and then format the text as you like. (You can even enter raw HTML code, by clicking the View HTML link.) Preview your formatted description by clicking the Preview Description button.

FIGURE 15.7
Enter a detailed description of your item.

Listing Designer

As you can see in Figure 15.8, eBay lets you create fancy listings without the need for additional listing creation software—for a paltry $0.10 per listing. It's a two-part process; you start by selecting a theme, and then choose what kind of picture layout you want. The themes are pretty simple, with different borders and colors. The layouts affect the placement of your pictures—on the left, right, top, or bottom. When you select a layout, it's previewed in a thumbnail to the right of the Theme list.

FIGURE 15.8

FIGURE 15.8

Creating a fancy listing with eBay's Listing Designer.

Visitor Counter

To display a hit counter (free, from Ándale) at the bottom of your listing, pull down the Visitor Counter list and select either Ándale Style or Green LED. If you don't want to display a counter, select the blank option from the list.

Selling Format and Price

Next, you need to determine what type of auction to launch, and for how long.

To select the auction type, pull down the first list shown in Figure 15.9. You can choose from several types of selling formats—although not options are displayed for all users. (For example, you only see the Store Inventory option if you have your own eBay Store.) The possible formats include:

FIGURE 15.9

Decide what type of auction listing to create.

- **Online Auction**. This is eBay's traditional auction format; you'll probably choose this option.

- **Fixed Price**. Choose this option only if you want to sell your item at a fixed price. (Items listed in eBay's Fixed Price Format appear in all item listings and searches, but users can't bid on them; they can only use the Buy It Now option.)

- **Store Inventory**. This option is available if you already have an eBay Store, and wish to add an item to its inventory.

- **Real Estate**. Choose this option if you want to create a real estate listing, instead of a typical auction.

Most users will choose the Online Auction option.

Now you have to set the starting (initial bid) price for your auction, as well as enter the reserve price or Buy It Now price (if you choose to use these options). For a normal, non-reserve, non-BIN (Buy it Now) auction, just enter a single price into the Starting Price box.

Enter the quantity you have to sell (typically "1"), and then pull down the Duration list and select how long you want your auction to run. The typical auction runs seven days, although you can choose from 1-, 3-, 5-, 7-, or 10-day auctions. (A 10-day auction costs $0.40 extra.)

Finally, you can choose to donate some of your auction proceeds to a designated non-profit organization. Select which non-profit you want and the percent you want to donate, then continue scrolling down the page.

> **note**
>
> Items listed in the Fixed Price Format are charged the same insertion and final value fees as regular auction items.

> **tip**
>
> Depending on how descriptive your title is, eBay may display information regarding the final selling prices of similar items. Use this information to help set your item's starting price.

Payment Methods Accepted

The next section, shown in Figure 15.10, is where you select which payment options you accept. You can opt for payment by PayPal, Money Order/Cashier's Check, Personal Check, or Other. (If you choose the Other option, be sure to describe your payment options in the Description section of your item listing.)

If you accept PayPal payments, you'll need to
enter your email address into the Email Address
for receiving Payment box. (PayPal identifies
members by their email addresses.) With this
information entered, eBay can route any credit
card payments to the correct PayPal account—
yours.

Shipping

Next up on the page is the Shipping section,
shown in Figure 15.11. This section is a bit of the
process, so follow along carefully:

- If you want to charge a flat shipping rate,
  pull down the Cost list, select Flat Same
  Cost to All Buyers, then click the Apply button. Then pull down the Domestic Shipping
  Services list, select a shipping service, and
  enter your shipping/handling cost into the
  adjacent box.

- If you want to charge a variable shipping
  rate based on the buyer's location—which
  displays eBay's Shipping Calculator in your
  listing—pull down the Cost list and select
  Calculated: Based on Buyer's Address and
  then click the Apply button. Next, pull down
  the Package Size list and select the type of
  package you have; pull down the Estimated
  Weight list and select the proper weight of
  the package; pull down the Domestic

" Mike Sez "

The most common
duration for an eBay
auction is 7 days. Unless you're in
a rush for cash (or are up against
some other deadline), there is no
reason to go for any auction lasting less than a week. On the
other hand, 10 days is probably
overkill, given that so much bidding takes place in the auction's
final minutes. The best option is
the 7-day auction, which exposes
your item to a week's worth of
bidders.

note

Learn more about
PayPal and other payment
methods in Chapter 19,
"Accepting PayPal and Other
Methods of Payment."

Shipping Services list and select which shipping service to use; then enter your added handling charge (if any) into the Package & Handling box.

If you plan on offering shipping outside the U.S., pull down the International Shipping Services list, select a shipper, and (if necessary) enter the shipping charge into the adjacent box. Make sure you check those regions to which you'll ship, in the Shipping Locations section.

Finally, if you have multiple items for sale and are willing to offer a shipping discount to anyone purchasing more than one item, check the Shipping Discount box.

Additional Information

Finally, we reach the bottom of the Describe Your Item page, shown in Figure 15.12. If you accept returns from your customers, check the Returns Accepted box, then enter/select the appropriate information regarding your returns policy.

When you're done, double-check your work on the page and click the Continue button.

note

Learn more about using eBay's Shipping Calculator—and determining shipping costs—in Chapter 23, "Packing and Shipping Your Items—Cheaply and Safely."

FIGURE 15.12

Enter your returns policy, if you have one.

Step 6: Review and Enhance Your Listing

The next page, shown in Figure 15.13, offers you the opportunity to enhance your auction listing in various ways, and then to review the results. Know, however, that these listing enhancements cost extra; choose too many and you'll wipe out your potential profit. To that end, Table 15.1 presents a list of the available listing enhancements, along with some advice as to which might be worth the money.

FIGURE 15.13

Choose various extra-charge listing enhancements.

Table 15.1 eBay Listing Enhancements

Listing Enhancement	Description	Cost	Recommendation
Gallery Picture	Displays a picture of your item on all search results pages	$0.35	Yes, especially if your item is highly visual
Subtitle	Displays a subtitle below the main title	$0.50	No, unless your item needs extra descriptive space
Gift Icon	Displays a gift icon beside your listing on all search results pages	$0.25	No, unless it's around the holidays and you offer gift wrapping and delivery to recipient's address
Bold	Displays your listing in bold on all search results pages	$1.00	No, very little bang for the buck
Border	Displays a border around your listing on all search results pages	$3.00	No, very little bang for the buck
Highlight	Displays a colored highlight behind your listing on all search results pages	$5.00	No, very little bang for your buck
Featured Plus!	Displays your item in the Featured Items section on the appropriate major category page, as well as in the Featured Items section at the top of any search results page	$19.95	No, unless the category is very crowded and you want (and can afford) premium placement
Gallery Featured	Periodically displays your item in the special Featured section at the top of the Gallery view	$19.95	No, unless the category is very crowded and you want (and can afford) premium placement
Home Page Featured	Periodically displays your item on eBay's home page	$39.95	No, too little exposure for a large expense

Below all the listing enhancements is the Review Your Listing section, shown in Figure 15.14. If you like what you see here, review your fees (below the preview) and click the List Item for Sale button. This will launch your auction.

FIGURE 15.14
Confirm your list-
ing before you
submit it.

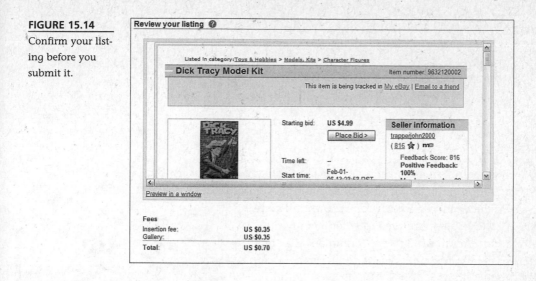

Step 7: You're Done!

When you're all done, eBay displays the Congratulations page. This page confirms your listing and presents you with important details about your auction—including your item listing's URL, in case you want to publicize your auction elsewhere on the Internet.

After you see the Congratulations screen, your completed listing should appear immediately on the eBay website—although it might take a few hours to be listed in the appropriate category listings.

Selling Commonly Sold Items with Pre-Filled Item Information

Back in step 4 we discussed the Choose a Listing Option page. If you recall, you had two options to choose from: listing the standard way or listing with pre-filled item information. Let's discuss that pre-filled option now.

eBay has created a huge database of commonly sold products—books, audio books, audiocassettes, CDs, DVDs, and various consumer electronics products. If you're selling one of these items, you can have eBay create your item description for you, using the information stored in its database—and add a stock photo of the item, as well. All you have to do is tell eBay what you're selling, and eBay will do the hard work for you. (Figure 15.15 shows an item listing with eBay's pre-filled information and product photo.)

FIGURE 15.15
Let eBay provide
the item informa-
tion for you.

Description

Black Cadillac [ECD]

Item Specifics - Music: CDs
Artist: **Rosanne Cash**   Release Date: **Jan 24, 2006**
Format: **CD**   Record Label: **Capitol/EMI Records**
Genre: **Rock & Pop**   UPC: **094634873802**
Sub-Genre: **--**   Album Type: **Full-Length CD**
                                      Condition: **New**

Stock Photo
Portions of this page Copyright 1948 - 2006 Muze Inc. **muze** All rights reserved.
Additional information

It all starts when you choose a product category for your listing. It the item you're selling is part of eBay's pre-filled information database, you'll see a Find Your Product window, like the one shown in Figure 15.16. You're prompted to enter identifying information, which—depending on what type of item you're selling—might be the item's model number, title, artist, director, author, UPC, or ISBN code. Enter the appropriate information, then click the Search button.

You now see a list of matching items, like the one in Figure 15.17. All items matching your search are displayed here; check your particular item, then click the Save Selection button.

> **tip**
>
> The most accurate way to search is via the item's UPC code—or, if you're selling a book, via the ISBN, which is typically found on the back or inside cover.

FIGURE 15.16
Enter identifying
information in
the Find Your
Product window.

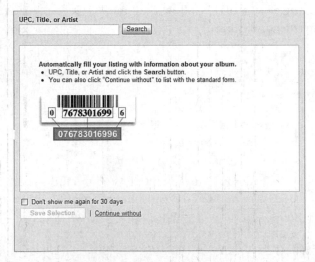

UPC, Title, or Artist
[   ] [Search]

Automatically fill your listing with information about your album.
• UPC, Title, or Artist and click the **Search** button.
• You can also click "Continue without" to list with the standard form.

```
0 | 7678301699 | 6
```
076783016996

☐ Don't show me again for 30 days
[Save Selection] | Continue without

FIGURE 15.17

Select the exact item you want to sell.

UPC, Title, or Artist		Sort	
rosanne cash	Search	Title: Ascending	

ⓘ Show: All albums

28 albums found for **Artist: rosanne cash**

○ **10 Song Demo**
Rosanne Cash
CD, 2003
UPC 724383239023

○ **Black Cadillac**
Rosanne Cash
CD, 2006
UPC 724357762724

☐ Don't show me again for 30 days

Save Selection | Continue without

eBay now moves to the standard Describe Your Item page, but with the item title and other details already entered. You'll want to review the pre-filled information to make sure it's accurate; you can choose to *not* include this information by unchecking the Include the Following Product Information in My Listing option.

You'll note that eBay adds its database information outside the standard item description area, which means you can still enter your item description into the Description box, if you want. I typically use the item description box to provide any personal details about the particular item I'm selling—if it's used, worn, damaged, or so on. From here, you should continue with the balance of the item listing process, as normal.

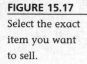

" Mike Sez "

I like using eBay's pre-filled item information, especially when I'm selling books, CDs, and DVDs. eBay's database includes a lot more information than I'm willing to type by hand—and it saves me from capturing and uploading a product photo. It's a real time-saver!

Dealing with Different Types of Auctions

As you've worked your way through eBay's item listing process, you've discovered that there are some variations on the main auction theme—in particular, reserve price and Dutch auctions. (There's also the option of including a Buy It Now price, which we'll discuss in Chapter 16, "Selling Items at a Fixed Price.") Each of these variations requires a slightly different listing approach, which we'll discuss next.

Set a Higher Minimum with a Reserve Price Auction

A reserve price auction is one in which your initial bid price really isn't the minimum price you'll accept. Even though bids might exceed the initial bid price, if they don't hit your reserve price, you don't have to sell.

Many buyers—especially those just getting started—don't like reserve price auctions, and shy away from them. That's probably because they appear more complicated than regular auctions (and they are, just a little), and also because the reserve price is never disclosed to bidders. In this case, lack of familiarity definitely breeds contempt, at least from a certain class of bidders.

But there's something to the confusion factor. Let's say you set a minimum price of $5 for an item (really low, to get a buzz going and attract some early bidders) but a reserve price of $50 (because that's what you believe the item is really worth). If the high bidder bids $25, that bid doesn't win—because it's less than the $50 reserve. Unfortunately, bidders have no idea how much more to bid to hit the undisclosed reserve price. Messy and confusing, eh?

Why, then, would you opt for a reserve price auction? There are two possible scenarios:

- When you're unsure of the real value of an item—and don't want to appear to be asking too much for an item—you can reserve the right to refuse to sell the item if the market value is below a certain price.

- When you want to use a low initial bid price to get the bidding going more quickly than if the true desired minimum price (now the reserve price) was listed; the reserve price still guarantees that you won't have to sell below a minimum acceptable price.

If you insist on running a reserve price auction, it's easy enough to do. On the Describe Your Item page, scroll down to the Selling Format section and enter a price (higher than your Starting Price) in the Reserve Price box. That's all you have to do; after that, the auction runs as normal—or as normal as a reserve price auction gets.

tip

If your auction ends and the high bid is below your reserve price, you don't have to do anything—you are not obligated to sell the item. However, you may want to use the Second Chance link on the item listing page to contact the high bidder and see whether he or she is willing to pay the reserve price for the item, or perhaps you can negotiate a fair price in between the high bid and your reserve. If you don't want to do this, you can always *relist* the item in a new auction, in the hope that a new round of bidders will push the price up to what you expect to receive. If you do relist, however, you might want to edit the item's description to make it more appealing, or even rethink your reserve price to make the item more affordable.

Remember, if no one bids the reserve price or higher, no one wins.

Sell Larger Quantities with a Dutch Auction

When should you place a Dutch auction? Simple: when you have more than one copy of an item to sell.

Dutch auctions are those in which you have more than one quantity of an identical item to sell. It's great if you have a dozen Scooby Doo PEZ dispensers, 10 copies of *Lord of the Rings* on DVD, or a hundred units of bright orange extra-large boxer shorts to sell.

To set up a Dutch auction, all you have to do is enter a quantity greater than 1 in the Quantity box in the Selling Format section of the Describe Your Item page. When you do this, eBay automatically registers your auction as a Dutch auction.

The way Dutch auctions work is a little complicated, so I'll refer you to the explanation in Chapter 8, "Bidding in Online Auctions." Suffice it to say that the highest bidder always wins something—but doesn't always have to pay the highest price. To be precise, all bidders pay the lowest winning price, even if they bid higher. (I told you it was complicated!)

In any case, eBay handles all the details automatically as long as you specify multiple quantities.

Managing Your Item Listing

When your listing is complete, the auction itself begins. But what if, for whatever reason, you need to make a change to your listing—or cancel the auction altogether?

Editing Your Listing

One thing I heartily recommend doing is to look over your ad carefully after you've posted it. Maybe you like it—great. Maybe you don't—not so great. Fortunately, if you don't like your listing, eBay lets you revise it.

If you haven't received any bids yet (and there's more than 12 hours left before the end of your auction), you can edit anything you want about your listing—the title, description, pictures, starting price, you name it. If the item *has* received a bid, you can only add information to your description—you can't change the existing description or other information. (And if there's less than 12 hours left, you're stuck—you can't change anything.)

To edit your listing, go to your item listing page and click the Revise Your Item link (located at the top of your listing, just below the item title). This leads you to an editing screen where you can change whatever information you want.

Canceling an Auction

What if your auction starts and you decide you really don't want to sell that item? You need a good excuse, but you *can* cancel eBay auctions.

Canceling an auction is a two-step process:

1. **Cancel any existing bids on your item.** Go to the Bid Cancellation page (offer.ebay.com/ws/eBayISAPI.dll?CancelBidShow—or go to the Site Map page and click Cancel Bids on Your Listing) and cancel the first bid on your item. Then return to this page as many times as necessary to cancel all the outstanding bids.

2. **Officially end your auction.** (You can't end an auction that has open bids, which is the reason you had to cancel all the bids first.) Go to the End My Listing page (cgi3.ebay.com/aw-cgi/ eBayISAPI.dll?EndingMyAuction—or go to the Site Map page and click End Your Listing) and enter the auction item number. Click the Continue button to proceed, and then click the End Auction button to officially cancel your auction.

Blocking Buyers

Here's something else you'll eventually run into. Not every member of eBay is worth dealing with. When you run into a deadbeat bidder or otherwise slimy customer in one of your auctions, you don't want to have to deal with that person *again*. The best way to remove this person from your life is to block that bidder from all your future auctions.

To block a bidder, you have to add that user to your Blocked Bidder/Buyer List. Follow these steps:

1. From the Site Map page, click the Block Bidder/Buyer list link (or go directly to pages.ebay.com/services/buyandsell/biddermanagement.html).

> **"Mike Sez"**
>
> You can also use the bid canceling feature to delete bids from undesirable bidders. Let's say you stipulated in your item listing that your auction is for U.S. bidders only, and you discover that someone from Japan has placed a bid. Just cancel the bid. (And maybe email the bidder and tell him why.) Or maybe you stated that you only wanted bidders with positive feedback, and a no-feedback newbie (or below-zero slime) places a bid anyway. Just cancel the bid. (And no emails are necessary!)

2. When the Bidder/Buyer Management page appears, click the Add an eBay User to My Blocked Bidder/Buyer List link.

3. When the Blocking a Bidder/Buyer page appears, as shown in Figure 15.18, add the buyer's user name to the list; separate multiple names with commas.

4. Click the Submit button when done.

FIGURE 15.18

Blocking unwanted bidders from your auctions.

Blocking a bidder/buyer:
Enter the User IDs of the eBay members you wish to block in the box below and click the Submit button.

Note:
- Separate User IDs with a comma, semicolon, blank space, or use the Enter key.
- You can block up to 1000 User IDs

Removing a bidder/buyer from your "blocked" list:
In the box below, delete the User ID(s) you wish to remove from the list, and click the Submit button.

Note:
- Inform the eBay members after lifting the block so that they can resume bidding on your items.

Blocked Bidder/Buyer list:

Submit

You can remove blocked buyers from your list at any time. Just return to the Blocking a Bidder/Buyer page and delete the user name you want to unblock, and then click Submit.

Relisting an Item

This is maybe getting a little ahead of things, but it's a good place to talk about the subject. What happens if your auction ends and you don't have any bidders?

The answer is simple: If at first you don't succeed, try, try again!

When you relist an unsold item, eBay automatically issues a refund for the second insertion fee, assuming the following conditions are met:

- You didn't receive any bids on a regular (no-reserve) auction or, in a reserve price auction, you didn't receive any bids that met or exceeded your reserve price.

  or

  The original buyer backed out of the deal, resulting in your filing an Unpaid Item alert.

- You are relisting an item within 90 days of the closing date of the first auction.

■ If you're relisting a reserve price auction, the new reserve price is the same as or lower than the original reserve price.

One last thing. If your item *doesn't* sell the second time, eBay won't waive the insertion fee. In other words, if you have a real loser item, eBay won't give you a free ride!

To relist an item, follow these steps:

1. Go to the item listing page for your completed auction, and click the Relist Your Item link.

2. Proceed through the normal listing creation procedure. Your information from the previous listing will already be entered, although you can make any changes you want for this new listing.

eBay will refund your listing fee for this second listing time, although you'll still be charged a final value fee if it sells. (That's only fair.) If your item *doesn't* sell the second time around, there's no third chance.

> **caution**
>
> You can't take advantage of the relisting offer if you tried to sell a fixed-price item at your eBay Store.

Five Common Selling Mistakes

You'll learn some tips for being a better seller in Chapter 26, "Secrets of Successful Sellers." But let's take a moment and examine some of the things you can do *wrong*—actions that can keep you either from selling your item or from getting the highest possible final price.

> **"Mike Sez"**
>
> If your item didn't sell the first time around, there was probably a good reason for it—maybe the starting price was too high, or the description stank, or you didn't include a picture. When you relist an item, take the opportunity to spruce up the listing, revisit the pricing, and so on, to try to make the item more attractive to potential bidders.

Mistake #1: List in the Wrong Category

You have to put your item where people will expect to see it. The problem is that eBay has all those categories—almost too many of them, especially if you're not sure just what it is you're selling.

If you list your item in the wrong category, many people looking for that type of item simply won't see it. Take the time to search for similar items currently on auction, and see what category they're listed in. Go where the others go—and, if you're still not sure, use the second category option to list in *two* different categories!

Mistake #2: Set Too High a Starting Price

I know that you want to get as high a price as possible for the item you're selling. But if you try to start the bidding at too high a level, you'll scare off potential bidders—especially if your idea of a fair price is higher than the going market price. It's better to start with a lower starting price and let the bidding take the price to its natural level. Or, if you honest-to-goodness don't want to sell at too low a price, use the reserve price option to protect yourself if the bidding doesn't go high enough.

Mistake #3: Don't Adequately Describe the Item

Let's face it. People shopping on eBay are bidding on items more or less sight unseen—so you have to help them feel comfortable about what they're bidding on. That means describing the item in words, to the best of your abilities. The better you describe the item, the more comfortable potential bidders will feel about it—and the more likely you'll be to sell the thing.

And describing the item also means describing its faults. If you're selling a used or distressed item, you better let potential bidders know about all the dings and dents. You most certainly don't want to misrepresent what you're selling—so be up-front about every little thing.

Mistake #4: Don't Include a Picture

It's a fact. Auction listings with pictures are more likely to sell than those without. Don't include a picture, and you start the auction with two strikes against you. Don't make this all-too-common mistake; get out your digital camera and start snapping—before you create your item listing!

Mistake #5: Don't Charge Enough Shipping and Handling

Oh, how many times I've been burned by not charging enough shipping and handling! This is probably *the* most common seller mistake. You want to include a flat shipping and handling charge in your item listing, so you do a little homework, weigh the item, look up the shipping rate on the postal service site, and enter a number. But when you take the item to the post office, you find your guesstimate to be off by a buck or two, and you end up eating that additional shipping cost. The difference might even be big enough that you end up losing money on the transaction.

How do you avoid this problem? First, be sure to weigh the item ahead of time—don't just guess at the weight. And don't stop at weighing just the item; you also have to weight the box you'll ship it in, and all the packing materials. (And that includes those Styrofoam peanuts or shredded newspapers you pack inside the box.) Then be sure to pick the appropriate shipping method (don't change your mind after you've placed the listing!), and the correct distance.

Ah, the correct distance—now there's a problem! You know your ZIP code, but you don't know the buyer's ZIP code—because you don't know who the buyer will be. This is one very good reason to use eBay's Shipping Calculator. As you'll learn in Chapter 23, the Shipping Calculator does the distance calculation for you, so you don't have to guess at a flat shipping and handling charge.

The lesson here? When it comes to shipping and handling charges, *don't guess!* Or if you absolutely, positively have to guess, guess high. The best answer, though, is to figure out the weight ahead of time, and then use the eBay Shipping Calculator.

The Auction's Over! Now What?

The days go by, and finally your auction is over. If you're fortunate, you've received a high bid that far exceeds your opening bid or reserve price—which means that you have a buyer.

The question is, now what do you do?

You've sat around watching the bidding for seven days or so, but now it's time to go to work. You need to contact the high bidder, figure out the final selling price (including shipping and handling), deal with the payment process, pack the darned thing up and ship it out, sit around for another couple of days hoping it gets to where it's going in one piece, and then leave feedback for the buyer. Whew! That sounds like a lot of hard work—and it is.

To learn about the post-auction process in more detail, turn to Chapter 21, "After the Sale: Concluding the Transaction." And to learn more about how to ship items to buyers, turn to Chapter 23, "Packing and Shipping Your Items—Cheaply and Safely."

THE ABSOLUTE MINIMUM

Here are the key points to remember from this chapter:

- Before you sell an item, you have to be a registered eBay user and have a credit card on file.

- To start an auction for an item, click the Sell link on the Navigation Bar, and work your way through the following pages to create your item listing.

- You can choose from 1-, 3-, 5-, 7-, or 10-day auctions—although the default 7-day auction is the most popular.

- You can opt to run a traditional online auction, or utilize the reserve price or Dutch auction options.

- If you're selling a commonly sold item, you can have eBay fill in the product details for you—all you have to do is enter the item's UPC/ISBN number or name.

- When the auction is over, you'll be notified by eBay; you then should contact the buyer and communicate payment and shipping terms and information.

16

SELLING ITEMS AT A FIXED PRICE

Most users buy and sell on eBay via the traditional online auction format. That doesn't mean you *have* to sell your items via the online auction format, however. eBay offers several different ways for you to sell items at a fixed price, without doing the whole auction thing. Read on to learn more.

Add Fixed-Price Selling to Your Auctions with Buy It Now

eBay's Buy It Now (BIN) option lets you add a fixed-price option to your auction list-ings. The way BIN works is that you name a fixed price for your item; if a user bids that price, the auction is automatically closed and that user is named the high bid-der. Note, however, that the BIN price is active only until the first bid is placed. If the first bidder places a bid lower than the BIN price, the BIN price is removed and the auction proceeds normally.

Why would you add the BIN feature to your auction? I find that many sellers who use BIN are retailers with a large quantity of similar inventory. That is, they're likely to place the same item up for auction week after week; in this scenario, the BIN price becomes the de facto retail price of the item.

You might also want to consider BIN around the Christmas holiday, when buyers don't always want to wait around seven days to see whether they've won an item; desperate Christmas shoppers will sometimes pay a premium to get something *now*, which is where BIN comes in.

You activate BIN when you're creating your item listing, in the Selling Format sec-tion of the Describe Your Item page, as shown in Figure 16.1. Just enter your BIN price into the Buy It Now Price box. And remember: Your BIN price should be higher than your Starting Price.

FIGURE 16.1

Enter a BIN price when creating an auction listing.

Know, however, that using the BIN option costs more than running a traditional auction. Adding a Buy It now price to your auction will cost

- an additional $0.05 for a BIN price between $0.01 and $9.99
- an additional $0.10 for a BIN price between $10.00 and $24.99
- an additional $0.20 for a BIN price between $25.00 and $49.99
- an additional $0.25 for a BIN price over $50.00.

Creating Fixed-Price Listings—No Bidding Required

eBay also offers the option of running straight fixed-price listings, with no bidding allowed. These listings look and feel pretty much like standard auction listings, and run for the same length as a standard auction, but feature only the Buy It Now purchase option. Potential buyers can't place bids on these items; they can only purchase the item at a fixed price by clicking the Buy It Now button.

To launch a fixed-price listing, start by creating a new item listing as you normally would. When you get to the Selling Format section of the Describe Your Item page, use the pull-down menu to select Fixed Price. Enter your desired selling price into the Buy It Now Price box, and then complete your listing as normal. That's all you have to do; the first buyer to click the Buy It Now button purchases the item.

> ## " Mike Sez "
>
> There's no sense using Buy It Now if you're not going to make any more money from it than you would a normal auction. If you want to use Buy It Now, set a BIN price 20% or so *above* your most wildly optimistic selling price. (So if you think your item might possibly, if all the stars align properly, sell for $10, set a BIN price of $12.) That way if an enthusiastic buyer does end your auction prematurely, you'll be well compensated for it.

Fixed-Price Selling with an eBay Store

If you have a lot of items for sale on a regular basis, you might want to consider opening an eBay Store. An eBay Store is a online storefront you can use to sell additional fixed-price merchandise, in addition to your regular auction items. If you're a heavy seller thinking of making the move into real honest-to-goodness online retailing, creating an eBay Store is a relatively painless way to start (see Figure 16.2).

FIGURE 16.2
The author's eBay Store.

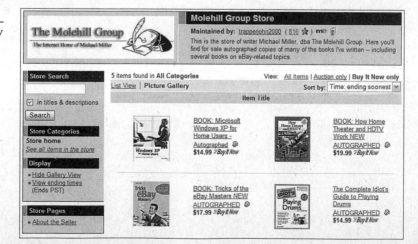

Do You Qualify?

Just about any seller can open an eBay Store. All you have to do is meet the following criteria:

- Be a registered eBay seller, with a credit card on file
- Have a feedback rating of 20 or more, or be ID verified
- Have a PayPal account (in order to accept credit-card sales)

Given these light requirements, you can see that you don't actually have to be a big traditional retailer to open an eBay Store. Any individual meeting the requirements can also open an eBay Store, thus making eBay Stores a great way for entrepreneurial types to get started in retailing.

Why would you want to open your own eBay Store? Well, it certainly isn't for casual sellers; you do have to set up your own web page, and keep the store filled with merchandise. But if you're a high-volume seller who specializes in a single category (or even a handful of categories), there are benefits to opening your own store. These include being able to sell more merchandise (through your store) than you can otherwise list in auctions; being able to display a special eBay Stores icon next to all of your auction lists; and being able to generate repeat business from future sales to current purchasers.

> **tip**
>
> Another benefit of selling merchandise in an eBay Store is that eBay will automatically advertise items from your store on the Bid Confirmation and Checkout Confirmation pages it displays to bidders in your regular auctions. These "merchandising placements" help you cross-sell additional merchandise to your auction customers.

> **" Mike Sez "**
>
> eBay Stores are great for small merchants who don't otherwise have a Web presence. They're overkill for the casual seller, however—and probably not worth the effort for larger retailers.

The Costs of Running an eBay Store

Naturally, it costs money to open an eBay Store. (eBay isn't in this for the betterment of mankind, after all.) You pay a monthly fee to be an eBay Store merchant, and there are three subscription levels to choose from, as shown in Table 16.1.

Table 16.1 eBay Stores Subscription Levels

Subscription	Price	Description
Basic	$15.95/month	Store listed in every category directory where you have items listed; position based on number of items listed; receive monthly store reports; send 100 emails a month to buyers; create 5 customizable pages; free subscription to eBay Selling Manager
Featured	$49.95/month	All features of Basic, plus store rotated through a special featured section on the eBay Stores home page; store receives priority placement in Related Stores section of search and listings pages; store featured within the top-level category pages where you have items listed; cross-sell products on view item pages; receive more detailed monthly reports; create 10 customizable pages; send 1,000 emails a month to buyers; and you get a free subscription to Selling Manager Pro and $30/month to spend on the eBay Keywords program
Anchor	$499.95/month	All features of Featured, plus premium placement in Related Stores section of search and listings pages; your store logo rotates through category directory pages (1 million impressions); send 4,000 emails a month to buyers; create 15 customizable pages; and you get dedicated 24-hour live customer support and $100/month to spend on the eBay Keywords program

You also have to pay eBay for each item you list and each item you sell—just as in a normal auction. The difference is you're not listing for a (relatively short) auction; you're listing for longer-term inventory. While eBay provides a detailed fee schedule, it pretty much boils down to paying $0.02 per month for each item listed in your eBay Store. If you list an item for 60 days, you pay $0.04; if you list an item for 90 days, you pay $0.06.

And, of course, for every item you sell in your eBay Store, eBay charges a final value fee. Table 16.2 lists the eBay Stores final value fees.

Table 16.2 eBay Stores Final Value Fees

Closing Value	Fee
$0.01–$25	8%
$25–$1,000	8% on first $25 *plus* 5% on remaining balance
$1,000 and up	8% on first $25 *plus* 5% on the part between $25.01 and $1,000 *plus* 3% on the remaining balance

eBay Stores also offers a full assortment of listing upgrades, just like the ones you can use in regular eBay auctions. These enhancements—gallery, bold, highlight, and so on—are priced according to the length of your listing. You can also offer multiples of the same item in Dutch auction format.

Setting Up Your eBay Store

Opening your own eBay store is as easy as going to the eBay Stores home page (stores.ebay.com), clicking the Open a Store button, and then following the onscreen instructions. There's nothing overly complex involved; you'll need to create your store, customize your pages (otherwise known as your virtual storefront), and list the items you want to sell. Just follow the onscreen instructions, and you'll have your own store up and running in just a few minutes.

> **note**
>
> Learn more about setting up your own eBay Store in my companion book, *Making a Living from Your eBay Business* (Que, 2005).

Fixed-Price Selling on Half.com

eBay isn't just eBay. The eBay corporation also owns a site called Half.com (half.ebay.com), which lets anyone sell certain types of merchandise in a fixed-price format. List your items for sale, wait for someone to buy them, and then collect the money. In this respect Half.com works a lot like the Amazon Marketplace—which, by the way, is another viable place for you to sell your stuff, if you're interested.

As you can see in Figure 16.3, Half.com specializes in specific types of merchandise: books, CDs, DVDs, videotapes, video games, and game systems. Buyers can purchase items from multiple sellers, and have all their purchases consolidated into a single shopping cart and checkout. They make one payment, then eBay deposits funds into each seller's account individually.

> **note**
>
> Learn more about Half.com from a buyer's perspective in Chapter 9, "Buying Fixed-Price Items."

To sell on Half.com, all you have to do is click the Sell Your Stuff link at the top of the page. When the Sell Your Items page appears, as shown in Figure 16.4, you can click a category link for your item, or enter the item's UPC, ISBN, or model number in the Quick Sell box and click the Continue button. Once you've entered the appropriate identifying information, Half.com then inserts pre-filled item information from a massive product database. (It's the same database that feeds eBay's pre-filled information in the same categories.) There are no listing fees, but you do have to pay Half.com a commission when an item sells. You'll pay a 15% commission on items under $50, and lower commissions as the price rises. Instead of a buyer paying you directly, Half.com collects the payment; the site sends you your payment every two weeks.

FIGURE 16.3
Items for sale on Half.com.

FIGURE 16.4
Getting ready to sell on Half.com

Finding Buyers with Want It Now

Another way to bypass the auction process is to go directly to buyers who want to buy what you have for sale. You can do this with eBay's Want It Now feature, where buyers create "wish lists" of specific items. You search the Want It Now listings, and when you find a match, you offer the item for sale to the interested buyer. (eBay still takes their normal cut, of course.)

Start by clicking the Want It Now link on eBay's home page. When the Want It Now page appears, as shown in Figure 16.5, you can browse through the listings by category, or use the Sellers search box to search for specific items that might be listed in the database. Click a particular listing for more detail from the interested buyer, like that shown in Figure 16.6.

FIGURE 16.5

Looking for prospective buyers with Want It Now.

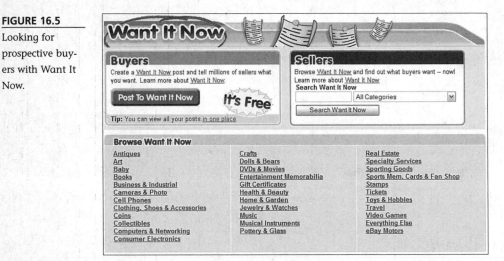

FIGURE 16.6

A hopeful buyer's Want It Now ad.

To respond to a request, click the Respond button to display the Respond page, shown in Figure 16.7. If you already have an item listed, enter the item number and click the Respond to Post button. If you haven't yet listed the item, click the Sell Your Item button, create an item listing, and then return to the Respond to a Post with a Listing page to enter the listing's item number.

FIGURE 16.7

Responding to a Want It Now request.

Want It Now: Respond	Help

1960 Filmation Superman Cartoons All Episodes DVD

Please note: The Want It Now post you are responding to is not a legally binding contract. There is no guarantee that the buyer will purchase your item. Learn more about Want It Now.

Haven't listed your item yet?	**or**	**Is the item already listed on eBay?**

1. Click the **Sell Your Item** button below.
2. List the item as you normally would.
3. Your item will be automatically added as a response to this post and an email will be sent to the buyer.

Sell Your Item >

Enter the item number of an item that is already listed for sale on eBay.

Item number

Don't know the item number? View the items you're selling in a new window.

Respond To Post >

The interested buyer is now emailed a message containing a link to your item listing. To place a bid on your item, all the recipient has to do is click a button.

THE ABSOLUTE MINIMUM

Here are the key points to remember from this chapter:

- You can add a fixed-price option to any auction listing by entering a Buy It Now price.

- Instead of running a traditional auction, you can create a fixed-price listing to sell your item at a specified fixed price, using the Buy It Now feature.

- Opening an eBay Store is a good way to sell quantities of fixed-price items through the eBay system.

- Half.com is an eBay site that lets anyone sell books, CDs, DVDs, and the like at fixed prices.

- You can use eBay's Want It Now feature to search for buyers who've expressed an interest in specific items.

17

CREATING MORE EFFECTIVE ITEM LISTINGS

Did you know that only about half the items listed on eBay at any given time actually sell during the current auction? That's right; in about half the current auctions, no one meets the minimum bid.

How do you increase the odds of *your* item selling? It's all about creating an effective item listing—in both content and appearance. That means writing a powerful title and detailed description, and then formatting your listing so that it packs a visual punch. It takes a bit of work to make your listing stand out, but it's worth it; the best-looking, most descriptive listings have higher sell-through rates and command higher selling prices. Spend the effort and reap the rewards!

Write a Title That SELLS!

When it comes to improving the effectiveness of your item listings, the best place to start is at the top—with the listing title. eBay lets you use up to 55 letters, numbers, characters, and spaces in your title, and you need to accomplish two things:

- Include the appropriate information so that anyone searching for a similar item will find your item in his search results.
- Make your title stand out from all the other titles on those long listing pages.

Do those two things, and you significantly increase your chances of getting your item noticed and sold.

Include Key Information

Let's tackle the first point first. You have to think like the people who will be looking for your item. Most users will be using eBay's search feature to look for specific items, so you want to put the right keywords into your item title, to make your item pop up on as many search results pages as possible.

As an example, let's say you have an original 1964 Superman model kit, manufactured by Aurora, still in its shrink-wrapped box. How do you list this item?

You have to make sure you get all the right keywords in your title. For this example, it's obvious that Superman should be a keyword, as should Aurora and maybe 1964. Then, it gets iffy-er. Should you call it a model kit or a plastic model kit or a plastic model? Should you call it unassembled or still in box or original condition?

When dealing with collectibles, you often can use accepted abbreviations and acronyms. (I'll list some of these acronyms later in this chapter.) In this case, you could use the abbreviation MISB, which stands for *mint in sealed box*. True collectors will know what this means, and it saves precious "real estate" in your title. (By the way, if this model wasn't in the box but was instead already assembled, you could use the abbreviation BU, for *built-up*.) Continuing this example, a title that included all the keywords users might search on would be 1964 Superman Aurora Plastic Model Kit MISB. (And this comes in at well under 55 characters!)

Note the inclusion of the year in the title. That's a good thing, because it helps to narrow down or better identify the item. Someone looking for a 1964 Superman model is not going to be interested in the 1978 or 2001 reissues, so including the date helps to narrow down your prospective customers.

> **tip**
>
> If you're unsure how best to word the title for your item listing, check out auctions for similar items and "borrow" their wording.

If your item has a model number or series name, that's definitely something to include. As an example, you might be selling a `14" Pearl Export Select Snare Drum with Case`. In this case, Pearl is the manufacturer and Export Select is the series or line. Another example might be a listing for a `1956 Gibson ES-175 Red Jazz Guitar`. This title gets in the year (1956), the manufacturer (Gibson), the model number (ES-175), the color (Red), and a brief description of what it is (a jazz guitar)—which pretty much covers all the bases.

Make Your Title Stand Out

Beyond including as many relevant facts as possible in your title, how do you make your title stand out from all the other boring listings? Obviously, one technique is to employ the judicious use of CAPITAL LETTERS. The operative word here is *judicious*; titles with ALL capital letters step over the line into overkill.

Instead, I advise you to think like an advertising copywriter. What words almost always stop consumers in their tracks? Use attention-getting words such as FREE and NEW and BONUS and EXTRA and DELUXE and RARE—as long as these words truly describe the item you're selling and don't mislead the potential bidder. (And don't bump more important search words for these fluffier marketing terms—that won't help your item show up in bidder searches.)

Try this one on for size: Which would you rather bid on, a `1964 Superman Model Kit` or a `RARE 1964 Superman Model Kit`? I'm betting you go for the second one—and mentally prepare yourself to pay more for it, too!

> **caution**
>
> Avoid the use of non-alphanumeric characters, such as !!! or ### or ***. eBay says that their use is prohibited, although that rule is seldom enforced. More important, eBay's search engine sometimes ignores titles that include too many of these nonsense characters—and could exclude your listing from buyers' search results.

In short, use your title to both inform and attract attention—and include as many potential search keywords as possible.

Write the Right Description

If the listing title is the headline of your ad, the listing description is your ad's body copy. Which means it's time to put on your copywriter's hat and get down to the nitty-gritty details.

Take All the Space You Need

What makes for good copy? First, you have all the space you need, so say as much as you need to say. Unlike with the title description, you don't have to scrimp on words or leave anything out. If you can describe your item adequately in a sentence, great; if it takes three paragraphs, that's okay, too.

When you're writing the description for your ad, be sure to mention anything and everything that a potential bidder might need to know. Note any defects or imperfections of the item. Include your desired payment terms and your preferred shipping methods. If the object is graded or evaluated in any way, include that assessment in your description. In other words, include everything you can think of that will eliminate any surprises for the buyer.

First Things First

You should probably put the most important and motivating information in your initial paragraph because a lot of folks won't read any farther than that. Think of your first paragraph like a lead paragraph in a newspaper story: Grab 'em with something catchy, give them the gist of the story, and lead them into reading the next paragraph and the one after that.

The Bare Necessities

There are certain key data points that users expect to see in your item description. Here's the bare minimum you should include:

- Name (or title)
- Condition
- Age
- Original use (what you used it for)
- Value (if you know it)
- Important measurements, contents, colors, materials, and so on
- Any included accessories (including the original instruction manual, if you have it)
- Any known defects or damage

If you don't know any of this stuff, that's okay—as long as you admit it. If you're not that familiar with the type of merchandise you're selling, just say so. Better to plead ignorance up-front than to have a more savvy buyer cause problems for you after the sale.

Describe It—Accurately

Because other users will be bidding on your item sight unseen, you have to make the process as easy as possible for potential bidders. That means describing the item as accurately as possible, and in as much detail as possible. If the item has a scratch or blemish, note it. If the paint is peeling, note it. If it includes a few non-original parts, note it. Bidders don't have the item to hold in their hands and examine in person, so you have to be their eyes and ears.

That's right; you need to describe the item in painful detail, and be completely honest about what you're selling. If you're *not* honest in your description, it will come back to haunt you—in the form of an unhappy and complaining buyer.

Stress Benefits, Not Features

Although you need to be descriptive (and in some collectibles categories, you need to be *obsessively* so), it doesn't hurt to employ a little marketing savvy and salesmanship. Yes, you should talk about the features of your item, but it's even better if you can talk about your product's *benefits* to the potential buyer.

Let's say you're selling a used cordless phone, and the phone has a 50-number memory. Saying "50-number memory" is stating a feature; saying instead that the phone "lets you recall your 50 most-called phone numbers at the press of a button" is describing a benefit. Remember, a feature is something your item has; a benefit is something your item does for the user.

Break It Up

You should include as much descriptive copy as you need in your listing, but you should also make sure that every sentence sells your item.

And if your listing starts to get a little long, you should break it into more readable chunks. Use separate paragraphs to present different types of information, or just to break one long paragraph into several shorter, more readable ones. You can even use eBay's formatting options to use different type sizes and colors for different portions of your listing description.

Don't Forget the Fine Print

Breaking up your description enables you to put a *lot* more info into your description. When it comes to informing potential buyers, it's impossible to be too complete. (And if you don't define a detail, the buyer will—in his or her mind.) Don't

caution

Don't forget to spell-check and proofread your listing. Bad grammar and misspellings can cause potential bidders to doubt your veracity and even to totally disregard your auction.

assume that buyers know *anything*; take the time to spell out all the details about payment and shipping and the like.

Here is some of the "fine print" you might want to include at the bottom of your item description:

- Bidding restrictions, such as "No bidders with negative feedback," "Bidders with positive feedback of at least 10 only," or "U.S. buyers only."
- Payment restrictions, such as "U.S. funds only," "No personal checks," or "Personal checks take two weeks to clear."
- Shipping/handling charges (if you know them) and restrictions, such as "Buyer pays shipping/handling" or "Shipping via USPS Priority Mail only."
- The grade of your item, if your item has been graded (discussed later in this chapter). Note that this information can also be included in the main body of the item description, as well as in the fine print section.
- Information about your other auctions.

Include Alternate Wording

The very last things you can put into your listing, at the bottom, are some extra words. Remember, not every person uses the same words to describe things. If you're selling a plastic model kit, for example, some users will search for model, others for kit, still others for statue or figure or styrene. Although you can't put all these variations into the item title, you *can* throw them in somewhere in the description—or, if all else fails, at the bottom of the item description. (Remember, they'll be picked up by eBay's search engine if they're *anywhere* in the description area.)

While you're at it, throw in any alternative spellings you can think of. For example, you might know that the correct spelling of Spider-Man includes the hyphen in the middle, but less-informed users might search for the unhyphenated Spiderman. Whichever variation you use in your title, throw the other one in at the bottom of the description.

Making the Grade

When you're selling items on eBay, it helps to know what kind of shape your items are in. For many categories of merchandise, that means grading the item's condition—according to some very formal rules.

Grading is a way of noting the condition of an item, according to a predetermined standard. Collectors use these grading scales to help evaluate and price items within a category. If you know the grade of your item, you can include the grade in the item's title or description, and thus more accurately describe the item to potential bidders.

Making a Mint

Unfortunately, there is no such thing as a "universal" grading system for all items; different types of collectibles have their own unique grading systems. For example, trading cards are graded from A1 to F1; stamps are graded from Poor to Superb.

That said, many collectible categories use a variation of the Mint grading system, as shown in Table 17.1.

Table 17.1   Mint System Grading

Grade	Abbreviation	Description
Mint	MT, M, 10	An item in perfect condition, without any damage or imperfections.
Very Fine	VF	Similar to mint.
Near Mint	NM, 9	An item with a very minor, hardly noticeable flaw. Sometimes described as "like new."
Near Fine	NF	Similar to near mint.
Excellent	EX, 8	An item considered above average, but with pronounced signs of wear.
Fine	F	Similar to excellent.
Very Good	VG, 7	An item in average condition.
Good	GD, G, 6	An item that has clear indications of age, wear, and use.
Fair	F	An item that is heavily worn.
Poor	P, 5	An item that is damaged or somehow incomplete.

Degrees between grade levels are indicated with a + or –. (For example, an item between Fine and Very Fine would be designated as F+.) Naturally, the definition of a Mint or Fair item differs by item type.

Getting Graded

If you're not sure what grade an item is, you may want to utilize a professional grading and authentication service. These services will examine your item, authenticate it (confirm that it's the real deal), and give it a professional grade. Some services will even encase your item in a sealed plastic container or bag.

Where can you get your items graded? Table 17.2 lists some popular websites for grading and authenticating collectible items.

Table 17.2   Grading and Authentication Services

Collectible	Site	URL
Autographs	OnlineAuthentics.com	www.onlineauthentics.com
	PSA/DNA	www.psadna.com
Beanie Babies	Peggy Gallagher Enterprises, Inc.	www.beaniephenomenon.com
Books	PKBooks	www.pkbooks.com
Coins	American Numismatic Association Certification Service	www.anacs.com
	Numismatic Guaranty Corporation of America	www.ngccoin.com
	Professional Coin Grading Service	www.pcgs.com
Comic books	Comics Guaranty	www.cgccomics.com
Jewelry	International Gemological Institute	www.e-igi.com
Sports cards	Professional Sports Authenticator	www.psacard.com
	Sportscard Guaranty, LLC	www.sgccard.com
Stamps	American Philatelic Society	www.stamps.org
	The Pilatectic Foundation	www.philatelicfoundation.org
	Professional Stamps Experts	www.psestamp.com

The cost of these authentication services varies wildly, depending on what you're authenticating, the age or value of the item, and the extent of the service itself. For example, Professional Sports Authenticator rates range from $5 to $150 per sports card; Professional Stamps Experts rates range from $15 to $500 per stamp. Make sure that the item you're selling is worth it before you go to this expense—and that you can recoup this expense in your auction.

tip

eBay provides a page of links to "authorized" authentication services at pages.ebay.com/help/community/auth-overview.html.

Other Ways to Describe Your Item

There are some other grading-related abbreviations you can use in your item listings. As you can see in Table 17.3, these abbreviations help you describe your item (especially in the title) without wasting a lot of valuable space.

Table 17.3 Grading-Related Terms

Abbreviation	Description	Meaning
ARC	Advanced readers copy	A pre-publication version of a book manuscript, typically released to reviewers and bookstores for publicity purposes
BU	Built up	For models and other to-be-assembled items; indicates that the item has already been assembled
CC	Cut corner	Some closeout items are marked by a notch on the corner of the package
CO	Cut out	Closeout item
COA	Certificate of authenticity	Document that vouches for the authenticity of the item; often found with autographed or rare collectible items
COC	Cut out corner	Same as CC (cut corner)
COH	Cut out hole	Some closeout items are marked by a small hole punched somewhere on the package
FS	Factory sealed	Still in the original manufacturer's packaging
GP	Gold plate	Item is gold plated
HC	Hard cover	Used to indicate hardcover (as opposed to softcover, or paperback) books
HE	Heavy gold electroplated	Item has heavy gold plating
HTF	Hard to find	Item isn't in widespread circulation
LE	Limited edition	Item was produced in limited quantities
LSW	Label shows wear	Item's label shows normal usage for its age
MCU	Might clean up	Might show a higher grade if cleaned or otherwise restored
MIB	Mint in box	Item in perfect condition, still in the original box
MIMB	Mint in mint box	Item in perfect condition, still in the original box—which itself is in perfect condition
MIP	Mint in package	Item in perfect condition, still in the original package
MISB	Mint in sealed box	Item in perfect condition, still in the original box with the original seal
MNB	Mint, no box	Mint-condition item but without the original packaging
MOC	Mint on card	For action figures and similar items, an item in perfect condition still in its original carded package

Table 17.3 (continued)

Abbreviation	Description	Meaning
MOMC	Mint on mint card	Item in perfect condition, still on its original carded package—which is also in mint condition
MONMC	Mint on near-mint card	Same as MOMC, but with the card in less-than-perfect condition
MWBMT	Mint with both mint tags	For stuffed animals that typically have both a hang tag and a tush (sewn-on) tag, indicates both tags are in perfect condition
MWBT	Mint with both tags	Same as MWBMT, but with the tags in less-than-mint condition
MWMT	Mint with mint tag	Mint-condition item with its original tag, which is also in mint condition
NIB	New in box	Brand-new item, still in its original box
NOS	New old stock	Old, discontinued parts in original, unused condition
NR	No reserve	Indicates that you're selling an item with no reserve price
NRFB	Never removed from box	An item bought but never used or played with
NWOT	New without tags	Item, unused, but without its original tags
NWT	New with tags	Item, unused, that still has its original hanging tags
OOP	Out of print	Item is no longer being manufactured
P/O	Punched out	Same as CC (cut corner)
RR	Re-release	Not the original issue, but rather a reissue (typically done for the collector's market)
SC	Soft cover	A paperback (non–hard cover) book
SS	Still sealed	As it says, still in the original sealed package
SW	Slight wear	Only minor wear commensurate with age
VHTF	Very hard to find	Self-descriptive
WOC	Writing on cover	Item has markings on front surface

The big problem with any grading system is that grading is subjective. Although there may be guidelines for different grading levels, the line between very good and excellent is often a fine one. You should be very careful about assigning your own grading levels; even better, supplement the grade with a detailed description and photographs so that bidders can make up their own minds as to your item's true value.

Apply Cool Templates with eBay's Listing Designer

Most of the item listings on eBay look the same: a paragraph or two of plain text, maybe a picture unceremoniously dropped in below the text. That's how a listing looks when you enter a normal, plain-text description for your item listing.

But then there are those ads that shout at you with colored text and different font faces and sizes and multiple columns and sizzling graphics and...well, you know the ones I'm talking about. How do you go about creating a dynamic listing like that?

The easiest way to create a listing that goes beyond plain text is with eBay's Listing Designer. This feature is available to all users, right from the Sell Your Item page— and it costs only $0.10 a listing.

Listing Designer provides over one hundred pre-designed templates, which eBay calls *themes.* You choose a theme when you're creating your item listing, in the Listing Designer section of the Describe Your Item page, a shown in Figure 17.1. Just select a theme from the Theme list, then choose a layout from the Photo Layout list. (Figure 17.2 shows a listing enhanced with a Listing Designer theme.)

FIGURE 17.1

Use eBay's Listing Designer to choose a template for your item listing.

FIGURE 17.2

An eBay item listing enhanced with a Listing Designer template.

Create Fancy Listings with Listing-Creation Tools

Listing Designer isn't the only option you have for creating fancy eBay item listings. There are many software programs and web-based services that offer pre-designed auction templates for your eBay listings. Most of these programs and services let you choose a design and fill in some blanks, and then they automatically write the HTML code necessary to create the listing. These programs and services are easy to use; some are free, some aren't.

Create-Your-Own Listing Websites

We'll start our tour of third-party auction templates by examining some of the most popular create-your-own listing websites. These sites are often referred to as code generators, because that's what they do—generate HTML code that you then insert into your eBay item listing.

Here are some of the most popular of these sites:

> **note**
>
> Want to learn more about creating great-looking auction templates—and get some free templates in the bargain? Then check out my companion book, *eBay Auction Template Starter Kit* (Que, 2006), available at bookstores everywhere. It comes with a CD full of ready-to-use auction templates!

- Antique Central's eZ Auction Advanced Template (www.antique-central.com/eztemplate.html)
- Auction AD Creator (www.auctionlotwatch.co.uk/auctionadcreator.html)
- Auction Insights code generator (www.auctioninsights.com/practice/auction-template.html)
- Auction Riches Free Auction Ad Creator (www.auctionriches.com/freead/create.pl)
- Auction Writer (www.auctionwriter.com)
- AuctionFlash (www.auctionflash.com)
- AuctionSpice (www.auctionspice.com)
- Bay Dream Design (www.bay-dream.com)
- BiggerBids (www.biggerbids.com)
- DeadZoom Auction Template Maker (www.deadzoom.com/auction-template/)
- K&D Web Page Design Custom Auction Creator (www.kdwebpagedesign.com/tutorials/tut_template.asp)
- ListTailor (www.listtailor.com/quickstart.html)
- Nucite Auction Templates (www.nucite.com/templates/)

■ RobsHelp.com FreeForm Builder (www.robshelp.com)

■ Two Wizards Designs Free Auction Template Creator (www.2wiz.net/dtemplates1.shtml)

■ Wizard's Free Auction Template Creation Form (www.ambassadorboard.net/hosting/free-form.php)

To give you an idea of what you can expect, Figures 17.3 and 17.4 show templates from two of these listing-generation sites, Auction Writer and Nucite.

FIGURE 17.3

An eBay item listing created with Auction Writer.

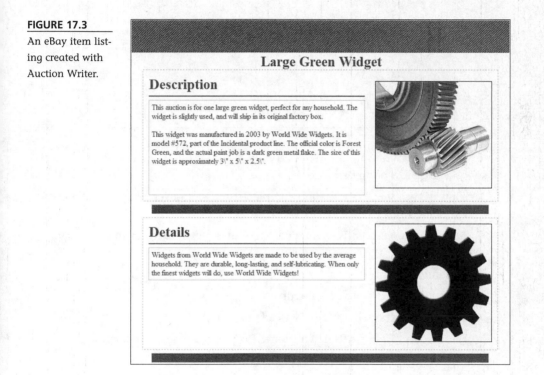

Downloadable Auction Templates

Online auction listing code generators are great, but what if you don't want to go to somebody else's website to design your eBay auction listings? If you prefer to work within the comfort and safety of your own computer desktop, consider using a downloadable auction template. These templates feature pre-designed color schemes and layouts; you have only to open them in any text editor program (such as Windows Notepad or WordPad) to insert your own auction information, and then copy the final code into your eBay item listing.

FIGURE 17.4

One of Nucite's
free auction
templates.

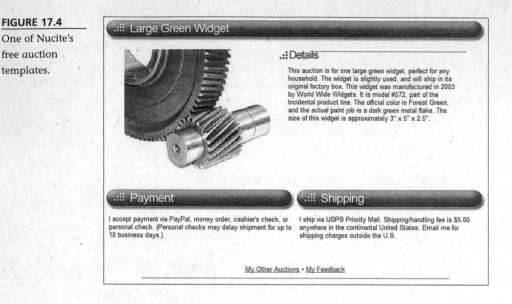

You can find all manner of both free and paid templates for your auction use; here are some of the most popular:

- Alou Web Design Free Auction Templates (www.alouwebdesign.ca/free-ebay-templates.htm)
- AuctionSupplies.com Free Auction Templates (www.auctionsupplies.com/templates/)
- Auction Template Center (www.auctiontemplatecentral.com)
- AuctionWraps (www.auctionwraps.com)
- DeSa C.S. Auction Templates (www.desacs.com)
- Free Auction Help Auction Templates (www.freeauctionhelp.com/free_auction_template.htm)
- K&D Web Page Design Custom Ad Creator (www.kdwebpagedesign.com/auction_templates.asp)
- SaverSites Custom eBay Auction Templates (www.saversites.com/services_ebay_auction_templates.htm)
- The Ultimate eBay Resource eBay Templates (www.sellingonebay.info/templates.html)
- Xample.net Free eBay Auction Templates (www.xample.net/templates.htm)
- Woo Woo Designs Auction Templates (www.woowoodesigns.com)

Auction Listing Services

An auction listing service is, quite simply, a website that lets you create eBay auction listings from within your web browser. You create the listings, apply some sort of pre-designed template (or perform your own custom formatting), and then have the service upload the listing to the eBay auction site. Depending on the service, your listings may be free; you may be charged a per-listing fee; or you may pay a flat monthly subscription charge. And, as part of the package offered by the site, you may have other auction management services available to you.

Here are some of the most popular of these third-party listing sites:

- Ándale (www.andale.com)
- Auction Hawk (www.auctionhawk.com)
- Auctiva (www.auctiva.com)
- ChannelAdvisor (www.channeladvisor.com)
- Hammertap (www.hammertap.com)
- inkFrog (www.inkfrog.com)
- SpareDollar (www.sparedollar.com)
- Vendio (www.vendio.com)

Figures 17.5 and 17.6 show item listings created by two of these listing services

Auction Listing Software

There are a few advantages to using a listing program instead of a web-based serv-ice. For one, using a software program lets you work offline, at your own pace; you can create your listings at any time of day or night, and upload them at your leisure.

Second, since you work offline, all your auction information is stored on your own computer—not on somebody else's website. That makes it easier to access past infor-mation when you're not online, and to manage it as you see fit. (Many sellers like to create their own sales reports using Excel or Access, which isn't always doable with web-based management services.)

Third, most web-based listing services charge you money for each listing you cre-ate—or sale that you make. That's not always the case with listing creation software; while some programs come with subscription plans, many are available as simple one-time purchases, just like most of the other software you have installed on your PC.

Here are some of the most popular listing-creation programs:

- Auction Lizard (www.auction-lizard.com)
- Auction Wizard 2000 (www.auctionwizard2000.com)
- AuctionSage (www.auctionsagesoftware.com)
- AuctionTamer (www.auctiontamer.com)
- eBay Blackthorne Basic and Pro (pages.ebay.com/blackthorne/basic.html)
- eBay Turbo Lister (pages.ebay.com/turbo_lister/)

FIGURE 17.6

An inkFrog item listing.

Description

This auction is for one large green widget, perfect for any household. The widget is slightly used, and will ship in its original factory box.

This widget was manufactured in 2003 by World Wide Widgets. It is model #572, part of the Incidental product line. The official color is Forest Green, and the actual paint job is a dark green metal flake. The size of this widget is approximately 3" x 5" x 2.5". Widgets from World Wide Widgets are made to be used by the average household. They are durable, long-lasting, and self-lubricating. When only the finest widgets will do, use World Wide Widgets!

Click to Enlarge

Payment Terms

I accept payment via PayPal, money order, cashier's check, or personal check. (Personal checks may delay shipment for up to 10 business days.)

Shipping Terms

I ship via USPS Priority Mail. Shipping/handling fee is $5.00 anywhere in the continental United States. Email me for shipping charges outside the U.S.

Format Your Listings with HTML

Here's a secret known to successful sellers: eBay lets you use HTML to spruce up your item listings. While this isn't a task for the faint of heart, writing your own code lets you create highly individualized item listings—much fancier than you can do with a template-driven listing creator.

How HTML Works

HTML coding might sound difficult, but it's really pretty easy. HTML is really nothing more than a series of hidden codes that tell web browsers how to display different types of text and graphics. The codes are embedded in a document, so you can't see them; they're visible only to your web browser.

These codes are distinguished from normal text by the fact that they're enclosed within angle brackets.

note

HTML stands for hypertext markup language.

Each particular code turns on or off a particular attribute, such as boldface or italic text. Most codes are in sets of "on/off" pairs. You turn "on" the code before the text you want to affect and then turn "off" the code after the text.

For example, the code <h1> turns specified type into a level-one headline; the code </h1> turns off the headline type. The code <i> is used to italicize text; </i> turns off the italics. (As you can see, an "off" code is merely the "on" code with a slash before it.)

Entering HTML Codes

You enter HTML codes while you're creating your item listing. When you reach the Description section of the Describe Your Item page, click the View HTML link. This displays eBay's HTML editor, shown in Figure 17.7. You can enter your raw HTML code into this form.

> **note**
>
> I present only a handful of the huge number of HTML codes available to you. If you want to learn more about using HTML in your eBay auction listings, I refer you again to my companion book, *eBay Auction Template Starter Kit* (Que, 2006). It will guide you step-by-step through the process of creating HTML-based item listings—no prior experience required!

FIGURE 17.7

Enter your own HTML code on eBay's Describe Your Item page.

Description

Back to Design View

Inserts

```
<P align=center><FONT face=times color=#ff0000 size=7><STRONG>Large Green Widget</STRONG></FONT></P>
<P align=center><STRONG><FONT face=arial size=5>Slightly used, in original box</FONT></STRONG></P>
<P align=center><FONT face=arial size=4>This auction is for one large green widget, perfect for any household. The widget is slightly used, and will ship in its original factory box.</FONT></P>
<P><FONT face=times>This widget was manufactured in 2003 by World Wide Widgets. It is model #572, part of the Incidental product line. The official color is Forrest Green, and the actual paint job is a dark green metal flake. The size of this widget is approximately 3" x 5" x 2.5". </FONT></P>
<P><FONT face=times>Widgets from World Wide Widgets are made to be used by the average household. They are durable, long-lasting, and self-lubricating. When only the finest widgets will do, use World Wide Widgets!</FONT></P>
<P><FONT face=times size=1><STRONG>Terms of Service:<BR></STRONG>I accept payment via PayPal, money order, cashier's check, or personal check. (Personal checks may delay shipment for up to 10 business days.) I ship via USPS Priority Mail. Shipping/handling fee is $5.00 anywhere in the continental United States. Email me for shipping charges outside the U.S.</FONT></P>
```

Preview description

Codes to Format Your Text

We'll start off with some of the most common HTML codes—those used to format your text. Table 17.4 shows some of these text-formatting codes you can use in your item description.

Table 17.4   HTML Codes to Format Text

Effect	On Code	Off Code
Bold	`<b>`	`</b>`
Strong (bold)	`<strong>`	`</strong>`
Emphasis (italic)	`<em>`	`</em>`
Italic	`<i>`	`</i>`
Underline	`<u>`	`</u>`
Center	`<center>`	`</center>`
First-level headline	`<h1>`	`</h1>`
Second-level headline	`<h2>`	`</h2>`
Third-level headline	`<h3>`	`</h3>`

Just surround the text you want to format with the appropriate on and off codes, and you're ready to go. For example, to format a piece of text as strong (bold), you'd write something that looks like this:

`<strong>this text is bold</strong>`

Codes for Font Type, Size, and Color

You can also use HTML to specify a particular font type or size, using the `<font>` code.

To specify a font type for selected text, use the `<font>` code with the `face` attribute, like this:

`<font face="xxxx">text</font>`

Replace the *xxxx* with the specific font, such as Arial or Times Roman—in quotation marks.

Another common use of the `<font>` code is to specify type size. You use the `size` attribute, and the code looks like this:

`<font size="xx">text</font>`

Replace the *xx* with the size you want, from –6 to +6, with –6 being the smallest, +6 being the biggest, and 0 (or no size specified) being "normal" size type.

You can also use the `<font>` code to designate a specific text color. In this instance, you use the `color` attribute, like this:

`<font color="#xxxxxx">text</font>`

note

If all you want to do is add some bold or color text to your listing, you don't have to learn HTML or use fancy listing-creation tools. eBay's standard text editor is available when you create your item listing with the Sell Your Item form. It lets you add HTML effects in a WYSIWYG environment, much the same way you add boldface and italics in your word processor. Just highlight the text you want to format and then click the appropriate formatting button. No manual coding necessary.

Replace the *xxxxxx* with the code for a specific color. Table 17.5 lists some basic color codes.

Table 17.5 Common HTML Color Codes

Color Name	Color Code
Black	000000
White	FFFFFF
Gray	808080
Silver	C0C0C0
Yellow	FFFF00
Orange	FFA500
Brown	A52A2A
Red	FF0000
Maroon	800000
Olive	808000
Fuchsia	FF00FF
Chartreuse	7FFF00
Green	008000
Lime	00FF00
Teal	008080
Aqua	00FFFF
Navy	000080
Blue	0000FF
Purple	800080
Violet	F080F0

caution

Just because you have a specific font installed on your computer doesn't necessarily mean that all the other web users who will be viewing your ad have the same font installed on their PCs. If you change fonts in your listing, change to a common font that is likely to be pre-installed on all Windows computers. Arial and Times Roman are always safe bets; choosing something more obscure could ensure an unpredictable display for your listing on many computers around the world.

Codes for Paragraphs

When it's time to start a new paragraph, you start the paragraph with a <p> code. Then, when the paragraph is done, you close it with a </p> "off" code. The code looks something like this:

```
<p>
This is a normal text paragraph. It consists
of multiple sentences. Like these.
</p>
```

note

For a complete list of the literally hundreds of different HTML color codes, check out the color charts at www.immigration-usa.com/html_colors.html and html-color-codes.com. Just choose a color and view the corresponding color code!

The `<p>` code can also contain the `align` attribute, which indicates how the paragraph is aligned—left, center, or right. Paragraphs are left-aligned by default, so if you want to center a paragraph, you'd use the following code:

```
<p align="center">
This is the paragraph to be centered. All the
text in the paragraph is aligned as
indicated.
</p>
```

Codes for Paragraphs, Line Breaks, and Rules

Some of the simplest HTML codes let you break your text into separate lines and add horizontal rules between paragraphs. These codes are inserted into your text just once; there are no matching ending codes.

Table 17.6 lists these "on-only" codes.

> **note**
>
> Earlier versions of HTML let you use the `<p>` tag to indicate the start of a new paragraph, without requiring the corresponding `</p>` "off" code at the end the paragraph. Current HTML standards encourage the use of the `<p>` and `</p>` codes as proper containers for the paragraph text. That said, you can probably get by without the `</p>` "off" code, although it's good practice to include it.

Table 17.6 HTML Codes for Lines and Paragraphs

Action	Code
Line break	` `
Horizontal rule (line)	`<hr>`

Codes for Graphics

As you'll learn in Chapter 18, "Using Pictures in Your Listings," adding pictures and other graphics to your listings really brings some excitement to the normally plain-text world of eBay. You can add pictures the eBay way (described in Chapter 18), which puts all your pictures at the end of your text description—or you can put a picture *anywhere* in your text, using HTML.

Before you can insert a graphic into your listing, you need to know the address of that graphic (in the form of a web page URL). Then you use the following code:

```
<img src="URL">
```

No "off" code is required for inserted graphics. Note that the location is enclosed in quotation marks—and that you have to insert the `http://` part of the URL.

As an example, if your graphic is the file graphic01.jpg located at www.webserver.com/mydirectory/, you insert this code:

```
<img src="http://www.webserver.com/mydirectory/graphic01.jpg">
```

The nice thing about inserting graphics this way is that you can include more than just pictures—you can add logos, starbursts, you name it. (And you can put the graphics *anywhere* in your text description.) You use the same technique to link to any graphic image anywhere in your item listing.

Codes for Links

You can use HTML to add links to your own personal web pages (a great idea if you have additional images of this specific item) or to related sites. Many sellers also like to provide a direct email link in case potential bidders have questions they need answered.

To insert a link to another web page in your item listing, you use the following HTML code:

```
<a href="URL">this is the link</a>
```

The text between the on and off codes will appear onscreen as a typical underlined hyperlink; when users click that text, they'll be linked to the URL you specified in the code. Note that the URL is enclosed in quotation marks and that you have to include the `http://` part of the address.

You can also create a "mail-to" link in your listing; users will be able to send email to you by simply clicking the link. Here's the code for a mail-to link:

```
<a href="mailto:yourname@domain.com">click
here to email me</a>
```

note

eBay allows links to pages that provide additional information about the item listed, additional photos of the item, and your other eBay auctions. eBay prohibits links to pages that attempt to sell merchandise outside eBay. Link at your own risk—eBay reserves the right to cancel any inappropriate listings.

Codes for Lists

Finally, if you have a lot of features to list for your item, you might want to format them in a bulleted list. Using HTML codes, it's easy to create a neatly bulleted list for your ad.

First, you enclose your bulleted list with the `<ul>` and `</ul>` codes. Then, you enclose each bulleted item with the `<li>` and `</li>` codes.

The code for a typical bulleted list looks like this:

```
<ul>
    <li>item one</li>
    <li>item two</li>
    <li>item three</li>
</ul>
```

Bulleted lists are great ways to run through a list of attributes or specifications; it's a lot cleaner than just listing a bunch of stuff within a long text paragraph.

tip

When you're dealing with complex coding like this, it's easier to understand what's going on if you indent the different levels of code.

THE ABSOLUTE MINIMUM

Here are the key points to remember from this chapter:

- Pack as much info into your item listing's title as possible, using common abbreviations and grading levels.

- The description of your item can be as long as you want—so take the space to include as much detailed information as is practical.

- Include all necessary fine print for your transaction at the bottom of the item description.

- Add visual appeal to your item listing by applying a template, or theme, with eBay's Listing Designer.

- You can also use third-party auction templates listing-creation programs and websites to create template-based item listings.

- eBay lets you use HTML code to customize the appearance of your item's description.

18

USING PICTURES IN YOUR LISTINGS

A picture in your listing greatly increases the chances of actually selling your item—and also increases the average price you will receive.

Adding a picture to your listing is a fairly easy process. Basically, you have to work through the following three steps:

1. Take a digital photo of your item.
2. Edit the image file (so that it looks pretty).
3. Upload your image file to a server somewhere on the Internet or use eBay's Picture Services.

We'll look at each of these steps individually, but first, here's a checklist of what you need in order to take effective pictures for your eBay listings:

Checklist: eBay Pictures

- ☐ Digital camera
- ☐ Lighting (built-in flash can work)
- ☐ Tripod (optional)
- ☐ Clean space with plain black or white background
- ☐ Scanner (for flat items)
- ☐ Graphics editing software
- ☐ Web picture hosting service (optional)

" Mike Sez "

Is there any time when you *don't* want to include a picture of an item? If the item is nothing more than a black box—or a blank book cover—there's not a lot of point in showing it. However, don't think that if an item is damaged you shouldn't show it—just the opposite! You want bidders to know what they're getting into, regarding damage and flaws, and showing a picture is the best way to do this.

Take a Picture—Or Make a Scan

It all starts with a picture. But it had better be a darned good picture, or potential bidders won't find it much use.

Tips for Taking Great Product Photos

Although this really isn't the place for a basic photography lesson, I can give you a few tips on how to take the right kinds of pictures to use in your eBay listings.

- ■ **Use a digital camera.** Although you can take pictures with a normal film camera, develop the film, and have your film processor transfer your photos to graphics files on a photo CD, it's a lot easier if you start with digital at the source—especially if you plan on listing a lot of items on eBay. You can pick up a good low-end digital camera for well under $200 these days, and going direct from camera to computer (and then to eBay) is a lot easier than any other method.

- ■ **Shoot in strong light.** One of the worst photographic offenses is to shoot under standard indoor room light. Although you

caution

Whatever you do, resist the temptation to simply copy someone else's picture file to use in your listing. Not only is this unethical, but it misrepresents the exact item you're selling. You could also find yourself on the wrong side of a copyright lawsuit if the owner of the photo takes particular offense.

can touch up the photo somewhat afterward (see the "Edit the Image File" section, later in this chapter), you can't put in light that wasn't there to begin with. Open all the windows, turn on all the room lights, use a flash (but judiciously—you want to avoid glare on your item), or just take the item outdoors to shoot—do whatever it takes to create a well-lighted photograph. (Figure 18.1 and Figure 18.2 show the same item shot in low light and with stronger lighting; Figure 18.2 definitely works best.)

> **"Mike Sez"**
>
> When you go shopping for a digital camera, look for one with a macro mode so that you can take close-ups of any small objects you might be selling. Also, invest another dozen bucks in a tripod so that you can take steady pictures in low light.

FIGURE 18.1
An item shot in low lighting—bad.

- **Avoid glare.** If you're shooting a glass or plastic item, or an item still in plastic wrap or packaging, or just an item that's naturally shiny, you have to work hard to avoid glare from whatever lighting source you're using—like that shown in Figure 18.3. This is one reason why I typically don't recommend using the type of single-point flash built into most of today's digital cameras—without any fill lighting, it produces too much glare. You avoid glare by not using a flash, using external lights (to the sides of the object), diffusing the lighting source (by bouncing the light off a reflector of some sort), or just turning the item until the glare goes away. A simpler solution is to shoot in an area with strong natural light—like outside on a nice day.

FIGURE 18.2
An item shot
in stronger
lighting—good.

FIGURE 18.3
A shrink-wrapped
item with glare
from a flash—
bad.

■ **Shoot against a plain background.** If you shoot your object against a busy background, it detracts from the main point of the photograph, as you can see in Figure 18.4. Hang a white or black sheet (or T-shirt) behind the item; it will make the main object stand out a lot better.

FIGURE 18.4

An ugly background detracts from the item you're shooting.

■ **Focus!** Okay, this one sounds obvious, but I see a lot of blurry pictures on eBay—like the one shown in Figure 18.5. Make sure you know how to focus your camera, or how to use the auto-focus function. Also—and this is particularly important if you're shooting in low-light conditions—remember to hold the camera steady. A little bit of camera shake makes for a blurry photo. Either learn how to steady the camera or buy a cheap tripod to hold the camera for you.

FIGURE 18.5

An out-of-focus photo—bad.

■ **Frame.** To take effective photographs, you have to learn proper composition. That means centering the item in the center of the photo, and getting close enough to the object so that it fills up the entire picture. Don't stand halfway across the room and shoot a very small object; get close up and make it *big!* (Figures 18.6 shows a poorly framed item—bad!)

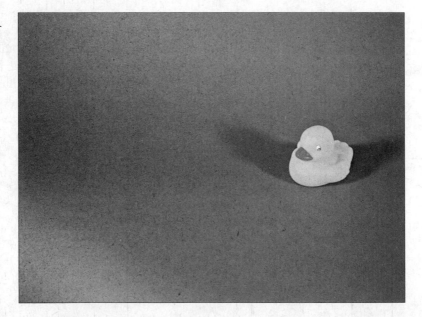

■ **Take more than one.** Don't snap off a quick picture and assume you've done your job. Shoot your item from several different angles and distances—and remember to get a close-up of any important area of the item, such as a serial number or a damaged area. You may want to include multiple photos in your listing—or just have a good selection of photos to choose from for that one best picture.

FIGURE 18.6

Bad composition— the object's way too small!

Scan Instead of Shoot

Of course, if you're selling relatively flat items (books, comics, CDs, and even small boxes), you might be better off with a scanner than a camera. (And remember that boxes have flat sides that can be scanned.) Just lay the object on a flatbed scanner and scan the item into a file on your computer. It's actually easier to scan something like a book or a DVD case than it is to take a good steady picture of it!

Use eBay's Stock Photos

If you're selling a book, an audio book, an audio cassette, a CD, a DVD, a VHS tape, or a video game, you might not need any photos at all. That's because eBay automatically inserts a stock product photo when you use the pre-filled item description option to create your item listing. (You learned about this back in Chapter 15, "Selling Items via Online Auction.") If the item you're selling is listed in eBay's product database—and you like the photo they provide—save yourself the trouble and let eBay insert the picture for you.

tip

When you're scanning compact discs, take the CD booklet out of the jewel case to scan.

Edit the Image File

After you've taken your digital photo (typically in a JPG-format file, the graphics file type of choice for eBay), you can do a little editing to "clean it up" for eBay use.

Things to Edit

What kinds of editing are we talking about? Here's a short list:

- Lighten up photos shot in low light.
- Correct the color and tint in poorly shot photos.
- Crop the picture to focus on only the subject at hand.
- Resize the image to fit better in your eBay listings. (Too big a picture won't fit within a normal Web browser window.)
- Decrease the resolution or color count to produce a smaller-sized file. (Files that are too big will take longer to load onto a bidder's PC—and may even be rejected by eBay.)

Graphics Editing Software

How do you do all this? You need an image-editing program. Although hard-core picture fanatics swear by the extremely full-featured (and very expensive) Adobe Photoshop CS, there are several lower-cost programs that perform just as well for the type of editing you'll be doing. These programs include the following:

- Adobe Photoshop Elements (www.adobe.com)
- IrfanView (www.irfanview.com)
- Paint Shop Pro (www.corel.com)

- Microsoft Digital Image Standard (www.microsoft.com/products/imaging/)
- Roxio PhotoSuite (www.roxio.com)

Most of these programs cost under $100 and have similar features. Or, if you'd rather not muck around with this sort of picture editing, you can always have somebody else do it for you; here again, FedEx Kinko's is a good place to start.

Resizing Your Photos

While you're editing, remember to resize your photo to best fit within your eBay listing. (Most pictures you take in a digital camera will come out too big to fit on a Web page without scrolling.) eBay recommends that you size your image to no more than 400 pixels wide by 400 pixels tall—unless you're using the Supersize option, which can accept photos up to 800 x 800.

Resizing Your Files

You should also reduce the amount of detail in your picture to keep the file size small—no more than 50KB for each picture. This keeps the loading time for each photo down to a reasonable level.

There are three ways to reduce the size of an image file. You can reduce the dots per inch (dpi); you can resize the width and height; or you can reduce the number of colors used. Depending on your pictures, you may need to use some or all of these techniques to get the file down to a workable size. Most image editing software lets you perform all three of these operations.

Your photo editing software should include settings that let you reduce both the physical size and the file size for your photographs. And, of course, the two go hand in hand: Reduce the physical size, and you'll also reduce the file size.

> 66 **Mike Sez** 99
>
> My favorite of these programs is Adobe Photoshop Elements—not to be confused with the much more expensive (and harder to use) Adobe Photoshop CS. The Elements program is extremely easy to use, with one-button operation for most common photo editing tasks. To learn more, check out my companion book *Bad Pics Fixed Quick* (Que, 2004).

> 66 **Mike Sez** 99
>
> Personally, I find 400×400 pictures to be a tad on the small side for some items. I see no harm in going up to 500 or even 600 pixels wide, especially if viewing the detail of the object is important. Note, however, that if you use a larger size for a picture hosted with eBay Picture Services, it will automatically be resized down to 400 pixels (on the longest side), which sometimes results in distorted images. So if you're using eBay Picture Services, stick with their 400×400 guideline; if you're using a different picture host, then you can use a larger picture size.

Upload Your Image File to the Internet—Or Use eBay Picture Services

When you have your photos ready, you need to do one of two things: Upload the photos to your own personal website or picture hosting service, or get ready to add these photos to your new eBay item listing.

You see, when it comes to photos, eBay gives you a choice. They can host your photos for you, or you can have someone else host your photos. Which one is the right solution for you?

> " **Mike Sez** "
>
> Probably the most effective way to reduce file size is to set a lower resolution (dots per inch). For photos that will be viewed exclusively over the Internet, set your dots per inch to 96 dpi—which just happens to be the standard resolution of a computer monitor connected to a Windows-based computer. (Mac monitors typically run at 72 dpi.) Any resolution higher than 96 dpi is overkill.

Using eBay Picture Services

When you have eBay host your photos, you have some choices to make. If you want to show only one picture, you're okay with eBay. If you want to show more than one photo, or if you want to show larger photos, you can still use eBay—you'll just have to pay for it.

Here's how eBay Picture Services' fee structure works:

- First photo: free.
- Each additional picture (up to six, total): $0.15 each.
- Picture show (multiple pictures in a slideshow format): Free.
- Supersize pictures (allow users to click a photo to display at a larger size): $0.75
- Picture pack (up to six pictures, supersized, with Gallery display): $1.00

If you like to get fancy with your pictures, those costs can add up pretty fast. Let's say you have two pictures of your item (front and back, perhaps) that you want to display in large format. You'll pay $0.90 for this privilege—the first picture is free, but you pay $0.15 for the second picture, plus $0.75 for supersizing.

If you frequently include multiple pictures in your auctions, it might be cheaper for you to find another site to host your pictures, which we'll talk about next. But if you typically include only a single photo, eBay Picture Services is both affordable (free!) and easy to use, especially for beginners. Here's how you do it:

1. Start the process to create a new item listing, and work your way to the Describe Your Item page.
2. Scroll to the Pictures section and click the Add Pictures button.
3. When the Add Pictures window appears, as shown in Figure 18.7, click the Add Pictures button in the first (top left) box.

FIGURE 18.7

Adding pictures via eBay Picture Services.

4. An Open dialog box now appears on your computer desktop; use this dialog box to locate and select the photo you want to use. Click the Open button when done; the photo you selected now appears in the Add Pictures window.

5. To insert an additional picture (for $0.15 extra), click the Add Picture button in the second box and repeat the instructions in step 4.

6. To insert even more pictures, click the Add Picture button(s) in the next box(es) and repeat the instructions in step 4.

7. When you're done adding pictures, select which picture options you want—Standard, Supersize Pictures, Picture Show, or Picture Pack.

8. Click the Upload Pictures button. This will upload the selected photos from your computer to eBay.

9. Back on the Describe Your Item page, scroll down to the Listing Designer section and (if you want to use the Listing Designer feature, which costs $0.10 extra), select a position for your photo from the Picture Layout list.

That's it. eBay will automatically upload the pictures from your hard disk to its picture hosting server, and automatically insert those pictures into your item listing.

> **tip**
>
> One plus to using eBay Picture Services is that you get a free picture of your item in the title bar of your item listing page—which you don't get if you host your pictures on another website.

Using Another Web Host

Many users are less than thrilled with eBay's picture hosting service. They find this service somewhat expensive (if you want to show a lot of pictures) and somewhat limited in how the pictures are displayed in your listing.

A better solution for some users is to use another Web hosting service to host their files. Here you have a lot of options.

First, if you have your own personal page on the Web, you can probably upload your pictures to that Web server. For example, if you have a personal page on Yahoo!, GeoCities, or Tripod, you should be able to upload your images to that site.

If you don't have a personal page but *could* have a personal page (via America Online or your Internet service provider), that's a potential place for you to upload picture files. If your company has a Web server, there's a chance it will let you use a little space there.

If you don't have any other options, you can go to a site that specializes in storing image files for eBay users. These sites include the following:

- Ándale Images (www.andale.com)
- Auction Pix Image Hosting (www.auctionpix.com)
- Photobucket (www.photobucket.com)
- PictureTrail (www.picturetrail.com)
- Vendio Image Hosting (www.vendio.com)

Most of these sites charge some sort of fee for hosting your pictures, either on a monthly basis for a certain amount of storage space or on a per-picture basis. Compare the fees at these sites with what you'll pay at eBay, and then make the smart choice.

After you have your pictures uploaded, you can add them to your new item listing. Just follow these steps:

> **tip**
>
> eBay now offers its own advanced picture hosting service, dubbed eBay Picture Manager. You get 50MB of storage for $9.99 per month; more storage is available for additional fees. Learn more at pages.ebay.com/ picture_manager/.

1. Start the process to create a new item listing, and work your way to the Describe Your Item page.
2. Scroll down to the Pictures section and click the Add Pictures button.
3. When the Add Pictures window appears, click the Host My Own Picture link at the bottom of the window.
4. When the next page appears, as shown in Figure 18.8, enter the full web address of your photo.

5. If you have multiple photos, check the Picture Show option and follow the onscreen instructions to add additional URLs.

6. Click the Save button.

7. Continue with the rest of the listing-creation process, as normal.

FIGURE 18.8

Pointing to a picture file uploaded to another hosting service.

Adding a Picture Within Your Item Description

Another picture option is available for more advanced users—especially if you're comfortable adding a little HTML code to your item descriptions. This option lets you insert images directly within your item description. (And eBay won't charge you for it, either!)

As you learned in Chapter 17, "Creating More Effective Item Listings," you can include HTML code in your item descriptions—and you can use this code to link to pictures you've already uploaded to a picture hosting service. This process isn't as hard as it sounds, assuming you've already found a hosting service, uploaded your picture file, and obtained the full URL for the uploaded picture. All you have to do is insert the following HTML code into your item description, where you want the picture to appear:

```
<img src="http://www.webserver.com/picture.jpg">
```

Just replace *www.webserver.com/picture.jpg* with the correct URL for your picture.

You'll also need to go through the process to add a picture to your listing, and from within the Add Pictures window click the Host My Own Picture link at the bottom of the window. When the next page appears, check the The Description Already Includes a Picture URL for My Item option. Your item will now display with the picture(s) you've selected—and you can expect the bids to start pouring in!

THE ABSOLUTE MINIMUM

Here are the key points to remember from this chapter:

- Adding a picture to your item listing will increase the number of bids you receive—and the value of those bids.

- The easiest way to take pictures of the items you want to sell is with a digital camera—unless you have a small, flat item, in which case scanning is probably better.

- Take the best picture possible, and then edit the picture (in a graphics editing program) to make it look even better.

- Make sure that the picture will fit on your item listing page, and that the file size of the picture isn't too large.

- You can choose to let eBay host your pictures (with some potential cost), or you can find a third-party hosting service (that might also charge a fee).

- You add photos to your listings when you're creating the item listing, on the Describe Your Item page.

19

ACCEPTING PAYPAL AND OTHER METHODS OF PAYMENT

When you're listing an item for auction on eBay, you can choose which types of payment you'll accept from the winning bidder. This may seem like an easy decision, but each type of payment needs to be handled differently on your end.

This chapter talks about the types of payment you can choose to use. As any experienced eBay seller will tell you, not all dollars are worth the same; a dollar paid by one method might actually be worth less (or be more risky) than a dollar by another method. And you *do* want the biggest dollar, don't you?

Fortunately, you're not forced to use any one payment method. For example, you can limit your payments to credit cards only; there's no law that says you have to accept cash or checks. So read on to learn which types of payment provide the biggest return for your efforts!

Accepting Credit Cards—via PayPal

There was a time that if you wanted to accept credit card payment for your auction items, you had to be a real retailer, complete with merchant account and bank-supplied charge card terminal. This limited the number of sellers who could accept credit card payment, which probably cut down on potential bidders, because many buyers like the convenience and relative safety of paying by credit card.

Today, however, just about any seller, no matter how small, can accept credit card payments. All you have to do is sign up to use an online payment service, such as eBay's PayPal. When a buyer uses his or her credit card to pay via PayPal, PayPal charges the credit card and then notifies you (via email) that you've been paid. Upon this notification, you ship the item and then access your account on the PayPal site and instruct PayPal to either cut you a check or transfer the funds into your bank account.

> **note**
>
> PayPal accepts payments by American Express, Discover, MasterCard, and Visa. Although it's primarily a U.S.-based service, it also accepts payments to or from 55 other countries.

Signing Up for PayPal

Before you can use PayPal as a seller, you must sign up for PayPal membership. You do this by going to the PayPal website (www.paypal.com), shown in Figure 19.1, and clicking the Sign Up Now button or Sign Up link.

FIGURE 19.1

The PayPal home page.

You can choose from three types of PayPal accounts:

- A **Personal** account is great for eBay buyers, but not quite enough for sellers. You can send money free, but can receive only non–credit card payments (for no charge, though). Also, sellers with Personal accounts aren't allowed to display the PayPal logo in their auction listings.

- A **Premier** account is the best way to go for most eBay sellers. You can still send money free, and you can now accept both credit card and non–credit card payments (for a fee).

- A **Business** account is necessary if you're receiving a high volume of payments. With this type of account, you can do business under a corporate or group name, and use multiple logins.

There is no charge for becoming a PayPal member—although there are fees for actually using the service. (The exception is the Personal account, which charges no fees for anything—but doesn't let you accept credit card payments.)

note

While I recommend you sign up for a PayPal account beforehand, you don't have to. You can simply choose PayPal as an accepted payment method when you're creating your eBay auction listing, and when a buyer chooses to pay via PayPal, you'll be prompted at that time to sign up for your PayPal account.

Paying for PayPal

The fee you pay to PayPal is separate from any other fees you pay to eBay. The way PayPal works is that the buyer doesn't pay any fees; it's the seller who is assessed a fee based on the *amount of money transferred*.

"Mike Sez"

I recommend you sign up initially for a Premier account. If your sales volume gets high enough, PayPal will automatically switch you to a Business membership.

This last point is important. PayPal charges fees based on the total amount of money paid, *not* on the selling price of the item. That means that if a $10 item has a $5 shipping and handling cost, the buyer pays PayPal a total of $15—and PayPal bases its fee on that $15 payment.

PayPal's fees range from 1.9% to 2.9%, depending on your monthly sales volume. Table 19.1 presents PayPal's fee schedule as of February 2006:

Table 19.1   PayPal Transaction Fees (U.S.)

Monthly Sales	Transaction Fee
$0–$3,000.00	2.9%
$3,000.01–$10,000.00	2.5%
$10,000.01–$100,000.00	2.2%
>$100,000.00	1.9%

You're also charged a flat $0.30 per transaction, regardless of your sales volume. All fees are deducted from your account with every transaction.

note

To qualify for the 2.5% or lower rate, you have to have a PayPal Business account.

Choosing PayPal in Your New Auction Listing

The easiest way to accept PayPal payments in your eBay auctions is to choose the PayPal option when you're creating an item listing. This is as simple as checking the PayPal box and entering your PayPal ID on the Describe Your Item page.

When you choose this option, a PayPal payments section is added to your item listing. PayPal will also appear as a payment option on your post-auction item listing page and in eBay's end-of-auction email to the winning bidder.

Collecting PayPal Payments

When a buyer makes a PayPal payment, those funds are immediately transferred to the seller's PayPal account, and an email notification of the payment is sent to the seller. In most cases, this email will include all the information the seller needs to link it to a specific auction and ship the item to the seller.

When you sign into the PayPal site, you're taken to the My Account tab, and the Overview tab within that. As you can see in Figure 19.2, this displays an overview of your recent PayPal activity, including payments made by buyers into your account. Click any item to view more detail about the activity.

In most cases, the buyers' payments come into your account free and clear, ready to be withdrawn from your checking account. The exception to this is an eCheck payment, in which a buyer pays PayPal from his or her personal checking account. Because PayPal has to wait until the "electronic check" clears to receive its funds, you can't be paid until then, either. PayPal will send you an email when an electronic payment clears.

FIGURE 19.2
An overview of
your PayPal
activity.

Withdrawing PayPal Funds

You can let your funds build up in your PayPal account, or you can choose (at any time) to withdraw all or part of your funds. You have the option of okaying an electronic withdrawal directly to your checking account (no charge; takes three to four business days) or requesting a check for the requested amount ($1.50 charge; takes one to two weeks). Just click the Withdraw tab (from the Overview tab) and click the appropriate text link.

Accepting Money Orders and Cashier's Checks

The good thing about accepting credit card payments via PayPal is that you get paid quickly; the bad thing is that it costs you (up to 2.9% plus $0.30 per transaction). For that reason, many sellers prefer alternate methods of payment, such as (and especially) money orders and cashier's checks.

When you receive payment via money order or cashier's check, you get to cash the entire check; there aren't any fees to deduct. However, you have to wait a bit for the buyer to send you the money order or cashier's check in the mail. That's a trade-off many sellers happily make.

> **" Mike Sez "**
>
> I prefer to empty my PayPal account to zero at the end of each day, via an electronic transfer to my checking account. I find this the fastest, no-hassle way to receive PayPal funds due.

The other good thing about money orders and cashier's checks is that you don't have to wait for the checks to clear, as you do with personal checks (discussed next). A money order or cashier's check is almost as good as cash; it's hard to get burned.

Accepting Personal Checks

Many buyers still prefer to pay for their purchases via personal check. Buyers like paying by check because it's convenient, and because checks can be tracked (or even canceled) if problems arise with the seller.

Sellers like personal checks a little less, because they're not instant money. When you deposit a check in your bank, you're not depositing cash. That $100 check doesn't turn into $100 cash until it tracks back through the financial system, from your bank back to the buyer's bank, and the funds are both verified and transferred. That can take some time, typically 10 business days or so.

Because some buyers still prefer paying by check, you should probably be prepared to handle this payment method. When you receive a check, deposit it as soon as possible—but do *not* ship the item. Wait until the check clears the bank (two weeks if you want to be safe—longer for checks on non-U.S. banks) before you ship the item. If, after that period, the check hasn't bounced, it's okay to proceed with shipment.

If you are on the bad end of a bounced check, all hope is not lost. The first thing to do is get in touch with your bank and ask them to resubmit the check in question. Maybe the buyer was just temporarily out of funds. Maybe the bank made a mistake. Whatever. In at least half the cases, bounced checks "unbounce" when they're resubmitted.

Whether you resubmit the check or not, you should definitely email the buyer and let him know what happened. At the very least, you'll want the buyer to reimburse you for any bad check fees your bank charged you. The buyer might also be able to provide another form of payment to get things moving again. (Credit cards are nice—as are money orders.)

> **caution**
>
> While cashier's checks and money orders are generally safe, there are some scams that you need to be aware of. In particular, beware of scammers who send you a money order or cashier's check in excess of the amount due, then ask you to send them the difference. That's a sure sign that the payment is fraudulent—and you make it worse by sending the scammer some of your money in return!

> **" Mike Sez "**
>
> If you ship an item on immediate receipt of a personal check and then a week later you get a notice from your bank that the check has bounced, you deserve to lose every single penny of that transaction. Eager shippers and personal checks just don't mix—and you *will* learn from your mistake.

Accepting C.O.D. Payments

Cash on delivery (C.O.D.) might sound good on paper. You ship the item, with the stipulation that the delivery man (or woman) collect payment when the item is delivered.

There are problems with this method, however. What happens if the buyer isn't home when the delivery is made? What if the buyer is at home, but doesn't have the cash? What if the buyer refuses to pay—and rejects the shipment? I've heard stories that up to 25% of all C.O.D. orders being refused, for one reason or another. And if the item is refused, you (the seller) have to pay postage in both directions.

Even worse, C.O.D. service often comes with a high fee from the carrier—and it's a fee that you, the seller, have to pay. The additional fee alone rules out C.O.D. for many sellers.

> **caution**
>
> If a check bounces, the depositor (you) will likely be assessed a fee from your bank. (The writer of the bad check will also have a fee to pay.) If the buyer who wrote the check offers to make good on the payment, make sure that they reimburse you for your bad check fee, over and above the final auction price.

All things considered, it's easy to see why few eBay sellers offer C.O.D. payment. The problems with this payment method tend to outweigh the benefits, and I can't recommend it.

Accepting Cash

As a seller, there's nothing better than opening up an envelope and finding a few crisp new bills inside. Unfortunately, sending cash through the mail is not one of the smartest things a buyer can do; cash is too easily ripped off, and virtually untraceable. While you can ask for cash payment, don't expect buyers to comply—especially since eBay recommends against this method of payment.

Which Way Is Best?

The more payment options you offer, the more potential bidders you'll attract. Still, some methods are better than others for different types of sellers; use Table 19.2 to determine which methods work best for you.

> **"Mike Sez"**
>
> In all my auctions, I accept personal checks, money orders, cashier's checks, and credit cards (via PayPal). Most buyers these days end up using PayPal, so I make sure to factor those charges into my cost of doing business.

Table 19.2   Payment Methods Rated

Payment Method	Pros	Cons
Credit cards (via PayPal)	Fast payment; buyers like paying via credit card; most popular form of payment today	Fees involved (up to 2.9% of total price plus $0.30 per transaction)
Money order/cashier's check	Almost as good as cash	Hassle for buyers; have to wait for the payment to arrive via mail
Personal check	Convenient for buyers	Slow; have to wait for payment to arrive via mail; have to wait for check to clear
C.O.D.	Cash payment	High noncompletion rate; lots of paperwork; high seller fees
Cash	Relatively fast payment, no hassles	Unattractive to buyers

The Absolute Minimum

Here are the key points to remember from this chapter:

- The fastest way to get your money is via credit card (using PayPal). You'll pay for the privilege, however—up to 2.9% of the total selling price, plus $0.30 per transaction.

- The slowest way to get your money is via personal check.

- If you do accept payment by personal check, remember to wait at least 10 business days for the check to clear before you ship the merchandise.

- The best compromise between speed and hassle is payment via cashier's check or money order. (And there are no fees involved.)

20

AUTOMATING YOUR LISTINGS WITH EBAY TURBO LISTER

As you learned in Chapter 15, "Selling Items via Online Auction," creating an item listing with eBay's standard selling process isn't that hard. However, if you have a lot of items to list, this page-by-page process can be time-consuming. Going through that cumbersome procedure for a dozen or more items isn't very appealing—trust me.

A better solution if you have a lot of items to list is to use a *bulk listing* program or service. These tools let you create a large number of item listings in advance, and even reuse saved listings—great if you run multiple auctions for similar items. You then schedule your auctions to launch at the time of your choosing, and you're done with it.

Several of these bulk listing tools are available, but the most popular one is available from eBay free of charge. This program is called Turbo Lister, and it also lets you create great-looking item listings through the use of predesigned templates.

Downloading and Configuring the Turbo Lister Software

Turbo Lister, shown in Figure 20.1, is a software program that you install on your own PC. When you run Turbo Lister, you can create your eBay item listings offline, at your leisure. Then, when you're ready, it uploads all your listings at once, with the click of a button. Creating multiple auctions couldn't be easier.

FIGURE 20.1

eBay's Turbo Lister bulk listing program.

Downloading Turbo Lister

To download the Turbo Lister software, go to pages.ebay.com/turbo_lister/. The program is free and there are no monthly subscription fees—which makes it the program of choice for cost-conscious sellers.

Configuring Turbo Lister

Before you use Turbo Lister, you need to configure it for your specific auction listings. You do this from the Options and Preferences dialog box, which you open by pulling down the Tools menu and selecting Options.

As you can see in Figure 20.2, the Options and Preferences dialog box is divided into two parts. The left side contains a menu tree of options; the specifics for the selected option are displayed on the right.

You'll want to go through each and every option to make sure that Turbo Lister is set up properly for your upcoming auctions. The options you set here determine the information used by default in your listings; you can always edit any piece of information when you create an individual auction.

> **note**
>
> The instructions in this chapter apply to the relatively new Turbo Lister 2. If you're using a previous version of the program, you should upgrade to the latest version at your earliest convenience.

FIGURE 20.2

Configuring Turbo Lister via the Options and Preferences dialog box.

Creating an Item Listing

The Turbo Lister software is quite easy to use. It uses a series of forms to request information about your listings. It also includes predesigned templates and a WYSIWYG (what you see is what you get) editor that lets you create great-looking listings.

You start out not by creating a listing, but rather by creating a new inventory item. After you've created the item, you then design a listing for that item. Here's how it works:

1. From the main Turbo Lister screen, click the New button and then select Create New Item.

2. When the Create New Item window appears, as shown in Figure 20.3, you fill out all the item information as you would when using the Describe Your Item page on the main eBay site. From top to bottom (and left to right), enter the following information:

FIGURE 20.3

Creating a new item listing.

- Item title, subtitle, and category
- Auction format, start price, reserve price (if any), Buy It Now price (if any), quantity available, and duration
- Picture(s)
- Item description
- Listing upgrades (gallery, bold, and so on)
- Shipping charges and services
- Inventory information (if you're listing in an eBay Store)

tip

If you're selling some common items (books, CDs, DVDs, video games, and the like), you have the option of using eBay's pre-filled information and stock photos. Read on to the "Creating Listings for Commonly Sold Items" section of this chapter to learn more.

■ Payment methods

■ Additional information, including
return policy

3. When you're done entering the item
information, click the Save button.

You've just created a new item listing—but you
haven't launched the auction yet. This new item
is added to your item inventory, which is what
Turbo Lister calls your database of item listings.
To turn this inventory item into a live auction,
you have to upload it to eBay—which you'll learn
how to do in the "Uploading Your Listings" section,
later in this chapter.

tip

To edit any listing you've
created, select the item on
the Inventory screen, and
then click the Edit button.
This opens the Edit Item
dialog box; make your
changes and then click the
Save button.

Creating Listings for Commonly Sold Items

As you learned back in Chapter 15, if you're selling commonly sold items—books,
audio books, audio cassettes, CDs, DVDs, video games, and various consumer electronics products—you can use eBay's pre-filled item description feature to automatically create item descriptions, complete with stock product photos. Turbo Lister
makes this feature even better by letting you create listings for multiple items at one
time; all you have to do is enter the name or number of your items, and Turbo Lister
will create multiple listings.

To create multiple listings of this type, follow these steps:

1. Click the New button and select Create Multiple Items with Pre-Filled
Information.

2. When the opening screen appears, click Next.

3. When the Enter Multiple Items screen
appears, as shown in Figure 20.4, pull down
the Select Product Type list and select which
type of items you're selling.

4. Still on the same page, pull down the Item 1
Search By list and select how you want to
search for the item (UPC or ISBN is most
accurate), and then enter the keywords or
number into the adjoining box. Repeat this
step to enter multiple items.

note

If you want to list
more than 10 items, click
the Add More Items button.

5. Still on the same page, pull down the Select
Selling Format list and select Auction, and then click Next.

FIGURE 20.4

Selling multiple commonly sold items.

6. Turbo Lister now connects to the Internet and searches for the items you entered. Select the items that correctly match the items you're selling, and then click Next.

7. Turbo Lister downloads the appropriate information for each of these items, and then displays the You're Almost Done! screen. Click the Save button to proceed.

8. You're now taken to the Inventory page in the main Turbo Lister window. Each of your newly created items is listed, along with a corresponding Edit button. You have to choose a listing category and enter auction details (such as starting price) for each item. Click the Edit button for each item to display the Edit Item screen; enter the required information and then click the Save button. Repeat this step for each item you've added.

When you've finished editing each of these new listings, they're ready to upload—which is what we'll do next.

Uploading Your Listings

Turbo Lister keeps all your item listings—past and pending—in an inventory list. To view the items in your inventory, click Inventory in the left-hand pane. This page lists all the items you've created; from here you can edit, delete, or create duplicate items.

When you have an auction that you're ready to launch, follow these steps:

1. Go to the Inventory page.

2. Select the item(s) you want to launch.

3. Click the Add to Upload button; this copies the item(s) to your upload list. (The original items still appear in your inventory listing, so you can reuse them for additional auctions later.)

4. Turbo Lister displays the Add to Upload dialog box; click the Go Upload button.

5. This action displays the Waiting to Upload screen, shown in Figure 20.5. (You can also select this screen manually, by clicking Waiting to Upload in the left-hand pane.) This screen shows all items waiting to be uploaded.

> **caution**
>
> Remember, just because an item appears in your inventory list doesn't mean that it has been launched as an eBay auction. You have to manually select which items you want to list, and then upload those items to eBay.

FIGURE 20.5

Items waiting to be uploaded to eBay.

6. To calculate your listing fees for these items, click the Calculate Fees button.

7. To change the starting time for an item, select the item and then click the Schedule button. When the Schedule Listing Start dialog box appears, make a new selection and then click OK. (Remember, you'll pay $0.10 per listing to schedule a later start time.)

8. When you're ready to upload these items, click the Upload All button.

Turbo Lister now connects to the eBay site and uploads the selected item listings. Those listings that are set to start immediately do so, and items with a future start time are sent to eBay's Pending Listings section. These auctions will go live at the time(s) you previously scheduled.

Pretty easy, huh? Just remember that you pay an extra $0.10 for every item you submit with Turbo Lister, due to the use of eBay's pay-per-use templates. (It's the same when you use these templates with the standard Listing Designer feature.)

THE ABSOLUTE MINIMUM

Here are the key points to remember from this chapter:

- You can use Turbo Lister to create multiple listings—complete with fancy formatting and templates—offline, and then upload all these listings at one time.

- The Turbo Lister software is available for downloading from eBay—and it's free!

- Before you use Turbo Lister, you have to configure it to display various default information for your auction listings.

- The listings you create are added to Turbo Lister's inventory list; you then have to upload these listings to eBay in order to start the auctions.

- You can also use Turbo Lister to create multiple listings for commonly sold items, using eBay's pre-filled item description feature.

21

AFTER THE SALE: CONCLUDING THE TRANSACTION

You've waited the requisite 7 (or 1 or 3 or 5 or 10) days, and your auction has finally ended. What comes next?

The post-auction process involves more work, in most cases, than the listing process. You have to contact the buyer, arrange payment, receive payment, pack the item, ship the item, and leave feedback. And that's if everything goes smoothly!

The post-auction process can also be a long one, depending on how the buyer pays. If the buyer pays by PayPal (or other credit card method) as soon as the auction ends, the post-auction process can be over that day or the next—as soon as you pack and ship the item. If, on the other hand, the buyer pays by check—and is a little slow in putting the check in the mail—the post-auction process can last two or three weeks.

That means, of course, that you need to remember this potential time lag when you're planning your auction activity. For example, if you're planning to go on vacation in two weeks, now is not the best time to list an item for auction. You need to allocate a full month, from beginning to end, when you're planning your auction listings. If your buyers help you complete the process faster, that's great. But there will always be that one last buyer who hasn't sent the check yet—and there goes your schedule!

The Post-Auction Process

What happens during the post-auction process is actually rather cut and dried. Put simply, you contact the winning bidder with a final price; he or she sends payment to you; you pocket the payment; you package and ship the item; the buyer receives the item; and you both leave feedback for each other.

In checklist form, here's what you have to look forward to:

Checklist: After the Auction

- ☐ Receive an end-of-auction email from eBay
- ☐ If the buyer doesn't pay immediately via PayPal, send an email or invoice to the high bidder (containing final price and payment information)
- ☐ Receive payment from the buyer—and wait for payment to clear, if necessary
- ☐ Package the item
- ☐ Ship the item to the high bidder
- ☐ Leave feedback for the buyer

Communicating with the Winning Bidder

Minutes after the conclusion of your auction, eBay will notify you by email that your auction has ended. This email message, like the one shown in Figure 21.1, will include the user ID and email address of the item's high bidder.

Several things can now happen:

- If you accept payment via PayPal and if the buyer opts to pay via credit card or bank debit, he can initiate payment from the end-of-auction email he receives. If the buyer pays immediately like this, you'll receive a second email informing you of the completed payment.
- If the buyer doesn't pay via PayPal, he can still go through eBay's checkout process, which then sends you an email notifying you of the buyer's intention to pay via check or money order or whatever, and providing you with the buyer's shipping address and other relevant information.

FIGURE 21.1

A typical eBay email notifying you of the end of your auction.

- If the buyer doesn't pay or check out immediately, you can send the buyer an invoice. Just click the Send Invoice link in the end-of-auction email you received (or on the closed auction page, or on your My eBay page) to display the Send Invoice to Buyer page, shown in Figure 21.2. Edit the payment information and instructions as necessary, and then click the Send Invoice button to email the thing.

- Alternately, you can choose to send your own personal end-of-auction notice directly to the buyer. If you opt for this method, include your name and address (so the buyer will know where to send the payment); your email address (so the buyer can contact you with any questions or issues); the total amount the buyer owes you (the final auction price plus shipping/handling); and your preferred method(s) of payment.

- You can also use various auction-management tools to handle all this post-auction messaging and processing for you. One of the most popular tools is eBay Selling Manager; learn more in Chapter 22, "Managing Your Sales with eBay Selling Manager."

note

eBay lets you combine multiple auctions into a single invoice, for those occasions where one buyer has made multiple purchases. The auctions are grouped by buyer, so all you have to do is select all the auctions from a single buyer to create a combined invoice. You can even manipulate the shipping/handling costs for the combined auctions, in order to offer a discount for multiple orders.

If the buyer doesn't pay immediately, he should at least respond to your invoice or end-of-auction email. If you haven't heard back from the buyer in a day or two, send another email. If, after three days, you still haven't been able to contact the buyer, you can consider that person a non-paying bidder. See Chapter 24, "Dealing with Non-Paying Buyers," to learn how to deal with this situation.

Accepting Payment

Now it's time to get paid. As recommended in Chapter 19, "Accepting PayPal and Other Methods of Payment," you've presumably determined how you want to get paid, and indicated so in your item listing. You need to repeat your preferred payment methods in your post-auction email to the high bidder, and then wait for that user to make the payment.

Whatever you do, do *not* ship the item before you've received payment! Wait until you've received a cashier's check or money order in the mail, or been notified by PayPal that a payment has been made, and *then* prepare to ship the item.

"Mike Sez"

It's important for sellers to know that the post-auction timeframe is when buyers feel the most vulnerable; the auction is final, their money is in the sellers' hands, and the merchandise that they bought sight unseen has yet to be delivered. Sellers need to understand buyers' concerns (especially those of new or inexperienced buyers) and offer excellent post-auction communication and customer service. I've found that the ultimate success of the transaction (and the likelihood of receiving positive feedback—and possible gaining a repeat customer) is directly proportionate to the amount of communication I have with the buyer. Put yourself in your buyer's shoes, and go that extra step in making him feel comfortable with his transaction.

When you receive payment, it's good business practice to email the buyer and let him or her know that the payment has been received. If you know when you'll be shipping the item, include that information in the email, as well.

And if the buyer never sends payment? Turn to Chapter 24 for my detailed advice.

caution

Remember, if you receive a payment via personal check, wait at least 10 working days for that payment to clear before you ship the item.

Packing and Shipping

One of the most crucial parts of the post-auction process is packing the item you've just sold. This process is so important, and so complicated, that I've devoted an entire chapter to it. So when you're ready to pack, turn to Chapter 23, "Packing and Shipping Your Items—Cheaply and Safely," for more information.

Finishing Things Up and Leaving Feedback

As you ship the sold item, there are two more things you need to do:

- First, send an email to the buyer, letting him or her know that the item is on its way. (You should note in your message when and by which method the item was shipped—and if you have a tracking or confirmation number, pass it along.)
- Second, you need to leave feedback about the buyer. Whether it was a good transaction or a bad transaction, you need to let your fellow eBay members know how things turned out.

To leave feedback for the buyer, follow these instructions:

1. Go to the listing page for the item you just sold and click the Leave Feedback link.

2. When the Leave Feedback page appears, indicate whether you're leaving Positive, Negative, or Neutral feedback, and then enter your comments (80 characters, maximum) in the Comment box.

3. Make sure you really want to leave the comments you've written, and then click the Leave Feedback button. Your feedback will be registered and added into the buyer's other feedback comments.

Reread Chapter 3, "Understanding and Using Feedback," for more information about the type of feedback to leave in different situations.

Handling Buyer Complaints and Problems

Not all auctions go smoothly. Maybe the item arrived damaged. Maybe it didn't arrive at all. Maybe it wasn't exactly what the buyer thought he was getting. Maybe the buyer is a loud, complaining, major-league son of a rutabaga.

In any case, if you have a complaining customer, you need to do something about it. Here are some of your options:

- Ignore them. If you specified "all sales are final" in your item listing, you don't technically have to do anything else at this point. Of course, complaining customers tend to leave negative feedback, and might even complain to eBay about you; this is not the option I'd recommend.

- If the item never arrived, put a trace on the shipment, if you can.

- If the item was insured, you can initiate a claim for the lost or damaged item. (See Chapter 21 for more information on filing insurance claims.)

- Negotiate a lower price for a damaged or disappointing item, and refund the difference to the buyer.

- Offer to refund the purchase price if the item is returned to you.

- Offer a full refund on the item, no questions asked, no further action necessary. (With this option, the buyer doesn't have to bother with shipping it back to you; this is the way Nordstrom would take care of it.)

> **" Mike Sez "**
>
> There are really no hard and fast rules for handling post-auction problems. You have to play it by ear and resolve each complaint to the best of your ability. Most eBay users are easy to deal with and just want to be treated fairly. Others won't be satisfied no matter what you offer them. You have to use your own best judgment on how to handle individual situations.

Most important are those complaints that escalate to the eBay level, via eBay's Item Not Received or Significantly Not as Described process. Under this process (described in Chapter 11, "Protecting Yourself from Shady Sellers"), a buyer can file a complaint if he doesn't receive his merchandise within 10 days of the end of the auction. The problem here is that many transactions will fall outside this arbitrary waiting period. For example, if a buyer pays by personal check and you hold the check for 10 business days before shipping, the buyer hasn't received his merchandise in 10 days and can technically file a complaint.

Fortunately, nothing major happens if the buyer files a claim at the 10-day mark. Once the buyer files a claim, eBay notifies you (the seller) of the claim and asks for a response; no formal action is taken until 30 days after the end of the listing. If, at that time, the buyer hasn't received the item (or the two of you haven't communicated and worked something out), then the buyer has the option of escalating the complaint into eBay's Standard Purchase Protection Program.

At that point eBay can get involved and refund the buyer's money (up to $200) and take action against you as a seller. That action could result in a formal warning, a temporary suspension, or an indefinite suspension. Of course, it's also possible that eBay could evaluate the situation and take no action against you. The outcome depends on the situation.

Obviously, if you're doing your job right, no complaint should escalate into the Standard Purchase Protection Program. If you do get an Item Not Received complaint, make sure you respond and inform the buyer why he or she hasn't received the item yet. The key here is communication—especially when you're dealing with inexperienced buyers.

What If You Don't Sell Your Item?

Not every item up for auction on eBay sells. (eBay's completion rate is right around 50%—which means that half the items listed at any given time don't sell.) If you reach the end of the auction and you haven't received any bids—or you haven't received high-enough bids in a reserve auction—you need to drop back ten and punt, and figure out what to do next.

Perhaps the easiest thing to do if your item didn't sell is to try again—by relisting your item. eBay makes this easy for you, by including a Relist Your Item link right on the original item listing page. Click this link to create a new item listing, based on the old item listing.

When you relist an item that didn't sell the first time, eBay still charges you a listing fee for the second listing. However, eBay will refund this second listing fee if your item sells the second time around. (But not if it doesn't.) You will, of course, have to pay the normal end-of-auction fee if the item sells the second time around. (And you only get this refund the first time you relist; if the item still doesn't sell, you'll have to ante up to keep it listed.)

" Mike Sez "

If you choose to relist your item, realize that there was probably something about the first listing that kept the item from selling. Maybe the starting price was too high; maybe the headline stank; maybe you didn't include a picture; maybe the description was too brief. (And maybe you just have an item that nobody wants to buy!) You need to figure out what was wrong with the first listing and change it on the relist—otherwise, you're probably doomed to another unsuccessful auction.

What If the Buyer Doesn't Pay?

To an eBay seller, the worst thing in the world is a high bidder who disappears from the face of the earth. When you never receive payment for an auction item, you're dealing with a non-paying bidder—and you're pretty much hosed. Still, you can report the bum to eBay, ask for a refund of your final value fee, and maybe offer the item in question to the second-highest bidder.

To learn more about how to handle a nonpaying buyer situation, turn to Chapter 24.

THE ABSOLUTE MINIMUM

Here are the key points to remember from this chapter:

- When the auction ends, eBay will contact you (and the high bidder) with end-of-auction information.

- You should then contact the high bidder with your final price and payment information.

- After you receive payment, pack and ship the item—and leave feedback for the high bidder.

- If an item doesn't sell, relist it—and if it sells the second time around, eBay will refund the second listing fee.

- If the high bidder is somehow dissatisfied or complains to eBay, try to work out a mutually agreeable solution.

22

MANAGING YOUR SALES WITH EBAY SELLING MANAGER

In the preceding chapter you learned how important it is to manage all your post-auction activity—sending out invoices to winning bidders, keeping track of who has paid and who hasn't, preparing items for shipping, leaving feedback, and the like. If you run only a few auctions at a time, you can probably manage this activity by hand. But if you're running a half-dozen or more auctions simultaneously, it gets tough to keep track of everything you need to do.

When your number of active auctions increases, you should think about using some sort of auction management tool to help you keep things in control. Although various third-party auction management services are available (which you'll learn about in Chapter 27, "Using Selling Management Services"), for many users the best tool is available from eBay itself. It's called eBay Selling Manager, and it's both easy to use and affordable.

Introducing eBay Selling Manager and Selling Manager Pro

eBay Selling Manager is one of eBay's official auction management tools. It's available in both basic and Pro versions; we'll discuss Selling Manager Pro later in this chapter.

The basic Selling Manager lets you keep track of current and pending auctions, as well as all your closed auctions; you can use Selling Manager to send emails to winning bidders, print invoices and shipping labels, and even leave feedback. Everything you need to do is accessed over the Web, on the eBay site, through your normal web browser. When you subscribe to Selling Manager, the All Selling page in My eBay is transformed into a Selling Manager page. From here, Selling Manager lets you manage all your post-auction activity.

To subscribe to eBay Selling Manager, go to pages.ebay.com/selling_manager/. The subscription cost for the basic version is $4.99 per month.

> **tip**
>
> You can switch the My eBay Selling Manager page back to the standard All Selling page by going to the Selling Manager Active Listings page and clicking the View My eBay Selling link in the lower left-hand corner.

How Selling Manager Works

To use Selling Manager, all you have to do is go to your My eBay page and click the new Selling Manager link. As you can see in Figure 22.1, the main Selling Manager page provides an overview of all your active and closed auctions.

The Summary page divides your auctions into six major categories (some categories not shown in Figure 22.1):

- **At a Glance**. This is a graph of your sales for the last 24 hours, 7 days, and 30 days.

- **Sold**. This section summarizes your recent sales activity—total sales, sales awaiting payment, sales awaiting shipment, sales sold and shipped, and those transactions being tracked via the Dispute Console.

- **Listing Activity**. This section summarizes your current sales activity—active listings, scheduled listings, and ended listings.

- **Cross Promotions**. This section summarizes your various cross-promoted items.

FIGURE 22.1

Access eBay
Selling Manager
from your My
eBay page.

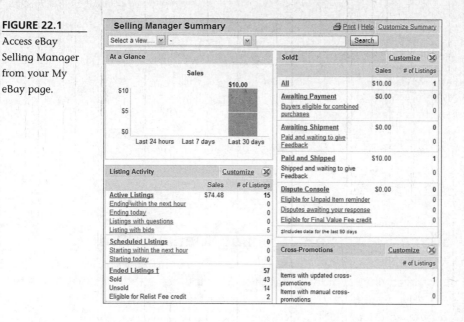

- **Picture Manager**. A visual representation of how many pictures and how much disk space you're using to store your digital photos.

- **Favorite Links**. Quick links to your eBay Preferences, My Messages, Manage My Store, PayPal, and Picture Manager Tools.

You use the links on this Summary page to display more detailed information about the items you have for sale. For example, when you click the All link in the Sold section, you display a list of completed auctions (shown in Figure 22.2), with the customer status indicated by a series of icons. You can select an individual auction to mark it paid or shipped, or to send it to your personal archive. You can also send various email messages to the winners of your auctions, as well as print invoices and leave feedback for multiple users in bulk.

"Mike Sez "

I find eBay Selling Manager an extremely useful tool if I have a moderate number of auctions running simultaneously. Running just a few auctions makes Selling Manager cost-prohibitive on a per-auction basis—and if I'm managing several dozen auctions, I come to curse its lack of batch email features. Still, for many sellers, Selling Manager does a fine job—and is a lot better than trying to manage post-auction activity manually.

FIGURE 22.2

Displaying a list
of your closed
auctions.

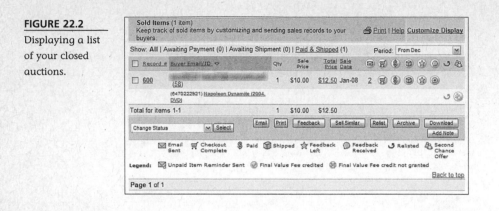

For Higher-Volume Sellers: eBay Selling Manager Pro

The basic Selling Manager product isn't perfect. One of its biggest problems is that
you pretty much have to manage one auction at a time—it lacks features that let
you effectively manage large numbers of auctions in bulk. If you're a high-volume
seller, a better solution is eBay's higher-end Selling Manager Pro, which offers better
bulk management and inventory mangagement features. For $15.99 per month,
Selling Manager Pro does everything the basic Selling Manager does, plus more:

- Manages individual inventory items, and issues restock alerts
- Offers free Listing Designer templates
- Generates a monthly profit and loss report, including all eBay fees and cost
  of goods sold

You can learn more about—and subscribe to—Selling Manager Pro at
pages.ebay.com/selling_manager_pro/.

Sending Buyer Emails

Probably the most useful feature of Selling Manager (Basic and Pro) is the capability
to send various end-of-auction email messages to winning bidders.

Selling Manager includes six boilerplate messages, all of which you can customize:

- Winning buyer notification
- Payment reminder
- Request shipping address
- Payment received
- Item shipped
- Feedback reminder

You typically send a winning buyer notification at the close of an auction, a payment reminder if the buyer hasn't paid within a week or so, a payment-received message when you get paid, and an item shipped message when you ship the item. The other messages are used only when necessary.

Sending a Standard Email Message

To send an email to a winning bidder, follow these steps:

1. Go to any of Selling Manager's Sold Listings pages.

2. Click a specific Buyer Email link.

3. When the Email Buyer page (shown in Figure 22.3) appears, select the type of message you want to send from the Template list.

4. If you want, edit the subject of the message in the Subject box.

5. If you want, edit the text of the message in the Message box.

6. If you want to receive a copy of this message, select the Send Me a Copy of This Email option.

7. Click Send to send the message.

tip

To view a list of emails you've sent to a specific buyer, click the number link in the email column next to the record # on the Sold Listings page. This opens an Email Log dialog box that lists all messages sent to that buyer.

FIGURE 22.3

Sending a post-auction email.

Email Buyer

Tip: You can also customize the End of Auction email sent to winning buyers from eBay. Learn more about customizing End of Auction emails.

Send | Preview | Cancel

Select an email: Winning buyer notification   Manage Email Templates

From: _____ Edit
To: _____
☐ Send me a copy of this email

Subject
Good news! eBay Item #6470222921 Napoleon Dynamite (2004, DVD)

Message
You are the winning buyer for the item below. Thank you for your business!

Item title: Napoleon Dynamite (2004, DVD)
Web address: http://cgi.ebay.com/ws/eBayISAPI.dll?
ViewItem&item=6470222921
Item number: 6470222921
Buyer User ID: _____
Seller User ID: trapperjohn2000

Your total is:
$10.00 per item
$2.50 shipping/handling

Editing an Email Template

Don't like Selling Manager's prepared email templates? Then customize them! Here's how:

1. From the Email Buyer page, click the Manage Email Templates link.

2. When the Manage Email Templates page (shown in Figure 22.4) appears, select the template you want to edit from the Template list.

3. Edit the text in the Subject and Message boxes, as desired.

4. Insert automated text (buyer name, buyer item number, and so on) into the message by selecting text from the Autotext list, then clicking the Insert button. The automated text (surrounded by curly brackets) now appears at the bottom of your message; cut and paste this text into its correct position within the message.

5. Click the Save Template button when done.

note

You can revert to the original template at any time by clicking the Reset to Default button.

FIGURE 22.4

Customizing a Selling Manager email template.

Manage Email Templates		
Create New Template		
Name	Last Modified	Action
Winning buyer notification	Oct-02-05 19:23:36	Edit
Payment reminder	--	Edit
Payment received notification	Oct-02-05 21:00:22	Edit
Request for shipping address	--	Edit
Feedback reminder	--	Edit
Shipping notification	--	Edit
Personalized email	--	Edit
Create New Template		

Receiving Payment

When you receive payment from a buyer, you want to update Selling Manager to reflect the payment, and to enter the buyer's shipping information. If a buyer pays via PayPal, this information is entered automatically. If the buyer pays by any other method (and doesn't go through the full checkout process), you'll need to enter this information manually. You do this from the individual Sales Record page, as described here:

1. On the Sold Listings page, click the Record # link for this specific auction.

2. When the Sales Record page appears, as shown in Figure 22.5, enter the buyer's name and address into the appropriate blanks.

FIGURE 22.5

Working with the buyer's Sales Record.

Sold Listing | Sales Record #600				*Help*
Buyer Details				

Buyer User ID

Buyer Email

Email addresses will be displayed for 45 days after a transaction ends.

Buyer Full Name

Street

City New Kingstown

State / Province PA

Zip / Postal Code 17072

Country United States

Phone Number (   )   -   ext.:

Fill in buyer's name and address

<< Move
Move >>

Optional: Copy and paste your buyers name and address into the box above. Use the Move buttons to move buyer details back and forth between the box and the form.

Transaction Details

Qty	Item #	Item Name	Price	Subtotal
1	6470222921	Napoleon Dynamite (2004, DVD)	$10.00	$10.00
		Subtotal:		$10.00
		Shipping & Handling: US Postal Service First Class Mail	$	2.50
		Shipping Calculator		

3. Scroll to the Sales Status & Notes section, shown in Figure 22.6, and check the Payment Received On box. The current date will be automatically inserted; you can edit the date if necessary.

4. Enter any other pertinent information, and then click the Save button.

At this time you should also send the buyer a payment-received message. You can access the Email Buyer page by clicking the Email Buyer button on the Sales Record page.

tip

If the buyer has paid with PayPal or used eBay's Checkout system, this information will be automatically entered for you. You can also cut and paste the buyer's address from an email message into the Fill In Buyer's Name and Address box, and then click the Move button to add the data into the Sales Record.

FIGURE 22.6

Marking an auction item paid.

Sale Status & Notes (will not be shown to buyer)

Status Summary (Sale Date: Jan-08-06)

- Checkout: Jan-08-06
- Last email sent: Jan-09-06 (2)
- Payment Date: Jan-08-06
- Feedback sent: **Yes**
- Shipment Date: Jan-10-06
- Feedback received: **Yes**

Payment Information

☑ Payment received on
01 / 08 / 2006

Paid with
PayPal

PayPal Transaction Details

Shipping Information

☑ Shipped on
01 / 10 / 2006

US Postal Service First Class Mail

Miscellaneous Information

Notes to yourself

600 characters left.

| Email Buyer | Print Invoice | Leave Feedback | Save | Cancel |

Printing Invoices and Shipping Labels

When you're ready to ship an item, you can use Selling Manager to print an invoice and shipping label. Follow these instructions:

1. On the Sold Listings page, click the Record # link for this specific auction.

2. When the Sales Record page appears, click the Print Invoice button.

3. When the Print page appears, select to print one of the following:

   - US Postal Service postage or UPS shipping label
   - Shipping (address) labels and invoice/packing slip combo
   - Invoice/packing slip
   - Invoice for your own records
   - All labels—shipping, invoice/ packing slip, and invoice
   - Store promotional flyer (if you have an eBay Store)

4. Click the Continue button to initiate printing.

tip

If you want to edit the information on the invoice, click the Edit Invoice Template link. This lets you edit your address or add a picture or additional text to the invoice.

At this time you should mark the item as shipped, and send the buyer an item-shipped message. You can do both of these from the Sales Record page.

After the Item Is Shipped

After you've shipped an item, you have some cleanup activities to do. In particular, you need to leave feedback about the buyer, and move the item listing into Selling Manager's archive.

Leaving Feedback

You can use Selling Manager to leave semi-automated feedback about a buyer. Just follow these steps:

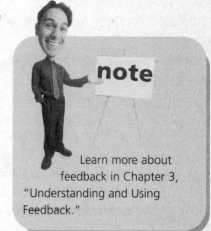

1. On the Sold Listings page, click the Record # link for this specific auction.

2. When the Sales Record page appears, click the Leave Feedback button.

3. When the Leave Feedback page appears, as shown in Figure 22.7, pull down the rating list and select positive, neutral, or negative ratings.

4. You now have the choice of using a stored comment or writing a custom comment. To use a stored comment, select the Use Stored Comments option and make a choice from the pull-down list. To enter a new comment, select the Use Custom Comment option and enter the comment into the adjacent box.

> **note**
>
> Learn more about feedback in Chapter 3, "Understanding and Using Feedback."

5. Click the Leave Feedback button to register your rating and comment.

FIGURE 22.7

Leaving feedback about a buyer.

Leave Feedback											
Choose from your stored comments or leave a customized comment for your buyer											
Invoice # Buyer Email			Qty	Final Price	Sale Date	Paid On	🛒	$	📦	☆	◯
600			1	$12.50	Jan-08	Jan-08	🛒	$	📦	☆	◉
(6470222921)Napoleon Dynamite (2004, DVD)											

Legend: 🛒 Checkout complete $ Paid 📦 Shipped ☆ Feedback left ◯ Feedback received
🖂 Unpaid Item Reminder Sent ◯ Final value fee ⊕ Final value fee credit not granted

Positive rating ▾

◉ Use stored comments   Great communication. A pleasure to do business with.   ▾

◯ Use custom comment   [   ]

[Leave Feedback]   [Edit Stored Comments]   [Cancel]

Archiving Completed Listings

After you've shipped the item and left feedback, you don't want this old listing cluttering up your Selling Manager page. Instead, you can store all completed auctions in the Selling Manager archive, where they're out of the way but you can still access them (if you ever need to). Just follow these steps:

1. On the Sold Listings page, select those auctions you want to archive.

2. Click the Archive button.

3. When prompted, confirm the archive action.

That's it. You're all done with this auction—thanks to eBay Selling Manager!

THE ABSOLUTE MINIMUM

Here are the key points to remember from this chapter:

- eBay Selling Manager is a web-based tool that helps you manage your in-process and closed auctions; it costs $4.99 per month.

- When you subscribe to Selling Manager, the All Selling page in My eBay is changed to a Selling Manager page.

- Selling Manager lets you send end-of-auction emails, print invoices and shipping labels, and leave feedback for winning bidders.

- If Selling Manager won't handle your auction volume, check out Selling Manager Pro; for $15.99 per month, it offers automated bulk management tools.

23

PACKING AND SHIPPING YOUR ITEMS—CHEAPLY AND SAFELY

The auction's over, you've received payment from the high bidder, and now it's time to pack your item and ship it off. If you don't have much experience in shipping items cross-country, this might seem a bit daunting at first. Don't worry, though; if you've ever wrapped a Christmas present or mailed a letter, you have all the skills you need to ship just about anything anywhere in the world.

Packing 101

Before you ship, you have to pack—which doesn't sound too terribly difficult. However, if you pick the wrong container, don't cushion the contents properly, don't seal it securely, or mislabel the whole thing, you could risk damaging the contents during shipping—or, even worse, sending it to the wrong recipient. Even if you think you know how to pack and ship, you still probably want to read the following sections. You never know; you might pick up a few useful tips!

Essential Packing Supplies

Before you do any packing, you need to have some basic supplies on hand. I'm not just talking boxes here; I'm talking about the stuff you stuff inside the boxes, and seal them up with.

Any halfway busy eBay seller needs to have these basic packing supplies on hand so that they're not constantly running off to the office supply store every time one of their auctions closes. These items should always be available and easily accessed.

Okay, so what supplies do you need to have at hand? Take a look at this checklist:

Checklist: Packing Supplies

- ☐ Packing tape—clear or brown
- ☐ Bubble wrap
- ☐ Styrofoam peanuts *or* old newspapers
- ☐ Scissors
- ☐ Box cutter or similar kind of knife
- ☐ Postal scale
- ☐ Black magic marker
- ☐ Large shipping labels
- ☐ Return address labels
- ☐ Other necessary labels: Fragile, This End Up, and so on
- ☐ Labels or forms provided by your shipping service of choice

Now for some elaboration. I recommend keeping both clear and brown packing tape on hand. Clear packing tape is best not just for sealing the box but also to tape over the address label and make it somewhat waterproof. Brown tape, on the other hand, can be used to tape over labels and logos when you reuse an old box. (And for normal box sealing, of course.)

When it comes to filler, I prefer peanuts to newspapers. That's because peanuts don't leave ink stains, and also because of the weight factor; using newspapers as filler can substantially increase your package weight, and thus your shipping costs. Of course, newspapers are free and peanuts aren't—but peanuts are cheaper than the added shipping costs you'll incur with newspapers. And you can reuse all those peanuts that come in the items you purchase online!

The other materials are somewhat self-explanatory—although you might ask why you need a knife when you're packing. I find myself using the knife primarily to slice off old shipping labels from boxes I reuse for my eBay shipping. Although some old labels tear off rather easily, most don't; to remove them, you have to cut (shallowly) around the label and then lift off the outermost layer of the cardboard box.

> **" Mike Sez "**
>
> I like to keep all my packing materials in a single, easy-to-access place—kind of like a ready-to-use packing station. For me, an otherwise-unused kitchen counter does the job; other users clear out a portion of their garage or home office for the same purpose.

Where to Find Boxes and Packing Materials

So where do you find all these packing materials and shipping containers? Lots of places.

First, some boxes are free. If you're shipping via the U.S. Postal Service, you can get free Priority Mail and Express Mail boxes, envelopes, and tubes. (Figure 23.1 shows some of the free boxes available for Priority Mail shipping.) Some post offices carry these free containers, or you can order in bulk (but still free) from the United States Postal Service (USPS) website at supplies.usps.gov.

Most post-office locations also sell various types of boxes, padded mailers, mailing tubes, and other packing materials, although their prices tend to be a little on the high side. (They must figure you're a captive customer at that point.) You can find better prices and a much bigger selection at any major office supply superstore (Office Depot, Office Max, Staples, and so on) or at specialty box and shipping stores.

Another good source of shipping supplies is eBay itself—or, more accurately, retailers who sell on the eBay service. There are several eBay Store sellers who specialize in packing supplies for other eBay sellers; go to stores.ebay.com and do a search for "shipping supplies" or "boxes."

> **note**
>
> Other carriers might or might not offer their own free shipping containers. FedEx, for example, offers certain sizes of envelopes and boxes for your (free) use. It's best to ask first—before you go buying an expensive new box.

Many eBay sellers also do a good job recycling old boxes. That's right, you can reuse boxes that were shipped to you, either from other eBay users or from online or direct mail retailers. (I'm a big fan of Amazon.com's boxes; they recycle quite nicely!)

You'd be amazed how many times a box can be reused. As long as the box is still structurally sound—and sturdy enough for whatever you're shipping—it can be pressed back into service. Just be sure to remove or cross out any old shipping labels and confirm that the box is in good shape, with no weak spots or cracks—and reinforce the box with new tape, as necessary.

Finally, don't forget your local merchants. These stores receive a lot of merchandise daily, and all those goods are packed in *something*. All those shipping boxes come into the store, and end up in the trash or recycling bin.

> **tip**
>
> Many of these eBay Stores operate their own websites as well; in particular, check out BubbleFAST (www.bubblefast.com) and eSupplyStore.com (www.esupplystore.com), two well-established supplies retailers.

What a retailer calls trash you might call reusable packing materials. Short of dumpster diving (which many eBay sellers are masters of), try making a deal with a local retailer to help dispose of those excess boxes and Styrofoam peanuts. You'll get free packing supplies, and the retailer gets a little less stuff to throw away.

Picking the Right Shipping Container

After you have all your shipping supplies assembled, all you need to do is put your item in a box and seal it up. Easy, right? Not really—and the consequences of choosing the wrong container can be both disastrous and unnecessarily expensive.

First, you have to decide whether to use a box or an envelope. If you have a very large item to ship, the choice is easy. But what if you have something smaller and flatter, such as a laser disc or a coin? Your choice should be determined by the fragility of your item. If the item can bend or break, choose a box; if not, an envelope is probably a safe choice.

Whichever you choose, pick a container that's large enough to hold your item without the need to force it in or bend it in an inappropriate fashion. Also, make sure that the box has enough extra room to insert cushioning material.

On the other hand, the container shouldn't be so big as to leave room for the item to bounce around. Also, you pay for size and for weight; you don't want to pay to ship anything bigger or heavier than it needs to be.

If you're shipping in an envelope, consider using a bubble-pack envelope or reinforcing the envelope with pieces of cardboard. This is especially vital if your item shouldn't be bent or folded.

If you're shipping in a box, make sure that it's made of heavy, corrugated cardboard and has its flaps intact. Thinner boxes—such as shoe boxes or gift boxes—simply aren't strong enough for shipping. When packing a box, never exceed the maximum gross weight for the box, which is usually printed on the bottom flap.

Although a bunch of different-sized boxes are available, sometimes you need something somewhere in between this size and that size box. When you face this situation, you have two choices.

First, you can take a larger box and cut it down. That means cutting through each corner of the box to make it shorter, and then cutting off the ends of the flaps accordingly. Sometimes it's difficult to fold unscored flaps, so you may want to make your own scores by slicing a knife (shallowly) where you want to bend the box closed.

Second, you can combine two smaller boxes. If your box is 16 inches long and your item is 20 inches, just take two boxes and insert the open end of one inside the open end of the other. You'll need to use sufficient packing tape to keep the boxes from sliding apart, but you'll have created a box custom-sized for the item you're shipping.

caution

Use the combination box technique judiciously, because it can significantly increase the weight of the package—and thus your shipping costs.

How to Pack

Here's what you don't do: Drop your item in an empty box and then seal it up. A loose item in a big box will bounce around and get damaged, guaranteed. (Imagine your box being tossed around by a bunch of gorillas in a parking lot, and you get an accurate picture of what most packages endure in the shipping process.) No, you need to carefully pack your item to minimize any potential damage from dropping and rough handling—and from various weather conditions, including rain, snow, and heat.

How do you pack your box? Professional shippers use Styrofoam peanuts, and lots of them; amateurs tend to use crumpled-up newspapers and other materials found around the house. Here's where you can learn something from the pros—peanuts are *much* lighter than newspaper. Weight is a factor in how much you'll pay for shipping, so anything you can do to lighten the weight of your package is important. Because peanuts cost...well, *peanuts*, they've become my preferred cushioning material. (And I used to be a crumpled-up newspaper kind of guy, until the latest increase in Priority Mail rates.)

As you might expect, packing needs vary for different types of items. You can use these packing tips when it's time to ship your next item:

- ■ If you have the item's original shipping box or packaging, use it! Nothing ships better than the original shipping container—assuming, of course, that the original box is made of shipping-grade cardboard.

- ■ If you're shipping a common item—DVDs, videotapes, books, and so on— look for item-specific shipping containers. For example, most office supply stores stock boxes and padded mailers specifically designed for CDs and DVDs. These containers typically do what they're advertised to do.

- ■ Always cushion your package contents, using some combination of shredded or crumpled newspapers, bubble wrap, or Styrofoam peanuts. (For example, when I ship a CD or DVD, I wrap it in bubble wrap and cushion it with peanuts.)

- ■ Whatever cushioning material you use, don't skimp on it. Pack your items tightly to avoid shifting of contents during transit, and make sure that the cushioning material covers all sides of the item.

- ■ Position the item toward the center of the box, away from the bottom, sides, and top. (This means placing peanuts *under* the item as well as on top of it.)

tip

You can also use plain (unbuttered!) air-popped popcorn for cushioning; it's inexpensive and environmentally friendly—and tastes good when you're watching a movie!

- If you're shipping several items in the same box, wrap each one separately (in separate smaller boxes, if you can), and provide enough cushioning to prevent movement and to keep the items from rubbing against each other.

- Not only should items be separated from each other in the box, but they also should be separated from the corners and sides of the box to prevent damage if the box is bumped or dropped.

- The preceding point argues for another technique: double-boxing items that are especially fragile, such as glass or ceramic items. That means packing the item tightly in a smaller, form-fitting box, and then placing that box inside a slightly larger, shock-absorbing box—with at least 3 inches of cushioning material between the boxes.

- If your item has any protruding parts, cover them with extra padding or cardboard.

- Be careful with the bubble wrap. Although it's great to wrap around objects with flat sides, it can actually damage more fragile figurines or items with lots of little pieces and parts sticking out. If the bubble wrap is too tight, it can snap off any appendages during rough handling.

- Stuff glassware and other fragile hollow items, such as vases, with newspaper or other packing material. This provides an extra level of cushioning in case of rough handling.

- When shipping jars and other items with lids, either separate the lid from the base with several layers of bubble wrap or tissue paper or (better still) pack the lid in a separate small box.

- When shipping framed photographs or artwork, take the glass out of the frame and wrap it separately. Do not let artwork come in direct contact with paper or cardboard.

- Wrap paper items (photographs, books, magazines, and so on) in some sort of plastic bag or wrap, to protect against wetness in shipment.

- When shipping electronic items (including toys and consumer electronics devices), remove the batteries before you ship. Wrap and place the batteries next to the items in the shipping container.

> ## " Mike Sez "
>
> When you're packing an item, watch the weight. I make it a point to have a postal scale at my packing station, and to weigh the item—shipping container and all—during the packing process. When I'm using Priority Mail, the difference between shipping a one-pound package and a one-pound, one-ounce package can be almost two dollars, depending on where it's going. Finding some way to cut that extra ounce of packing material can save almost two bucks in shipping costs—which is why I want to know the weight before I seal the package.

■ When shipping computer parts—circuit boards, video cards, memory chips, and so on—pad the item well and pack it in an Electro Static Discharge (ESD) bag to prevent damaging static buildup. And *don't* use peanuts for filler—all that Styrofoam can carry a damaging static charge.

After you think you're done packing, gently shake the box. If nothing moves, it's ready to be sealed. If you can hear or feel things rattling around inside, however, it's time to add more cushioning material. (If you can shake it, they can break it!)

Packing for International Customers

Packing for international customers shouldn't be any different from packing for domestic customers—as long as you do it right. Foreign shipments are likely to get even rougher treatment than usual, so make sure that the package is packed as securely as possible—with more than enough cushioning to survive the trip to Japan or Europe or wherever it happens to be going.

What *is* different about shipping internationally is the paperwork—and the shipping costs. I cover all this in Chapter 28, "Selling Internationally," so turn there if you have a non-U.S. buyer to deal with.

How to Seal the Package

After your box is packed, it's time to seal it. A strong seal is essential, so always use tape that is designed for shipping. Be sure to securely seal the center seams at both the top and the bottom of the box. Cover all other seams with tape, and be sure not to leave any open areas that could snag on machinery.

What kind of sealing materials should you use?

■ **Do** use tape that is designed for shipping, such as pressure-sensitive tape, nylon-reinforced kraft paper tape, glass-reinforced pressure-sensitive tape, or water-activated paper tape. Whichever tape you use, the wider and heavier, the better. Reinforced is always better than non-reinforced.

■ **Don't** use wrapping paper, string, masking tape, or cellophane tape.

One last thing: If you plan to insure your package, leave an untaped area on the cardboard where your postal clerk can stamp "Insured." (Ink doesn't adhere well to tape.)

Labeling 101

You've packed the box. You've sealed the box. Now it's time for the label.

Buying the Right Kinds of Labels

For most purposes, you can't beat the standard 4-inch×6-inch blank white label. Anything smaller is tough to work with, and anything larger just leaves a lot of wasted space. Stick with 4-inch×6-inch and you'll be happy. You can purchase these labels at any office supply store, or even get free versions (for Priority Mail shipping) at your local post office.

If you want to splurge, you can even purchase labels with your name and return address preprinted at the top. This is a good idea if you do a lot of shipping (a dozen or more items a week); otherwise, it's probably not cost-efficient.

You can also purchase or create your own return address labels, to use in conjunction with your main shipping labels. It's easy enough to print a full page of smallish labels in Microsoft Word; most printing firms (such as FedEx Kinko's) can also do up a roll of address labels for a nominal charge.

If you use computer-generated labels, you can program your label-making program to include your return address when it prints the label. This is a good (and lower-cost) alternative to using preprinted labels.

tip

If you're unsure what label to use, go with Avery; just about every software program out there supports Avery labels. Plus, Avery offers its own label-making software and templates, downloadable for free from www.avery.com.

How to Create an Idiot-Proof Label

The best-packed box won't go anywhere if you get the label wrong. For fast and efficient delivery, keep these points in mind when addressing your package:

note

If you don't use a preprinted label, you'll want to hand-print your return address on the shipping container, or use some sort of return address label.

- Write, type, or print the complete address neatly.
- Always use complete address information, such as the suffixes Dr., Ave., St., and Blvd.
- Include the recipient's apartment or suite number, if applicable.
- Always use correct directions, such as N, S, E, W, or SW.
- Use the correct ZIP code—and, when possible, use the four-digit add-on, ZIP+4 (example: 46032-1434). Be sure to hyphenate the ZIP+4.
- Always use the proper two-letter state abbreviation.

- When addressing to a P.O. Box or rural route destination, include the recipient's telephone number on the label.
- When shipping outside the U.S., include a contact name, telephone number, and postal code on the label—and don't forget to include the country name!
- Always include your return address information.
- If you're using any special services of the U.S. Postal Service (Priority Mail, First Class Mail, insurance, and so on), note this above the destination address and below and to the right of the return address.
- Place the delivery label on the top (not the side) of the box. To avoid confusion, place only one address label on the box. If using a packing slip, place it on the same surface of the box as the address label.
- Do not place the label over a seam or closure or on top of sealing tape.
- To avoid ink smudges and rain smears, place a strip of clear packing tape over the address label. (Notable exception: Do *not* tape over any bar codes on a label with pre-paid postage; bar code readers have trouble reading through tape.)
- If you're reusing a box for shipping, remove or block out all old address labels or markings on a used box.

And here's one last tip. Make a duplicate of your shipping label and stick it *inside* the box, before you seal it. This way if the original shipping label gets torn off or destroyed, anyone opening the box can read the duplicate label and figure out where the box is supposed to go.

> **tip**
>
> Don't know the ZIP code for the address you're shipping to? Then look it up at the U.S. Postal Service's ZIP Code Lookup at www.usps.com/zip4/.

Printing Labels and Postage on Your Own Computer

Here's a real time-saver. If you're shipping via the U.S. Postal Service or UPS, you can print labels on your home printer—including labels with prepaid postage. When you print your own prepaid postage, you don't have to make a trip to the post office. Just print the label—including postage—on your own printer, attach the label to your package, and hand it to your postman. No more standing in line at the post office!

You can print these labels directly from eBay, and pay for them using your PayPal account. Here's how to do it:

1. Go to your closed item listing page and click the Print Shipping Label button. (You can also find this option on your My eBay All Selling page.)
2. You're now taken to the Select Shipping Carrier page on the PayPal site. Select either USPS or UPS shipping, then click the Continue button.

3. When the Create Your Shipping Label page appears, as shown in Figure 23.2, scroll down to the Shipment Information section and select the desired shipping service.

4. Fill in the rest of the necessary information and click the Continue button.

5. View the information on the confirmation page and authorize payment from your PayPal account.

6. Follow the onscreen instructions to print the label on your own printer.

7. The label prints on half of a sheet of paper. Cut off the label side of the paper and affix it to your package.

Once you've affixed the label, your work is done. You can drop your package in the mail, or hand it to your local postal worker when he makes his daily rounds. There's no need to visit the post office—or if you do, you can bypass the long lines and drop the pre-paid package off at the nearest counter.

Shipping 101

How often do you frequent your local post office? When was the last time you visited a UPS shipping center? Do you even know where your local FedEx branch is located?

note

One plus to printing your own USPS labels is you get Delivery Confirmation included, at no charge.

If these questions make you nervous, you're not alone. For many users, the scariest part of the entire auction process is shipping the item. Not packing, not labeling, but actually taking the box to the shipping center and sending it on its way.

That's because when it comes to shipping, there are so many choices involved. Which carrier do you use? Which specific service offered by a carrier should you choose—the fastest one or the cheapest one? And what about all those extras, such as insurance and delivery confirmation? With all those choices, how do you avoid making the wrong decisions?

If shipping is somewhat foreign to you, don't worry. It isn't quite as difficult as it seems, and it will become old hat after just a few trips to the shipping center.

Examining the Major Shipping Services

You have several choices when it comes to shipping your package. You can use the various services offered by the U.S. Postal Service (regular mail, Priority Mail, Express Mail, Media Mail, and so on) or any of the services offered by competing carriers, such as UPS or Federal Express. You can deal directly with any shipping service or use a local shipping store to handle the shipping (and even the packing)—but at a cost.

As you've no doubt gathered, there are some significant differences in shipping costs from one shipping service to another. The cost differential is typically based on a combination of weight and distance; the heavier an item is and the farther it has to go (and the faster you need to get it to where it's going), the more it costs. As an example, the costs of shipping a two-pound box from New York to Los Angeles run from less than two bucks to more than $30. For this reason, it's a good idea to "shop" the major shipping services for the best shipping rates for the types of items you normally sell on eBay.

Of course, cost isn't the only factor you want to consider. You also want to compare how long it takes the package to arrive, what kind of track record the shipping service has, and how convenient it is for you to use. If you have to drive 20 miles to get to a UPS office, and you have a post office just down the street, that might offset a slightly higher cost for Priority Mail.

All that said, which shipping service should you use? That's a good question, but not always an easy one to answer. Ultimately, you have to strike a compromise between cost, convenience, and speed.

> **" Mike Sez "**
>
> Which shipping services do I use? For small items, I default to USPS Priority Mail; it's inexpensive and relatively fast, plus I get free packing materials from my local post office. For books, I use USPS Media Mail, which is cheaper and almost as fast. For really big items (over 10 pounds or so), I go with UPS. But I find that, nine times out of ten, Priority Mail or Media Mail does the job for me.

Using the U.S. Postal Service

The USPS offers several shipping options:

- **Priority Mail**. This is the preferred shipping method for many experienced auction sellers, if only for its relative convenience. Although Priority Mail used to be predictably low-cost (with flat fees based on weight, not distance), recent price increases have left the service less competitive than before. (You also have to factor distance into the pricing equation, for packages over one pound.) There's also the advantage of getting a flat rate on small packages shipped in one of their flat-rate envelopes—just $4.05 to go anywhere in the U.S. Service is typically in the one-to-three–day range, and the postal service has lots of free Priority Mail boxes you can use. And you can print out Priority Mail shipping labels and postage on your own PC, direct from eBay/PayPal, as we discussed previously.

- **Express Mail**. This is the USPS's fastest service, offering guaranteed next-day delivery 365 days a year, including weekends and holidays. Merchandise is automatically insured up to $100. Express Mail is considerably more expensive than Priority Mail.

- **First Class Mail**. This is an option if your item fits into an envelope or small package. It also provides the benefit of shipping directly from your mailbox, without necessitating a trip to the post office—assuming that you can figure out the correct postage. Delivery is similar to Priority Mail, typically three days or less.

- **Parcel Post**. This used to be known as the "slow" USPS service for larger packages, but it has gotten faster of late—and it's priced lower than Priority Mail. Still, shipping something Parcel Post from coast to coast might take seven to nine days, as opposed to Priority Mail's two (or three) days.

- **Media Mail**. This is what USPS used to call "book rate"; it can be used to ship books, DVDs, videotapes, compact discs, and other printed and prerecorded "media." The rates are much cheaper than those for Priority Mail, although delivery is typically in the Parcel Post range—seven to nine days. Still, this is a good, low-cost way to ship many popular items; the cost for shipping a typical hardcover across the country is less than two bucks, compared to $4.05 for Priority Mail.

caution

Media Mail is reserved for publications without advertising—so you can't use it to ship magazines, newspapers, or comic books.

You can find out more about USPS shipping at the USPS website, located at www.usps.gov. This site includes a postage calculator (postcalc.usps.gov) for all levels of service.

Using UPS

UPS is a good option for shipping larger or heavier packages but can be a little costly for smaller items. UPS offers various shipping options, including standard UPS Ground, Next Day Air, Next Day Air Saver, and 2nd Day Air.

You can find out more about UPS shipping—and access a rate calculator—at the UPS website, located at www.ups.com.

Using FedEx

FedEx is probably the fastest shipping service, but it can also be the most costly. FedEx tends to target the business market (which can afford its higher rates), so it isn't widely used for auction or retail shipping—with one significant exception: FedEx Ground.

FedEx Ground is a terrific choice when you're shipping out larger items. It's designed for bigger and/or heavier packages, and its rates are well below similar services offered by the Postal Service and UPS. I use FedEx Ground to ship DVD players and various audio equipment, and it's extremely cost effective. For example, FedEx charges almost $5 less than Priority Mail to ship a five-pound item from coast to coast. That's a big savings!

FedEx is also a convenient choice for many sellers, especially since you can now ship from any FedEx Kinkos location. You can find out more about FedEx shipping at its website, located at www.fedex.com, and can access the company's rate finder directly at www.fedex.com/us/rates/.

tip

USPS, UPS, and FedEx are the three most popular shipping services in the U.S., but they're not the only services available. Two other services you can use to ship your eBay merchandise are DHL (www.dhl.com) and Purolator Courier (www.purolator.com).

Using a Professional Packing and Shipping Service

If you're new to this packing and shipping thing, you might want to do your packing and shipping through a professional shipping store. These stores—such as The UPS Store (www.theupsstore.com) or FedEx Kinkos (www.fedexkinkos.com)—will handle the entire process for you. Just bring them the item you want to ship, and they'll find the right-sized box, pack it up for you, and fill out all the shipping paperwork.

Of course, all this work comes at a cost. Make sure you find out how much you'll have to pay for this service, and add that cost to your shipping/handling charges in your auction item listing.

How to Reduce Shipping Weight—And Shipping Costs

Because weight is an important part of the shipping equation, here are a few tips for bringing down the weight of the items you ship:

- Use peanuts instead of paper for cushioning; peanuts are *much* lighter—and don't leave ink stains on the merchandise.

- Even better, use air instead of peanuts—in the form of those air-filled bags that Amazon.com uses to cushion their packages—also available from some packing materials retailers.

- Use less heavy-duty boxes, if you can. (This is generally an option only when you're shipping light objects.) You'd be surprised at the difference in weight between similarly sized boxes, based on the thickness of the cardboard.

- Don't use oversized boxes. If the box is too large, either trim down the unused portion of the flaps or move to a smaller box.

Finally, be sure to include the weight of the box and the cushioning material when you weigh your item for shipment. A big box with lots of crumpled paper can easily add a half-pound or more to your item's weight—excess weight you'll have to pay for.

Shipping Large or Heavy Items

Some items are just too big to ship via conventional means. Suppose you just sold an old pinball machine, or a roll-top desk, or a waterbed. How do you deal with items that big?

Assuming that the item is too big even for UPS, you have to turn to traditional trucking services. Some of these services will pack or crate the item for you (for a fee); others require you to do all the crating. In addition, some of these firms require you to deliver the item to their shipping terminal, and for the buyer to pick it up from their dock. (Other firms offer door-to-door service—again, sometimes for a higher fee.) In any case, it helps to make a few calls and ask for specifics before you decide on a shipper.

For shipping oversized items, here are some of the trucking services that other eBay sellers have used. Check with each firm for information on fees and shipping policies.

- AAA Cooper Transportation (www.aaacooper.com)

- Forward Air (www.forwardair.com)

> **caution**
>
> Most of the standard shipping services I mentioned earlier in this chapter, such as the U.S. Postal Service, won't handle packages that weigh more than 70 pounds, or have a combined length and girth of more than 130 inches.

- Vintage Transport Services (www.vintagetransport.com)
- Yellow Freight (www.yellowfreight.com)

In addition, eBay itself offers a Freight Resource Center (ebay.freightquote.com) for shipping large items; you can obtain freight quotes and initiate shipping directly from this page. You can also contact Freightquote.com via phone, at 888-875-7822.

How to Price Shipping and Handling for Your Item Listings

Let's think back to the start of the auction process. You probably remember that I recommended you include your shipping and handling charges up front so that bidders know what to expect.

But how do you figure shipping costs before you know where the item is going?

Working with Flat Fees

The solution is easy if you're shipping something that weighs (packaging included) less than a pound. For these lightweight items, you can use USPS Priority Mail, which ships one-pound packages anywhere in the U.S. for a single price ($4.05 at the time of writing). Because you can also use free boxes (provided by the postal service), you know that your cost to package and ship a one-pound item will be $4.05. Easy.

If you're shipping books, CDs, or videos, you also have it easy—if you choose to ship via USPS Media Mail. These rates are so cheap that you can do some creative rounding of numbers and say that any item weighing two pounds or less can ship anywhere in the U.S. for $2.00. The actual Media Mail rate might be $1.56 or $1.84 or whatever, but $2.00 makes a convenient number to state up front; the gap between actual and projected shipping can go toward the purchase of an appropriate box or envelope.

tip

Another option is to use of the post office's flat-fee boxes or envelopes, which let you ship items of any weight anywhere in the U.S. for a single flat fee.

Working with Variable Fees

When you're shipping items that weigh more than a pound, the calculation gets much more complex. The fact is that if you're selling an item that weighs, let's say, four pounds, the actual shipping costs (via Priority Mail) can range from $5.60 to $10.90, depending on where you are and where the buyer is. That's

tip

When you're shipping light items, such as a single CD, check with your post office for the best rate. Sometimes First Class can be cheaper than Media Mail!

because Priority Mail rates—most shipping rates, actually—vary by distance. So there's no way to quote an exact shipping cost until the auction is over and you get the buyer's ZIP code.

That said, there are three ways you can deal with this situation in your auction listings.

First, you can calculate an *average* shipping cost for your item, figuring a cost halfway between the minimum and the maximum possible costs. Using our four-pound example, the minimum cost for Priority Mail shipping is $5.60 and the maximum is $10.90, so you would charge the buyer the average of these two numbers, or $8.25. (Or maybe you would round up to $9.00.) The theory here is that you lose money on some shipments and make it back on others, so over the long term it's a wash. Of course, nearby buyers might complain that they're paying too much (which they are, because they're in fact subsidizing sellers who live farther away). You'll have to decide whether you can live with the occasional complaint—or refund the difference if it's too large.

Next, you can simply state that buyers will pay actual shipping cost based on location, which will be calculated at the conclusion of the auction, and not include a flat shipping and handling charge in your listing. If you take this approach, you have to request the buyer's ZIP code at the end of the auction, refer to various rate charts to figure the shipping cost, and then relay that cost to your buyer. It's a bit of work, but it gets the job done. (It's also made easier by the fact that eBay is now including the buyer's ZIP code—when available—in its end-of-auction notification emails.)

Using eBay's Shipping Calculator

Finally, and this is my new preferred method, you can choose to include eBay's Shipping Calculator in your item listings. The Shipping Calculator, shown in Figure 23.3, is a great tool; it lets buyers enter their ZIP code on the auction listing page, and then calculates the actual shipping cost, based on the shipping service you selected. (You can also choose to have the Shipping Calculator add a predetermined *handling charge* for each shipment, which we'll discuss in a minute.) When buyers use eBay Checkout at the end of an auction, or choose to pay via PayPal, they can also use the Shipping Calculator to automatically add shipping and handling fees to their total.

You can activate the Shipping Calculator when you're creating a new item listing on the Describe Your Item page. Just follow these steps:

1. Work your way through the sell your item process until you reach the Describe Your Item page, then scroll down to the Shipping section.

2. Pull down the Cost list and select Calculated: Based on Buyer's Address and then click the Apply button. The Shipping section now changes to reflect the calculated shipping option, as shown in Figure 23.4.

FIGURE 23.3

Add eBay's
Shipping
Calculator to
your item listings
so that buyers
can automati-
cally determine
shipping and
handling fees.

3. Pull down the Package Size list and select the type of package you have.

4. Pull down the Estimated Weight list and select the total weight of the package (including the box and all packing materials).

5. Pull down the Domestic Shipping Services list and select which shipping service you want to use.

6. Enter your added handling charge (if any) into the Package & Handling box.

You can now proceed with the rest of the listing creation, as normal.

FIGURE 23.4

Activating eBay's
Shipping
Calculator from
the Describe Your
Item page.

Because the Shipping Calculator can be added to your item listings free of charge, there's no reason not to use it—especially because it greatly simplifies the task of calculating exact shipping charges to your customers.

Determining the Handling Charge

Aside from the pure shipping costs, you should consider adding a handling charge to the shipping fees your customers pay. After all, you need to be sure that you're compensated for any special materials you have to purchase to package the item. That doesn't mean you charge one buyer for an entire roll of tape, but maybe you add a few pennies to your shipping charge for these sorts of packaging consumables. And if you have to purchase a special box or envelope to ship an item, you should definitely include that cost in your shipping charge. (This argues for planning your shipping before placing your item listing—which is always a good idea.)

So you should have no compunction against "padding" your shipping fees with an additional handling charge. In fact, eBay's Shipping Calculator lets you add a separate handling charge to its calculations. It's an accepted part of doing business online.

How to Track Your Shipment

If you think the package might be lost in transit (it's taking too long to arrive), you can always avail yourself of the tracking services provided by UPS, FedEx, and other major carriers. These services typically provide tracking numbers for all packages shipped. In most cases, you can track your package by entering the package's tracking number into the carrier's website.

The one major shipping service that doesn't offer tracking (by default) is the U.S. Postal Service. What you can get from the postal service (at a cost of from $0.50 to $0.60—or free, if you print your own electronic postage labels) is *delivery confirmation*. USPS confirmation, however, does not confirm that an actual person received the package; it confirms only that the mail carrier delivered it (stuck it in the mailbox, that is).

> **tip**
>
> If you have multiple items for sale, there is every possibility that a single buyer will purchase more than one item. If that happens, you don't need to pack two or more separate boxes for that buyer; you can easily pack all the item purchased in a single box, which will reduce shipping costs. You should pass on that savings to your customer, in the form of a combined shipping and handling fee for all items purchased. If you're inflexible in adjusting your shipping and handling for multiple purchases, you're ripping people off—and will lose customers for it.

> **" Mike Sez "**
>
> When I'm supplying quality packaging for a shipment, I find that a handling charge of $1 or $2 (depending on the cost of the item itself) meets with little or no objection from my customers. If I'm using free Priority Mail packaging, I charge less.

If you want a signature confirmation on a USPS shipment, you need to send your item with either Signature Confirmation or the certified mail option. Signature Confirmation costs $1.90 ($1.35 if you print electronic postage labels), while certified mail costs $2.40. Both require the recipient to sign on delivery, and are good options if you're shipping something extremely valuable.

When to Recommend Insurance

If you're shipping a moderately expensive item (over $50, let's say), it might be worth the expense to insure it. You can always give the buyer the option of buying insurance—or just do it yourself and include the costs in your normal shipping and handling fee.

As to cost, the U.S. Postal Service charges $1.35 to insure items up to $50, $2.30 for items between $50 and $100, and $2.30 plus $1.05 for each additional $100 for higher-priced items. UPS includes $100 worth of insurance in its basic rates; additional insurance can be purchased for additional cost.

What to Do When Things Go Wrong

If the package never arrives—or arrives damaged—you have some work to do. If you insured the package, you have to file a claim with the carrier. Information for claim filing appears on most of the shipping services' websites, but you might have to visit your carrier's local office to obtain the proper claim forms.

Note, however, that the procedure for filing a claim can be long and involved. Take the example of the U.S. Postal Service. The process starts with the buyer, who must take the package (merchandise, box, peanuts, and all) to their local post office to fill in half of a claim form (PS 1000). After this form is processed, the post office sends you (the seller) the half-filled-out form, via the mail. You then fill out the rest of the form and take it (along with your original insurance receipt) to *your* local post office for processing. When enough time goes by the USPS will (or won't, if you filled in something wrong) send a check for the insured amount directly to the buyer.

tip

You can speed up this process by obtaining the claim form yourself, filling in your part, and then sending the claim form and the original insurance receipt to the buyer—and let him deal with the post office through the rest of the process.

Other shipping services work differently, and some even send the insurance check to you instead of to the buyer. However it works, you need to communicate with the buyer while you're waiting for the claim to be paid so that both of you are in the loop about what's going on. If you receive the insurance check, you'll then need to refund the buyer's money; if the buyer receives the check, he should notify you when he's been paid.

Tips for Less-Painful Shipping

To wrap things up, here are some additional tips you can use to take some of the hassle out of shipping your eBay items:

caution

If you didn't insure your package—or if the carrier didn't offer automatic insurance—then you have a situation. eBay protocol has it that the seller is responsible for any losses in shipment, so you might end up refunding the buyer's money out of your own pocket.

- When you're using the U.S. Postal Service for shipping, try to time your visits to avoid long lines. That means avoiding lunch hour and the last half hour or so before closing; avoiding Mondays; and avoiding peak shipping periods around major holidays, such as Christmas and Valentine's Day. Early morning and mid-afternoon are typically low-volume times.

- Don't feel obligated to ship every single day of the week. Save up your shipments and go to the post office just one or two days a week.

- When you have a lot of packages to ship, don't go to the post office by yourself. Take a helper—and, if large shipments are common, invest in a small hand truck to help you cart all those boxes to the counter.

- If you're a heavy shipper, consider setting up an account with a single shipper and arranging daily pickups from your home. Pickup service will cost you a little more but can be more than worth it in time savings. (Most carriers will also pick up single items if you arrange so in advance—but at a much higher fee.)

- You may need to factor weather conditions into which type of shipping you choose. If it's summertime and you're shipping something that might melt in extreme heat (like an old vinyl LP), pick the fastest shipping method possible.

The Absolute Minimum

Here are the key points to remember from this chapter:

- Pack your item so that it doesn't rattle when you shake it.

- Pack your item so that the package is as light as possible.

- Calculate shipping costs based on the weight of the item being shipped and the packaging—including the box and cushioning material.

- Get free boxes for Priority Mail shipping from the post office, or from the USPS website.

- Don't be afraid to reuse boxes you receive from other sources—as long as they're still in serviceable shape and you remove all previous labels.

- Make sure that your label is neatly printed and includes a full address and ZIP code.

- You can print U.S. Postal Service labels with pre-paid postage direct from the eBay site, on your own computer and printer.

- Place a layer of clear tape over the delivery label (but not over any bar codes) so that it doesn't get smeared in transit.

- For most packages, the U.S. Postal Service is a good shipping option, either via Priority Mail, Media Mail, or Parcel Post.

24

DEALING WITH NON-PAYING BUYERS

A non-paying buyer—sometimes called a *deadbeat bidder*—is someone who wins an auction but never follows through with the transaction. Not only should you leave negative feedback about these unreliable buyers, but you also should request a credit from eBay for your final value fee.

What do you do when you have a non-paying buyer in one of your eBay transactions? Fortunately, you still have the merchandise, which you can relist and (hopefully) sell again. You are out some eBay fees, however—although you can probably get them refunded when you report the non-paying buyer to eBay.

When eBay receives what it calls a Non-Paying Bidder Alert, the service automatically sends a warning to the user in question. If the buyer is found at fault, he receives an Unpaid Item strike against his account. After three such strikes, he's indefinitely suspended from the eBay service.

So there!

How to Handle Bum Buyers

If you are unfortunate enough to get stuck with a non-paying buyer, there is a set procedure to follow, as you can see in the following checklist:

Checklist: Dealing with Deadbeat Bidders

☐ Contact the non-paying bidder

☐ File an Unpaid Item Dispute

☐ Close out the dispute to receive a final value fee credit

☐ Leave negative feedback on the deadbeat bidder

☐ Offer the item in question to the second-highest bidder

or

Relist the item

Contacting an Unresponsive Bidder

It's on your shoulders to go to whatever lengths possible to contact the high bidder in your eBay auctions. This should start with the standard post-auction email, of course. If the buyer hasn't responded within three days, resend your original email with an "URGENT" added to the subject line. You should also amend the message to give the buyer a deadline (two days is good) for his response.

If another two days go by without a response, send a new message informing the buyer that if you don't receive a response within two days, you'll be forced to cancel his high bid and report him to eBay.

If a full week goes by and you still haven't heard from the buyer, you can assume the worst. Which means it's time to let eBay know about the bum.

tip

In some instances, you may have more luck trying to contact a member via phone or snail mail than via email. To obtain a member's real-world contact information, click the Advanced Search link to the right of the eBay toolbar; when the Find Items page appears, click the Find Contact Information link in the left-hand column. When the Find Contact Information page appears, enter the user's ID and the item number of the auction in question. eBay will then email you the bidder's contact info.

Filing an Unpaid Item Dispute

The way you notify eBay about a deadbeat bidder is to file an Unpaid Item Dispute. You have to file this form (and wait the requisite amount of time) before you can request a final value fee credit on the auction in question.

An Unpaid Item Dispute must be filed between 7 and 45 days after your auction ends. You file the dispute by going to eBay's Security & Resolution Center (pages.ebay.com/securitycenter/), shown in Figure 24.1. Check the Unpaid Item option, then click the Report Problem button. When the Report an Unpaid Item Dispute page appears, enter the auction's item number, click the Continue button, and follow the onscreen instructions.

FIGURE 24.1

Begin the dispute process in eBay's Security & Resolution Center.

Asking eBay to Refund Your Fees

After an Unpaid Item Dispute has been filed, eBay sends a message to the bidder requesting that the two of you work things out. (It's not a very strong message, in my humble opinion, but it's what it is.) You then have to wait 7 days before you can request a refund of your final value fee. You have to make the request no later than 60 days after the end of your auction, and your claim has to meet one of the following criteria:

- The high bidder did not respond to your emails or backed out and did not buy the item.
- The high bidder's check bounced or a stop payment was placed on it.
- The high bidder returned the item and you issued a refund.

■ The high bidder backed out, but you sold the item to another bidder at a lower price.

■ One or more of the bidders in a Dutch auction backed out of the sale.

If your situation fits, you're entitled to a full refund of eBay's final value fee—but you must request it. To request a refund, go to your My eBay page and click the Dispute Console link. When the Dispute Console page appears, click through to the item in dispute and select the I No Longer Wish to Communicate With or Wait For the Buyer option. eBay then issues a final value fee credit, and your item is eligible for relisting.

caution

eBay's policy is to not refund insertion fees— although if you have a really special circum- stance, there's no harm in asking. (And, besides, if you relist the item, eBay will refund you the second insertion fee if the item sells the second time around.)

Leaving Negative Feedback

Naturally, you want to alert other eBay members to the weasel among them. You do this by leaving negative feedback, along with a description of just what went wrong—no contact, no payment, what- ever. Be descriptive but professional; there's no rea- son to resort to insults and name-calling. Just state the facts, and you'll be fine.

To leave negative feedback, go to the item listing page, click the Leave Feedback to Bidder link, and when the Leave Feedback About an eBay User page appears, check Negative and enter your com- ments. Click the Leave Feedback button when done.

note

Learn more about feedback in Chapter 3, "Understanding and Using Feedback."

Giving Other Bidders a Second Chance

When a bidder backs out of an auction, you're stuck with the merchandise you thought you had sold. Assuming that you still want to sell the item, what do you do?

eBay offers the opportunity for you to make what it calls a Second Chance Offer to other bidders in your failed auction. This lets you try to sell your item to someone else who was definitely interested in what you had to sell.

You can make a Second Chance Offer to any of the under-bidders in your original auction. The offer can be made immediately at the end of the auction, and up to 60 days afterward.

To make a Second Chance Offer, return to your original item listing page and click the Second Chance Offer link. When the Second Chance Offer page appears, follow the onscreen instructions to fill out the form and make the offer.

tip

Second Chance Offers can also be used, in a successful auction, to offer duplicate items to nonwinning bidders.

Note that when a bidder accepts your Second Chance Offer, eBay charges you a final value fee. You are not charged a listing fee. Buyers accepting Second Chance Offers are eligible for eBay's normal buyer protection services.

Relisting Your Item

If you don't have any takers on your Second Chance Offer, you can always try to sell the item again by relisting the item. See Chapter 21, "After the Sale: Concluding the Transaction," for more details.

THE ABSOLUTE MINIMUM

Here are the key points to remember from this chapter:

- If 7 days go by with no contact from the high bidder in your auction, you probably have a deadbeat on your hands.
- After you've made all reasonable effort to contact the buyer, file an Unpaid Item Dispute with eBay.
- Wait another 7 days, and then close out the dispute to receive a final value fee credit from eBay.
- You can try to sell the item in question by making a Second Chance Offer to other bidders, or by relisting the item in a new auction.

LETTING A TRADING ASSISTANT SELL YOUR ITEMS FOR YOU

Maybe you find the whole eBay process a little intimidating. You have some things you'd like to sell, but don't want to bother with the online auction process. What do you do?

If you don't want to sell your own stuff on eBay, you can let someone else sell it for you. In essence, you let another seller sell your goods on consignment. If the items sell, you pay the consignment seller a percentage of the final price. The consignment seller handles all the eBay stuff for you—taking photographs, creating item listings, managing the auctions, collecting payments, and packing and shipping the items. All you have to do is deliver the merchandise to the seller, and let him do all the work for you.

eBay calls this type of consignment seller an eBay Trading Assistant, and there are lots of them. Many individual sellers operate as Trading Assistants; there are also numerous local and national businesses that operate eBay consignment stores.

An eBay Trading Assistant is known as a TA.

Finding a Trading Assistant

eBay Trading Assistants are everywhere. Almost every locality has one or more individuals or businesses that will take your goods on consignment and sell them on eBay for you. But how do you find a Trading Assistant near you?

It's simple, really, thanks to eBay's Trading Assistants Directory, which lists TAs by location and specialty. To search the directory, all you have to do is go to eBay's Trading Assistants hub (pages.ebay.com/tahub/), shown in Figure 25.1, and click the Find a Trading Assistant link or the Find a Seller button. When the Trading Assistants Directory page appears (as shown in Figure 25.2), enter your street address, city, state, and ZIP code. Pull down the I Need Help Selling list and select a category for what you want to sell, then check whether you want a TA with a drop-off location or one that offers a pick-up service. Click the Search button to begin your search.

FIGURE 25.1

eBay's Trading Assistants hub

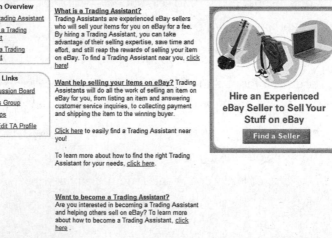

FIGURE 25.2

Searching the
Trading
Assistants
Directory.

When the list of Trading Assistants in your area appears, click a link to view the
Trading Assistant's profile. (Figure 25.3 shows a typical TA profile.) If you like what
you see, click the Contact Assistant button to send a message to the Trading
Assistant and get the process going.

FIGURE 25.3

Viewing a
Trading
Assistant's
profile—and
making contact.

When researching Trading Assistants, there are a few things you want to look for. First, make sure the TA's fees are competitive; compare fees from more than one TA in your area, just in case. You should also look to see how many listings the seller has placed on eBay over the last few weeks. Look at their listings. Are they professionally done? Do they list reasonable shipping fees? Do they ship outside the country? Do they have experience selling a variety of items, or do they specialize in a very specific area?

You may also want to consider convenience. Some Trading Assistants offer merchandise pick-up services; others have staffed drop-off locations. You can fine-tune your search for either type of Trading Assistant.

note

A Trading Assistant with a retail drop-off location is called a Trading Post.

Finally, know that not all Trading Assistants are individual sellers. eBay consignment selling has become a big business, with lots of stores opening their doors in communities all across America. Locally owned consignment stores can be found in your local Yellow Pages. Some of the largest national chains include AuctionDrop (www.auctiondrop.com), iSold It (www.i-soldit.com), and QuikDrop (www.quikdrop.com); visit their websites to find a location near you. (Figure 25.4 shows the AuctionDrop website.)

FIGURE 25.4

AuctionDrop, a national Trading Assistant chain with drop-off locations at UPS Store locations.

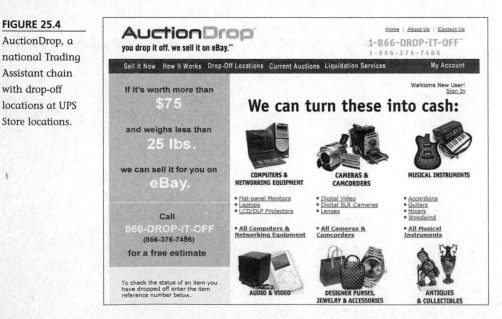

What to Expect from a Consignment Sale

The great thing about using a Trading Assistant to sell your items on consignment is that the TA handles all the details for you—taking photographs, creating item listings, managing the auctions, collecting payments, and packing and shipping the items. All you have to do is deliver the merchandise to the seller (or have him pick it up from you); he'll do all the rest of the work for you.

When you hand over your merchandise to the TA, he'll take a quick inventory of the items and their condition. A good TA will also do a little research to determine the items' probable resale value; he wants to make sure you have realistic expectations as to whether the items will sell, and for how much.

Most legitimate TAs will present a consignment sale contract for you to sign. Make sure everything is in order, and pay particular attention to how and when you'll get paid. Naturally, you won't be reimbursed until the TA is paid; some TAs only write checks once a month, or wait a specified amount of time after the auction close to pay their clients.

You should also review the TA's complete fee schedule. The TA's fees may range anywhere from 10% to 50% of the final selling price; some TAs also charge an initial listing fee, or a fee if the item fails to sell. You'll also be expected to pay all necessary eBay and PayPal fees on the transaction.

When the TA has the merchandise in hand, he'll use a digital camera to take professional-looking photos of the items. He'll then use his research to help write the item description. This description and the product photos will be used to create the item's auction listing, which the TA will then post to eBay at an appropriate time. (You may have to wait a week or so for the TA to launch the auction; TA's have their own auction-listing schedules to adhere to.)

Once the auction is underway, the TA should email you with details about the auction—including the auction's URL, so you can follow along with the auction progress. Expect another email when the auction closes, notifying you of the sales status and final selling price. Don't be shy about contacting the TA with any questions you may have—but try to remain patient during the course of the auction itself!

caution

Some TAs will only accept higher-priced items for consignment sale. It may not be worth their time to try to sell items priced under $50 or so.

note

If you'd like to become a Trading Assistant yourself, see Chapter 29, "Opening a Trading Assistant Business.

THE ABSOLUTE MINIMUM

Here are the key points to remember from this chapter:

- If you don't want to sell your items yourself, you can use a Trading Assistant to sell your items on a consignment basis.

- Trading Assistants can be individual eBay sellers, small businesses, or franchise stores in a national chain.

- All registered Trading Assistants are listed in eBay's Trading Assistants Directory; you can search this directory for a TA near you.

- Some Trading Assistants will pick up items for sale at your location; others offer a drop-off location that you can visit with your merchandise.

- A Trading Assistant will handle all aspects of the auction process, including taking digital photos, writing the item description, launching the auction, and packing and shipping your item to the winning bidder.

- Expect to pay from 10% to 50% in commissions to the Trading Assistant, based on the item's final selling price.

26

Secrets Of Successful Sellers

You have things to sell. You want to make sure that you actually sell them and that you get the highest price possible. But you're also competing with millions of other items up for auction at the same time. How do you stand out from the crowd, attract a bunch of bidders, and goose up the high bids?

If you're looking for extra-special selling secrets, this chapter is for you. Discover the secrets and strategies that will help you be a successful online auction seller!

Secrets for Selling and Promoting Your Items

We'll start by presenting some practical sales and promotional strategies. Follow this advice to maximize your sales—and your final selling price!

Secret #1: Research Your Price

Don't sell without doing your homework first; make sure you know the true value of an item before you put it up for auction. Before you price your item, search for similar items in eBay's closed auctions. What was the starting bid price? What was the final selling price? You should also research the price of similar items offline; sometimes you can get a feel for relative value if you compare your item to a newer version of the same. Be informed, and you won't set the price too high or too low; you'll set it just right.

Secret #2: Go Long...

When it comes time to choose the length for your auction, go for the 7- or 10-day option. The longer your item is up for auction, the more potential bidders who will see it—and the more potential bidders, the better your chances of selling the item for a higher price. Don't cheat yourself out of potential sales by choosing a shorter auction.

Secret #3:...Or Create a Short-Term Frenzy

On the other hand, if you have something really hot, create a bidding frenzy by choosing a very short auction length. If you do this, play it up in your item's title: `3 Days Only!` works pretty well.

Secret #4: There's No Reason to Reserve

I don't know of a single bidder who likes reserve price auctions. Why use something that scares some bidders away? (Remember, many beginning users don't understand reserve price auctions, and thus don't bid in them.) Set a realistic minimum, and get on with it.

Secret #5: Single Items Are Best...

If you're looking for the highest total dollar, don't group items together. Multiple-item lots seldom bring as much money as multiple items sold individually.

Secret #6:...Although You Can Unload Some Dogs in a Pack

On the other hand, if you have a lot of things to sell, selling in lots can reduce your personal overhead, as well as help you unload some less attractive items that you probably couldn't sell individually. (Plus, you get hit for only a single insertion fee!)

Secret #7: Don't Compete Against Yourself

If five people are looking to buy footstools today, don't give them five choices all from one person (you). If you have five footstools to sell, don't sell them all at once. Sell one this week, one next week, and one the week after that. Spread it out to create an illusion of scarcity, and you'll generate more total revenue.

Secret #8: Start and End in Prime Time

When you *start* your auction is important—because that affects when your auction *ends*. If you start a seven-day auction at 6:00 p.m. on a Saturday, it will end exactly seven days later, at 6:00 p.m. the following Saturday.

Why is it important when your auction ends? Because some of the most intense bidding takes place in the final few minutes of your auction, from snipers trying to steal the high bid at the last possible moment. To take advantage of last-minute bidders, your auction needs to end when the most possible bidders are online.

If you end your auction at 3:00 in the morning, everyone will be asleep and you'll lose out on any last-minute bids. Instead, try to end your auction during early evening hours, when the most users are online.

Remember, though, that you're dealing with a three-hour time-zone gap between the East and the West coasts. So, if you time your auction to end at 7:00 p.m. EST, you're ending at 4:00 p.m. PST—when most potential bidders are still at work. Conversely, if you choose to end at 9:00 p.m. PST, you just hit midnight in New York—and many potential bidders are already fast asleep.

The best times to end—and thus to *start*—your auction are between 9:00 p.m. and 11:00 p.m. EST, or between 6:00 p.m. and 8:00 p.m. PST. (Figure the in-between time zones yourself!) That way you'll catch the most potential bidders online for the final minutes of your auction—and possibly generate a bidding frenzy that will garner a higher price for your merchandise!

Note, however, that the best time to end an auction can be influenced by the type of item you're selling.

note

eBay operates on Pacific (West Coast) time. If you're in another time zone, be sure to do the math to determine the proper time for your area.

For example, if you're selling an item that appeals to grade-school or high-school kids, try ending your auction in the late afternoon, after the kids get home from school and before they head off for dinner. Items with appeal to housewives do well with a late morning or early afternoon end time. And business items sell best when they end during normal business hours.

Secret #9: End on a Sunday

When you end your auction on a Sunday, you get one full Saturday and *two* Sundays (the starting Sunday and the ending one) for a seven-day item listing. Sunday is a great day to end auctions because almost everybody is home—no one is out partying, or stuck at work or in school. End your auction on a Sunday evening, and you're likely to get more bids—and higher prices.

There are exceptions, however.

As with the time you end your auction, your ending day might also be influenced by the type of item you're selling. If you're selling an item of interest to college students, for example, you might be better ending on a night during the week, because a lot of students travel home for the weekend; you'll catch them in the dorms on a Wednesday or Thursday night. Items targeted at churchgoers might also be better ending during the week so that you don't catch bidders when they're at Sunday evening church services.

Secret #10: Don't End on a Friday or Saturday Night

If Sunday is normally the best night of the week to end your auction, what's the worst night?

Friday and Saturday are probably the worst nights to end most auctions, because a lot of eBay users are out partying on these non-school nights. End an auction for any item (especially youth-oriented items) on a Friday or Saturday night, and you eliminate a large number of potential buyers.

You should also try not to end your auction right in the middle of a hit television series—some potential bidders might find it difficult to tear themselves away from the old boob tube. That means avoiding "Must-See TV" Thursdays, and any block-buster sporting events or award shows.

Secret #11: Slow Down in the Summer

For whatever reason, eBay traffic slows way down in the summertime. (Lots of potential buyers are on vacation, and even more are outside enjoying the sunshine.) If you want to maximize your bids, you'll get a higher price when fall and winter come along.

Secret #12: Avoid Premature Cancellation

Know that many bidders wait until the very last minute to place a bid. (It's called sniping, and it really works.) If you cancel an auction early, you'll miss out on the bulk of the potential bids. So don't cancel!

Secret #13: Avoid Deadbeats

You don't have to sell to just anybody. You can stipulate that you won't sell to bidders with negative feedback or with feedback ratings below a certain level. If you receive bids from these potential deadbeats, cancel them. If the deadbeats continue to bid (after being warned off via email by you), block their bids. You want to sell to someone who will actually consummate the transaction and send you payment; bidders with negative feedback are more likely to leave you high and dry.

Secret #14: Accept Credit Cards—Via PayPal

One of the easiest ways to increase the number of bids in your auction is to accept payment via credit card. Unless you're a real business with a merchant bank account, this means signing up for PayPal—which is extremely easy to do.

Secret #15: Use a Middleman for Expensive Items

If you're selling a high-priced item, consider offering the buyer the option of using an escrow service. It's a good deal for you; the buyer pays for the service (in the neighborhood of 5%, typically), it provides a level of peace of mind for the buyer, and it lets you accept credit card payments that you might otherwise not accept.

Secret #16: Promote Your Auctions

Let people outside eBay know about your auction. Mention your auction in relevant newsgroups and mailing lists, feature it on your personal website, and send emails about it to all your friends. Include your item listing's URL in everything you do so that anyone interested can click the link to view your auction. Do anything you can think of to draw traffic to your listing—and thus increase your chances of selling it.

Secret #17: Promote Yourself with Your About Me Page

eBay's About Me page is the perfect way to provide more background information about you as a seller, and to drive potential bidders to your other live auctions. Be sure to create an About Me page—and use it to help "sell" yourself and your other items.

Secrets for Creating More Effective Item Listings

Now let's look at some secrets you can use to make better-looking, more effective item listings. And, as we all know, the better-looking your listing, the more sales you'll have!

Secret #18: Make Your Listing Stand Out

Do everything in your power to make your item listings stand out from all the other listings currently online. Work on both the title and the description, and consider using a listing-creation tool (or using HTML formatting) to create a more dynamic ad.

> **note**
>
> Learn more about eBay's About Me pages in Chapter 6, "Creating Your Own Personal About Me Page."

Secret #19: Get All the Buzzwords in the Title

Make sure you have the right words and phrases in the title of your item listing. If your audience looks for "compact discs," say compact disc; if they look for "CDs," say CD. If they look for both, use both. Use all possible words (up to your auction's character limit) to hit all possible keywords your potential bidders might be searching for—even if some of the words are redundant.

> **note**
>
> See Chapter 17, "Creating More Effective Item Listings," for more ideas about creating eye-catching item listings.

Secret #20: Be Descriptive

Include as much descriptive text about your item as you can. The better you describe your item, the fewer mid-auction emails you'll get asking about it and the greater the chance that your ultimate buyer won't get any unpleasant surprises. In addition, you never know when that single "unimportant" detail is just the thing a specific bidder is looking for—so don't overlook any detail, no matter how small.

Secret #21: Reuse Text That Sells

After you find a winning formula, reuse it! This is especially so if you sell a lot of similar items. Cut and paste descriptive text from your successful listings into additional listings, or use eBay's Relist Similar Item function so you're not always starting from scratch. If nothing else, this gives you a head start when creating new item listings!

Secret #22: A Picture Says a Thousand Words

Nothing increases your chances of selling an item like including a picture of it in your listing. Take a photo of your item, scan it in, upload it, and include it with your listing—even if it's just a plain text listing. (And when you take your picture, make sure that it's a good one—there's no point in posting a picture if the item is too small and out of focus.)

Secret #23: Include Shipping and Payment Details

Don't forget to include all the details about shipping and handling (how much and who pays), payment methods, and the like. (That means estimating shipping and handling up front, if you can.) Don't leave anything open to interpretation.

Secret #24: Remember All Your Shipping Costs

When figuring your shipping and handling costs, be sure to factor in all your costs—not just the shipping itself, but also the cost of the packaging, the labels, and the packing tape. Don't gouge your buyer (this isn't meant to be a profit center), but don't cheat yourself, either. If actual shipping costs are $3.50, think about charging the buyer $4 to cover your additional costs.

And, when you're figuring the item's shipping weight, remember that you don't just ship the item—you also ship the box and all cushioning materials. These items have weight and must be included when you're weighing your item for shipment. (Those free Priority Mail boxes are especially heavy—and can easily increase your cost of shipping.)

Secret #25: Be Honest

Be honest in your description of the item. If the item has a few flaws, mention them. If there's damage or the item is otherwise imperfect, make note of it. Misleading a buyer will only cause you grief.

Secrets for Managing Your Auctions

If you run a lot of auctions at once, managing all those auctions can be a pain in the posterior. Take advantage of these secrets to take some of the pain out of your day-to-day auction management.

Secret #26: Use Turbo Lister to Create Your Listings

If you list a lot of items for auction, take advantage of eBay's free bulk-listing tool. Turbo Lister is great for listing multiple items at one time, but also makes it easier to create great-looking listings for just an item or two. Besides, there's no reason *not* to use it—it's free!

Secret #27: Use My eBay to Track Your Auctions

Don't let your auction activity get away from you. Use My eBay to look at all your auctions daily, or use auction management software to track your auctions automatically.

You can also use My eBay to track your favorite auction categories, as well as your feedback ratings and account status. Personalize your My eBay page the way you like and then bookmark it; it's a great home page for the heavy auction trader.

Secret #28: If You Sell a Lot, Use eBay Selling Manager

My eBay is great for tracking your auctions, but when it comes to managing your end-of-auction activities, consider subscribing to eBay Selling Manager. For just $4.99 per month you get assistance in sending emails, printing invoices and packing slips, and leaving feedback. It's great if you run a lot of auctions simultaneously.

Secrets for After the Auction

Once the auction is concluded, the real work begins—sending emails, packing and shipping, leaving feedback, and the like. Here are some secrets to make the post-auction process quicker and easier.

Secret #29: Communicate Quickly—And Clearly

When your auction ends, get in touch with the high bidder *immediately*. Don't wait until the next day; send your post-auction email within minutes of the auction close. Remember, the faster you notify the high bidder, the faster you'll get paid.

note

Learn more about Turbo Lister in Chapter 20, "Automating Your Listings with eBay Turbo Lister."

note

Learn more about My eBay in Chapter 5, "Managing Your eBay Activity with My eBay."

note

Learn more about Selling Manager in Chapter 22, "Managing Your Sales with eBay Selling Manager."

And here's something the best sellers do. Email the buyer again when you receive payment and once more when you're ready to ship the item. The more everyone knows, the fewer surprises there are.

Also, remember that not everyone reads his or her email daily, so don't expect an immediate response. Still, if you don't receive a response, send another email. If you're at all concerned at any point, get the buyer's phone number or physical address from the auction site and call or write him. A good phone conversation can clear up a wealth of misunderstandings.

Secret #30: Wait for the Check to Clear

The reality is that many buyers still prefer to pay by check. That's okay, as long as you wait a good 10 business days for the check to clear. Don't be stupid and ship an item before the check proves good—you're bound to get burned!

Secret #31: Ship Promptly

Ship promptly after you've received payment (and after the check has cleared). Nobody likes to wait too long for something they've paid for—and you don't want to gain a reputation as a slow shipper.

Secret #32: If Nobody Buys, Relist—With a Different Description

If you didn't sell your item the first time, try it again. eBay lets you relist unsold items at no additional listing charge (though listing it a third and subsequent times will result in additional listing fees); even if you have to pay again, you still want to sell the item, right? But remember that if it didn't sell the first time, there was proba-bly a reason why. Was your asking price too high? Was your description too vague? Was the title too boring? Should you have included a picture or used HTML to spice up the listing? Whatever you change, change something to increase your chances of selling your item the second time around.

Secret #33: If You Get Stiffed, Ask for a Refund

When your high bidder does a vanishing act, file an Unpaid Item Dispute and request a refund of the auction's final value fee. There's no sense paying eBay for something you didn't get paid for!

Secret #34: Don't Forget About Number Two

If you run up against a nonpaying bidder, you can try to sell the now-unsold item to the next highest bidder, if he or she is still interested. It never hurts to ask, in any case; just use eBay's Second Chance Offer feature and see whether the bidder bites.

Secrets for Any eBay Seller

We'll end this chapter with some general selling secrets that any eBay seller can use. Read and learn!

Secret #35: Document Everything

In case something goes south, it helps to have good records of all aspects of your transaction. Print copies of the confirmation email, plus all email between you and the buyer. Be sure to write down the buyer's user ID, email address, and physical address. If the transaction is ever disputed, you'll have all the backup you need to plead your case.

Secret #36: The Customer Is Always Right...

Although many sellers take a hardball attitude and refuse any discussion of refunds, I recommend a more customer-friendly approach. When I have a dissatisfied buyer, I offer a full refund. Yeah, some buyers might try to take advantage of you, but most are honest. So if you have a buyer with a complaint, you can generally assume that it's a legitimate beef. You'll get better feedback—and sleep easier at night—if you have the customer return the item and refund the purchase price. It's the right thing to do!

> **caution**
>
> If you do offer a refund, don't send the money until you've received and examined the item in dispute. Some smarmy buyers might try to dupe you by sending back a different item than the one you shipped!

Secret #37: ...Or All Sales Are Final

If you choose *not* to offer a "satisfaction guaranteed" policy, be sure to state that "all sales are final" in your item listing. (Alternatively, you can say that your item is "sold as-is" or that there are "no returns.")

Secret #38: If It's a Business, You Pay Taxes

This book isn't meant to offer tax advice (and you'd be foolish to consult me for such!), but larger eBay sellers need to be aware of the tax issue. In general, if you're an individual who classifies as a casual eBay seller, you probably don't have to worry about collecting sales taxes or reporting

> **note**
>
> Learn more about running a full-fledged eBay business (and paying taxes!) in my companion book, *Making a Living from Your eBay Business* (Que, 2005).

taxable income. However, if you're a business or an individual at the power seller level, the Internal Revenue Service will want their share. The best advice here is that no matter what level your eBay sales, you should consult your accountant or a similar tax expert—and never, never try to fool Uncle Sam.

Secret #39: Join the eBay Community

Here's a tip of value to both sellers and buyers. When you have questions or problems with your eBay auctions, you can get *tons* of help from other eBay users, via eBay's community discussion boards. Just click the Community link on the eBay Navigation Bar (or go directly to hub.ebay.com/community), and you'll see eBay's Community hub, as shown in Figure 26.1. Click the Discussion Boards link to see all the different boards available.

caution

As helpful as the board members are, they probably can't answer all the questions you might have. In particular, don't expect these users to reveal their personal buying/selling secrets, merchandise suppliers, or other proprietary information. So be realistic about the help you can get—and make sure you thank those who answer your questions!

FIGURE 26.1

Get help and support from other members of the eBay community.

eBay offers discussion boards for individual product categories, as well as more general boards for buying, selling, and creating auction listings. The users who frequent these boards are extraordinarily helpful, and can answer just about any question you pose.

Secret #40: Be Nice

Whenever you're communicating with a buyer, remember that you're dealing with another human being, someone who has feelings that can be hurt. A little bit of common courtesy goes a long way. Say please and thank you, be understanding and tolerant, and treat your trading partner in the same way you'd like to be treated. Follow the golden rule; do unto other auction traders as you would have them do unto you.

> **tip**
>
> Want even more advice? Then check out my companion book, *Tricks of the eBay Masters, 2nd Edition* (Que, 2006). It's filled with 600 tricks and tips that any eBay seller can use!

THE ABSOLUTE MINIMUM

Here are the key points to remember from this chapter:

- Research your listing beforehand.
- Take the time and effort to create an attractive and descriptive auction listing.
- For best results, time your auction to end on a Sunday evening in prime time.
- Never end an auction on a Friday or Saturday night, or on a holiday.
- When the auction's over, communicate with the buyer—the more often, the better.
- Get help and support from other eBay users, in eBay's discussion boards.
- Treat your auction sales as a business, and your buyers as customers; and remember, the customer is always right!

PART

BECOMING A POWER SELLER

USING SELLING MANAGEMENT SOFTWARE AND SERVICES

Throughout this book I've mentioned several third-party software programs and services you can use to automate various parts of the online auction process. This chapter is where you get the complete list of products and services, along with some personal comments and recommendations about which are the best to use.

So if you want to make selling on eBay a little easier—particularly important if you're a high-volume power seller—this chapter is for you!

Selling Management Software

If you're running a lot of auctions at one time, you need some way to keep track of which auctions are still open, which have closed, which need emails sent to high bidders, which need to be shipped out, and so on. It also helps if you can somehow automate the listing process itself, and create great-looking HTML-based listings to boot.

Making life easier for eBay power sellers has become somewhat of a cottage industry. There are a large number of software programs and web-based services that handle some or all of the eBay selling process—from ad creation to post-auction management.

We'll start by focusing on those standalone software programs that help to automate the selling management process. Read on to learn more.

> ## " Mike Sez "
>
> Remember to factor the costs of these programs and services into your overall auction costs. If a service charges $20 a month and you list only 20 auctions, you've just added a buck to the cost of each of your auctions. Same thing if a service charges on a per-listing basis, or as a percentage of your selling fee. Believe me, these costs add up fast—especially if you're a relatively small seller!

All My Auctions

All My Auctions (www.rajeware.com/auction/) is a basic auction management software program. It includes template-based listing creation, live auction management (including the capability to track competitors' auctions), end-of-auction email notification, and report generation. The price is $39.95 for a one-year license.

Auction Lizard

Auction Lizard (www.auction-lizard.com) is an easy-to-use listing-creation software program. It creates great-looking HTML-based listings using forms and templates. Auction Lizard is shareware, with a $29 registration fee.

Auction Wizard 2000

Auction Wizard 2000 (www.auctionwizard2000.com)—that's *wizard*, not *lizard*—is an auction management software program that includes an image editor, a listing creator, a report generator, an FTP manager, and an auction database. Auction Wizard 2000 costs $75 for the first year (and $50 for each subsequent year) with no monthly subscription fees.

AuctionSage

AuctionSage (www.auctionsagesoftware.com) is a software program that lets you post and manage your eBay auction transactions. It also includes email and bulk feedback functions. Cost is $29.95 for 3 months, $49.95 for 6 months, or $79.95 for a year.

AuctionTamer

AuctionTamer (www.auctiontamer.com) is an all-in-one auction management software program for both sellers and bidders. For sellers, it lets you create auction listings, schedule delayed auction listings, manage your live auctions, send post-auction emails, and print shipping labels. Cost is $22.95 per month or $149.95 for a year.

eBay Blackthorne

Although Turbo Lister is eBay's recommended listing creation software, the site also offers another program called eBay Blackthorne (formerly known as eBay Seller's Assistant). ebay Blackthorne is available in two different versions: Basic and Pro.

Blackthorne Basic (pages.ebay.com/blackthorne/basic.html) is best for casual users, offering HTML-based listing creation (using forms and templates), auction tracking, and basic post-auction management (including automatic email notification and feedback generation). The software is available on a per-month subscription; you'll pay $9.99 each month, no matter how many listings you create.

Blackthorne Pro (pages.ebay.com/blackthorne/pro.html) is a more powerful software-based tool for high-volume sellers. This program is essentially SA Basic on steroids, with many more post-auction management features. In particular, you get inventory management, sales management and reporting, bulk feedback posting, and the ability to print invoices and shipping labels—in addition to the standard bulk listing creation and end-of-auction emails. The program costs $24.99 per month, and comes with a free subscription to eBay Selling Manager Pro. Use it with eBay's standard checkout feature, and you're in business.

eBay Turbo Lister

eBay Turbo Lister (pages.ebay.com/turbo_lister/) is eBay's official software program for the bulk uploading of multiple auctions. Although Turbo Lister doesn't offer any auction tracking features, it excels at bulk uploading—and it's free! Many sellers use Turbo Lister to create their listings and Selling Manager to manage their auctions; it's a good combination.

note

Learn more about eBay Turbo Lister in Chapter 20, "Automating Your Listings with eBay Turbo Lister."

HammerTap

HammerTap (www.hammertap.com) offers various auction management software and services, all priced separately. Their software tools include the following:

- BidderBlock—Software for managing blocked bidder lists
- DeepAnalysis—Auction research tool
- FeeFinder—Software for calculating eBay, PayPal, and shipping fees

Each of these tools is priced separately, so you can pick and choose among those you actually need.

Shooting Star

Shooting Star (www.foodogsoftware.com) is a software program designed to manage the end-of-auction process. It uses what it calls a "workflow system" to move you through various post-auction operations, including email notification. Price is a one-time $60.00.

Selling Management Services

Even more popular than selling management programs are selling management services, offered by a variety of third-party websites. Although many of these sites offer similar features, there are a lot of important differences, so pay attention. And know that most of these sites cost real money to use—in some cases, the kind of serious bucks that only big-volume sellers can afford.

Ándale

Ándale (www.andale.com) is a site that offers various services for eBay sellers. In fact, it's the only site that offers the full range of tools from pre-auction research to post-auction management.

Ándale's auction tools are first-rate, and they're extremely easy to use. Here's a short list of what's available:

- Ándale Checkout—Provides one-stop customer checkout, as well as automatic end-of-auction emails
- Ándale Counters—Free traffic counters for your item listings
- Ándale Counters Pro—More advanced counters with traffic reports and related statistics

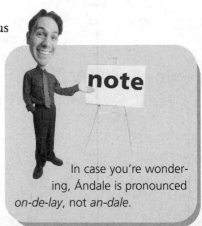

note

In case you're wondering, Ándale is pronounced *on-de-lay*, not *an-dale*.

- Ándale Customer Manager—Enables you to mine your customer list for additional sales
- Ándale Gallery—Displays other items you have for sale
- Ándale Images—Image hosting
- Ándale Lister—Bulk listing creation with predesigned templates
- Ándale Lister Pro—Offline bulk listing creation
- Ándale Reports—A suite of business management reports for analyzing your eBay sales
- Ándale Research—A collection of eBay sales analysis reports
- Ándale Sales Analyzer—Detailed analysis of your eBay sales
- Ándale Suppliers—Identify and contact suppliers for specified types of merchandise
- Ándale Stores—Your own branded fixed-price online storefront
- Ándale What's Hot—Reporting of eBay's hottest product categories

You have the option of using—and paying for—each of these tools separately; you're not locked into the complete toolkit, unless that's what you want. Although some of these tools can be used free of charge, most carry either a per-month or a per-transaction charge. The individual fees might seem reasonable, but they can add up very quickly. In fact, the thing I like least about Ándale is the cost; depending on which services you subscribe to, you could end up spending more money here than at any other site.

Auction Hawk

Auction Hawk (www.auctionhawk.com) is a web-based service with affordable pricing. The site offers various tools in its main service, including image hosting, bulk listing creation, end-of-auction checkout with automated winning-bidder email, bulk feedback posting, and profit-and-loss reporting.

One nice aspect of Auction Hawk's services is that it doesn't charge any per-transaction or final value fees. In addition, all its services are included in a single price, so you're not nickel-and-dimed to death with a la carte pricing. The full-service monthly plans range in price from $12.99 (for 110 listings) to $89.99 (unlimited listings). At these prices, it's worth checking out.

Auctiva

Auctiva (www.auctiva.com) offers a variety of different services, including bulk listing, image hosting, auction tracking and management, and a showcase photo gallery—all available at no charge whatsoever. Auctiva's services are first rate, and you get them for free!

ChannelAdvisor

ChannelAdvisor (www.channeladvisor.com) offers a fairly affordable suite of auction management tools—as well as services for bigger online merchants. The service you want to look at is ChannelAdvisor Pro, which is actually HammerTap Manager in disguise. This service is a surprisingly easy-to-use collection of auction management tools, quite reasonably priced at a flat fee of just $29.95 per month. If you're doing more than 50 auctions a month, it's definitely worth considering—even more so if you're a heavier lister.

eBay Selling Manager

As you learned in Chapter 22, "Managing Your Sales with eBay Selling Manager," Selling Manager (pages.ebay.com/selling_manager/) lets you manage your pending, in-process, and closed auctions right from within My eBay. It's a fairly complete service, equal to that offered by many third-party providers. It includes predefined email templates and automatic feedback forms, automatically tracks buyer checkout and payment, and lets you print shipping labels, invoices, and reports. At $4.99 per month, it's a pretty good deal—definitely worth checking out if you have a lot of auctions to manage.

eBay Selling Manager Pro

The more robust Selling Manager Pro (pages.ebay.com/selling_manager_pro/) adds features of value to power sellers, including bulk listing and relisting, bulk email, inventory management, report generation, and the capability to create and print shipping labels. The subscription fee is $15.99 per month.

HammerTap

HammerTap (www.hammertap.com) offers various auction management software and services, all priced separately. Their primary web-based tool is HammerTap Manager, which offers auction posting and management. (In fact, HammerTap Manager is the same service as ChannelAdvisor Pro, just under a different name.) The basic HammerTap Manager service runs a flat $29.95 per month.

inkFrog

inkFrog (www.inkfrog.com) is a cute name for some heavy-duty web-based auction management services. inkFrog offers auction listing, tracking, and management, along with image hosting and listing creation and design. Various plans are offered, starting at $7.95 per month.

ManageAuctions

ManageAuctions (www.manageauctions.com) offers web-based listing creation, auction tracking, email notification, shipping label printing, feedback generation, and other post-auction management. Pricing is on an a la carte basis; listings cost $0.06 each and post-sale management is $0.06 per auction. There's a minimum monthly charge of $5.95, and a maximum of $29.95; image hosting is extra.

Marketworks

Marketworks (www.marketworks.com), formerly known as Auctionworks, is one of the oldest and most established third-party auction management services. The site offers various professional auction tools, including inventory management, a bulk listing creator, traffic counters, image hosting, automatic end-of-auction emails, a checkout system, reciprocal feedback posting, web-based storefronts, and customizable reports.

Marketworks charges no monthly fees for its service, instead opting for a 2% fee on each successful transaction, with a $0.20 minimum. The site caters to high-volume sellers, however; their minimum monthly fee is $29.95.

SpareDollar

SpareDollar (www.sparedollar.com) is low-priced auction service, ideal for small or occasional sellers. It's extremely affordable, with everything offered for a flat $8.95 per month price.

SpareDollar's auction tools include the following:

- sdCounter—Traffic counters for your item listings
- sdGallery—Photo gallery of all your auction items
- sdImage—50MB of image hosting
- sdLister—Bulk listing creation with predesigned templates
- sdTracker—Post-auction tracking and emails

While SpareDollar is attractively priced, its services might prove too limited for really high-volume sellers. That said, many high-volume sellers do use SpareDollar, and are quite happy with the results. Give it a try to see if it fits your particular eBay business.

Vendio

Vendio (www.vendio.com), formerly known as Auctionwatch, offers the Vendio Sales Manager set of listing creation and auction management tools. You can use Sales Manager not only to create new item listings, but also to manage all of your current and post-auction activity. Sales Manager will automatically generate end-of-auction emails, print invoices and packing slips, and upload customer feedback to eBay.

Vendio offers Sales Manager in both Inventory and Merchandising Editions; the mix of features is a little different between the two, but the pricing is the same. The company tries to appeal to different types of sellers by offering a mix of fixed and variable priced monthly subscriptions.

For example, the Sales Manager Pay as You Go Plan carries no fixed fee, although you'll pay $0.10 per transaction and a 1% final value fee. On the other hand, the Sales Manager Variable Rate Power Plan costs $29.95 a month, but with no listing fee and a 1.25% final value fee; and the Flat Rate Power Plan costs $39.95 a month, with a $0.10 per-transaction charge but no final value fee. Confusing? You bet—but it does let you choose the type of payment (flat versus variable versus per-transaction) that best suits your needs.

I like Vendio's tools almost as much as Ándale's— although the range of tools isn't quite as wide. (No research, for example.) The variable-rate pricing is actually a little more attractive to me, especially because my sales volume varies from month to month. And I like the fact that Vendio doesn't nickel-and-dime me to death. All in all, a service definitely worth your consideration.

> **" Mike Sez "**
>
> Of all these auction management tools, I still like the combination of eBay Turbo Lister/Selling Manager, especially for small sellers. For more active eBay sellers, I like either Ándale, Auctiva, SpareDollar, or Vendio, all of which offer a wide variety of very professional tools.

THE ABSOLUTE MINIMUM

Here are the key points to remember from this chapter:

- Many big websites offer news, education, community, and auction management services for online auction users—particularly for power sellers.
- If you're a power seller (listing dozens of auctions every week), check out sites like Ándale or Vendio.
- If you're a smaller seller (listing a half-dozen or fewer auctions a week), eBay's combination of Turbo Lister and Selling Manager does a good job at an affordable price.

28

SELLING INTERNATIONALLY

If you're a seller doing any amount of volume on eBay, you will sooner or later be faced with an interesting situation: someone from outside the U.S. bidding on one of your items. Becoming an international seller sounds exotic and glamorous, but the honor comes with an increase in paperwork and effort on your part. Although you might be able to increase the number of potential bidders by offering your merchandise outside the U.S., you also increase your workload—and, more important, your risk.

Should you sell internationally? And if so, how do you handle payment and shipping and all those other niggling details? Read on to learn more about international sales via eBay—as well as hear my own opinion on the subject.

Pros and Cons of Selling Internationally

Let's start with the big question: Should you sell internationally? The answer to this isn't a simple one. It depends a lot on your tolerance for differences (in money, in language, in routine), and your ability to deal with unusual post-auction activity—especially in regard to payment and shipping.

The pros of opening your auctions to non-U.S. bidders include the following:

- You might be able to attract additional bidders—and thus sell more items at (presumably) higher prices.
- You can offset some of the seasonality of the U.S. market; when it's winter here, you can still be selling swimsuits to the summer market in Australia.
- You establish a reputation as a hard-working global trader.
- It's fun (sometimes) to interact with people from different countries and cultures.

The cons of selling outside the U.S. include the following:

- You might run into difficulties communicating with bidders from outside the United States.
- You might have to deal with payment in non-U.S. funds, on non-U.S. banks.
- You'll have to put extra effort into the packing of an item to be shipped over great distances.
- You probably won't be able to use your standard shipping services—which means investigating new shipping services and options.
- Shipping costs will be higher than what you're used to—and will need to be passed on to the buyer.
- You'll need to deal with the appropriate paperwork for shipping outside the U.S.—including those pesky customs forms.
- If there are any problems or disputes with the item shipped, you have an international-sized incident on your hands.

Just looking at this list, it may appear that the cons outweigh the pros. That might not always be the case, however—especially if you're a real "people person." Many eBay sellers get great joy from interacting with people from different cultures, sometimes turning foreign buyers into lasting friends. I can vouch from my limited personal experience that most non-U.S. buyers I've dealt with are exceedingly polite and tolerant of the extra effort required to complete an international transaction.

If you decide to sell outside the U.S., you'll want to state this in your auctions, along with a line indicating that "shipping and handling outside the U.S. is higher," "listed shipping charge is for U.S. only," or something to that effect. If, on the other hand, you decide *not* to sell internationally, state that in your ad also—with a "U.S. bidders only" type of notice.

Selling Outside the U.S.

If you decide to take the leap and open your auctions to an international audience, you need to be prepared for a new world of activities—no pun intended. Selling outside the U.S.—especially the shipping part of the process—is much different from selling to someone in New York or California. Although I can't prepare you for all the issues you might encounter, I will point out some of the bigger hassles to look out for.

Communicating with International Bidders

One of the joys—and challenges—of selling internationally is communicating with non-U.S. bidders. Although citizens of many countries speak English, not all do—or do so well. This means you're likely to receive emails in fractured English, or in some language that you might not be able to easily translate.

The solution to this problem isn't always easy. It's one thing to say you should send non–English-language emails back to the buyer, requesting communication in English. But if the buyer can't read or write English, how is he supposed to read your request? This problem is a tricky one.

I have found, however, that communication goes more smoothly if you keep your written communications short and simple. Use straightforward wording and avoid slang terms and abbreviations, and you stand a good chance of being understood.

In addition, you have to deal with the time difference between the U.S. and many other countries. If you're dealing with a buyer in the Far East, you're sleeping while he's sending emails, and vice versa. This introduces an unavoidable lag into the communication that can sometimes be problematic.

The only advice I can give you here is to be aware of the time differences, and plan accordingly. Don't expect an immediate response from someone on a different continent, and try to avoid the kind of back-and-forth communications that can go on for days and days.

Accepting Foreign Payments

One of the issues with selling outside the U.S. is in dealing with foreign currency. First, you have to convert it to U.S. dollars. (How many lira to the dollar today?) Then you have to receive it in a form that is both secure and trusted. (Do you trust a personal check drawn on a small Spanish bank?) Then you have to find a way to deposit those funds—and convert them to U.S. dollars. (Does your bank handle foreign deposits?)

The currency issue is simplified somewhat when you specify bidding and payment in U.S. funds only. This puts the onus of currency conversion on the buyer, which is a plus.

The payment process can be further simplified when the buyer pays by credit card—or, even better, by PayPal. PayPal is now active in 55 countries (including the U.S.) and can handle all the payment, conversion, and deposit functions for you.

tip

When you need to convert foreign funds, use the Universal Currency Converter (www.xe.net/ucc/).

Shipping Across Borders—And Oceans

The biggest difficulty in selling to non-U.S. buyers is shipping the item. Not only are longer distances involved (which necessitates more secure packaging—and longer shipping times), but you also have to deal with different shipping options and all sorts of new paperwork.

Chances are your normal method of shipping won't work for your international shipments. For example, you can't use Priority Mail to ship outside the U.S.—not even to Canada or Mexico. This means you'll need to evaluate new shipping methods, and possibly new shipping services.

If you want to stick with the U.S. Postal Service, you can check out Global Priority Mail (reasonably fast and reasonably priced), Global Express Mail (fast but expensive), Airmail (almost as fast, not quite as expensive), or Surface/Parcel Post (slow but less expensive). In addition, UPS offers its Worldwide Express service, FedEx offers its FedEx Express service internationally, and DHL is always a good option for shipping outside the U.S. Be sure to check out your options beforehand, and charge the buyer the actual costs incurred.

tip

Given the increased chances of loss or damage when shipping great distances, you should consider purchasing insurance for all items shipping outside North America.

You'll also have to deal with a bit of paperwork while you're preparing your shipment. All packages shipping outside U.S. borders must clear customs to enter the destination country—and require the completion of specific customs forms to make the trip. Depending on the type of item you're shipping and the weight of your package, you'll need either Form 2976 (green) or Form 2976-A (white). Both of these forms should be available at your local post office.

When you're filling out these forms, describe the item in terms that ordinary people can understand. That means using simple, generic terms. An "Alicia Keyes greatest hits CD compilation" becomes "compact disc." A "SimCity extension pack" becomes "video game." And so on.

You should also be honest about what you're shipping. Some buyers will try to talk you into describing the item as a gift so that they can save on duties or tax on their end. That's lying, and you shouldn't do it.

In addition, there are certain items you can't ship to foreign countries—firearms, live animals and animal products, and so on. (There are also some technology items you can't ship, for security reasons.) You need to check the government's list of import and export restrictions to see what items you're prohibited from shipping outside U.S. borders. Check with your shipping service for more detailed information.

Finally, note that shipping across borders takes longer than shipping within the U.S. This is especially true if an item is held up at customs. Make sure your international buyers know that shipping times will be longer than what you might state for domestic buyers.

note

Customs forms aren't required on non-duty items that weigh less than 16 ounces.

tip

eBay offers several pages of advice for international trading at pages.ebay.com/globaltrade/.

eBay's International Marketplaces

To better participate in marketplaces outside the U.S., eBay has established separate sites for 26 foreign countries. Each of these sites lists items in the country's native language, using the local currency. (You can see this in Figure 28.1, which shows the eBay China site.)

The list of eBay's international sites includes the following:

- Argentina (www.mercadolibre.com.ar)
- Australia (www.ebay.com.au)
- Austria (www.ebay.at)
- Belgium (www.ebay.be)
- Brazil (www.mercadolivre.com.br)
- Canada (www.ebay.ca)

FIGURE 28.1
One of eBay's many international sites: eBay China.

- China (www.ebay.com.cn)
- France (www.ebay.fr)
- Germany (www.ebay.de)
- Hong Kong (www.ebay.com.hk)
- India (www.baazee.com)
- Ireland (pages.ebay.ie)
- Italy (www.ebay.it)
- Korea (www.auction.co.kr)
- Malaysia (www.ebay.com.my)
- Mexico (www.mercadolibre.com.mx)
- Netherlands (www.ebay.nl)
- New Zealand (www.ebay.com/nz/)
- Philippines (www.ebay.ph)
- Poland (www.ebay.pl)
- Singapore (www.ebay.com.sg)
- Spain (www.es.ebay.com)
- Sweden (www.ebay.se)
- Switzerland (www.ebay.ch)
- Taiwan (www.tw.ebay.com)
- United Kingdom (www.ebay.co.uk)

Although these sites were designed for trading within a specific country, there's nothing keeping you from searching them for items to buy—which will put you on the opposite side of the international buyer/seller argument!

THE ABSOLUTE MINIMUM

Here are the key points to remember from this chapter:

- When dealing with non-U.S. buyers, be sure to specify payment in U.S. funds—ideally via PayPal or an international money order.

- Shipping outside the U.S. requires the completion of customs forms (available at your local post office) and the use of special international shipping services.

- eBay offers 26 country-specific online auction sites (in addition to the main U.S. site), for trading within each local region.

29

OPENING A TRADING ASSISTANT BUSINESS

If you want to become a high-volume eBay seller, you have to find a steady stream of merchandise to sell—more than what you have stashed away in the attic or garage. Many eBay sellers purchase merchandise for resale from liquidation or wholesale sites, but this isn't the only way to go. That's because it's possible to become a high-volume seller by selling other people's stuff, as an eBay Trading Assistant.

A Trading Assistant is, quite simply, a consignment reseller. You find clients who want to sell their items on eBay, but don't want to go through all the hassles themselves, and then you handle all the eBay activities needed to sell the items. You take possession of the merchandise, research it, photograph It, write up an item description, and create and launch the auction listing. You manage the auction and collect the buyer's payment when it sells; then you pack it and ship it out to the buyer. You also pay all applicable eBay fees (although you pass them on to the client as part of your fees to him). Your client, the owner of the merchandise, doesn't have to do a thing.

Of course, you get compensated for all this work. Many Trading Assistants receive some sort of flat fee up front (in case the item doesn't sell), as well as a percentage of the final selling price. Most sellers also pass through eBay's fees to the client.

How to Become an eBay Trading Assistant

All eBay Trading Assistants are consignment sellers, but not all consignment sellers are Trading Assistants. That is, you don't have to be an official TA to consignment sell on eBay. Nothing in eBay's rules and regulations prohibits a regular member from reselling merchandise for other people. In fact, if you're just testing the waters, there's no real reason to bother with joining the TA program. Test the waters with a few "unofficial" consignment auctions before you decide to launch your own boat.

Once you decide to become a full-blown consignment seller, however, there's no reason not to join the TA program. It doesn't cost you anything, and you get the benefit of being listed in eBay's Trading Assistants Directory—which is how many users find TAs to sell their items for them.

Joining the TA program doesn't have any really stringent requirements. Here's all that eBay requires:

- You've sold at least ten items in the past 90 days.
- You have a feedback rating of at least 100.

That's it. To join up, just go to the Trading Assistants hub (pages.ebay.com/tahub/) and click the Become a Trading Assistant link. When the Become a Trading Assistant page appears, as shown in Figure 29.1, click the Click Here button below the Sell It For Others! graphic. Follow the onscreen instructions from there and you'll be ready to go.

FIGURE 29.1

Getting ready to join eBay's Trading Assistant program.

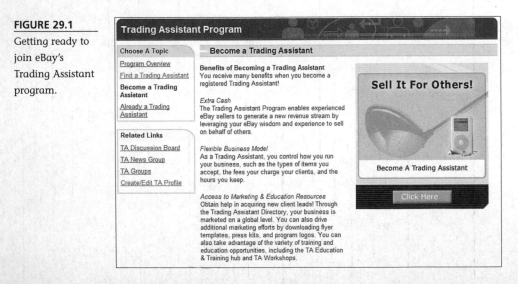

Setting Up Shop—and Setting Prices

Once you've joined eBay's Trading Assistant program, it's time to set up your business—which is as simple as establishing a selling procedure, writing up a contract, and then going out and finding clients. Let's take a quick look.

Create a Consignment Contract

All serious Trading Assistants should create a contract for their clients to sign. This contract spells out exactly what it is you are and are not responsible for, and clarifies your legal position in terms of ownership of the product.

Your contract should include the following items:

- The names and contact information for both parties (you and your client)
- The purpose of the contract—that you will offer the items owned by the client for sale on eBay
- The services you, the reseller, will offer—writing the listing, taking photos, listing the item, managing the auction, handling payment, packing the item, shipping the item, and so on
- Who takes possession of the merchandise during the transaction (typically you) and who retains ownership of the merchandise (typically the client)
- How and when the client can cancel the transaction
- What happens if the item doesn't sell (relist, return the merchandise to the client, whatever)
- Who handles customer complaints and returns (probably you, but not necessarily)
- Fees

Obviously, both you and your client need to sign this contract before you can begin the selling process.

Set Your Fee Schedule

As a Trading Assistant, you make your money from the fees you charge for your services. There are no set guidelines for these fees; you can charge pretty much whatever you want, or whatever the market will bear.

First, consider establishing a flat fee of $5 or $10 for every transaction, in addition to a selling commission. This fee, typically paid up front, ensures that you get paid something whether the item sells or not. It also helps to weed out lower-priced and lower-potential items; if clients have to pay a little up front to get in the game, they might think twice about the salability of what they bring to the table.

As to the selling commission, you'll find sellers charging anywhere from 10% to 50% of the final selling price. The average fee seems to be in the 25% range. That is, you take 25% of what the item sells for; if you sell an item for $100, your fee is $25.

Then you have all the various eBay and PayPal fees to consider. Most consignment sellers pass on these fees to the client, in the form of additional charges. So on your $100 item, you'll take out your $25, plus eBay's listing and final value fees, plus the PayPal or merchant credit card fees (if any).

Consider Opening a Drop-Off Location

Many eBay Trading Assistants work out of their home. If you go this route, you'll either have to pick up items from your clients' homes or have your clients drop off items at your home. While some clients might like this homey touch, others might be a little nervous about dealing with a business that doesn't look like a business.

A more professional (and more expensive) option is to rent your own retail storefront for merchandise drop-offs. Chances are you'll attract more clients with a drop-off location, and not only because your signage will provide added visibility; many people will be more comfortable leaving their merchandise at a retail location than at some stranger's house or apartment. You also get lots of added space to store the consigned merchandise and conduct your business.

The downside of this, of course, is you have additional costs—the rent and utilities for your store, plus signage and the like. And you'll pay those bills every month, no matter how much auction business you do. But you don't need a *big* store, and it doesn't have to be in a high-rent location. Any type of storefront or office space will do.

note

eBay calls a Trading Assistant with a drop-off location a *Trading Post*. To qualify for official Trading Post status, you must offer a staffed drop-off location with regular hours, have a feedback rating of 500 or higher (with at least 98% positive), and have monthly eBay sales of at least $25,000.

Go the Franchise Route

Another option is to buy into one of the several eBay drop-off franchise operations that are starting to bloom. With a franchise you get lots of help getting started; the main office will help you choose a retail site and negotiate your lease, plan your store layout, and market your operation. You'll also get training and ongoing operations support, plus the value of the franchise name. For all this, you pay a large upfront fee and a percentage of your monthly revenues.

Is a franchise a good idea? Maybe, especially if you're new to this or generally inexperienced in running a business. Maybe not, if you're an experienced seller, know how to run a business, and prefer to work for yourself (and keep all the profits yourself). If you're interested in doing the franchise thing, definitely check out several different franchises, visit a few of the stores, and talk to some of the franchise owners. Know what you're getting into before you sign that first check.

Some of the more popular eBay drop-off franchises include

- e-Powersellers (www.e-powersellers.com)
- iSold It (www.i-soldit.com), shown in Figure 29.2
- NuMarkets (www.numarkets.com)
- The Online Outpost (www.theonlineoutpost.com)
- QuikDrop (www.quikdropfranchise.com)
- Snappy Auctions (www.snappyauctions.com)

FIGURE 29.2

The home page for the iSold It franchise.

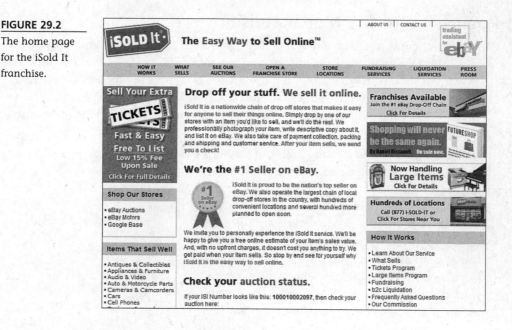

Remember, before you enter into any franchise agreement, do your homework: Check out the franchisor's finances and history, talk with other franchisees, and compare franchise fees with other franchises.

Running Your Trading Assistant Business

Running an eBay Trading Assistant business is just like running your own auctions—with the additional responsibility of finding clients who have merchandise they want to sell. Let's take a look at what a typical consignment business involves.

Finding Clients

To sell items on consignment, you first have to find some clients. Now, if you have a drop-off location, you can sit behind your counter and wait for your clients to come to you. (Although a little advertising and promotion probably wouldn't hurt, of course.) If you're running your consignment business out of your home, however, you'll need to do a little advertising and promotion—and make sure you're listed in eBay's Trading Assistant Directory.

Taking Possession of the Merchandise

When you agree to sell an item for a client, you need to take that item into your possession. You're in the consignment business, after all; you need to have the item in your possession in order to sell it. Plus, if you don't have it, you don't know for sure that it exists—or that your client hasn't disposed of it elsewhere. Remember, it's your name on the eBay auction; you'll be held responsible if the item isn't actually available for sale.

If you're running your Trading Assistant business out of your home, you'll probably make your initial contact with a client over the phone. One phone call is all it takes to get a feel for the client, find out what he or she wants to sell, and determine whether it's worth your time. You should also take this opportunity to tell your prospective client about you and your business, discuss fees, and work out any other details. Then, if all goes well on the phone, you can arrange for the client to drop off the merchandise—or for you to pick it up.

While you can try to get all your clients to drop off their items at your home, chances are you'll have to do some merchandise pickup yourself. Going to a stranger's home can get a little dicey, so you'll want to play it as safe as you can. If you have a relative who happens to play football, take him along with you. Otherwise, judge the location

note

You don't have to accept everything that your clients want you to sell. It's okay to turn away goods that you think you'll have a hard time selling or that you think are worth considerably less than the client does—or that you think may have been obtained illegally.

carefully, and if you're at all nervous, arrange to meet the client at a neutral (and safer) location, like a local coffeehouse or fast-food joint.

Managing the Auction Process

Once you have the merchandise in your possession, selling it is just like running any auction. You'll need to do a little research to learn more about the item and determine the appropriate starting price. You'll also need to photograph the item and write the item listing. There's nothing special you need to do at this point.

Packing and Shipping—and Settling with the Client

At the end of the auction, you receive payment just as you would with any other auction. (The payment comes to you, not to your client.) Then you pack and ship the item, and get ready to settle things up with your client.

Once you've received payment from the buyer, you need to calculate your final fees and create an invoice for the client. Start with the final selling price, subtract your commission, subtract all the eBay and PayPal fees, and the balance is what you pay the client. If it's an occasional client, cut a check right then (or within the time frame specified in your contract). If you have an ongoing relationship, you may want to arrange payment for all that client's auctions at the end of each month.

That's really all there is to it. You run your TA auctions just like you do your personal auctions. The only difference is that you're selling somebody's else's items, and you're only taking a percentage of the final selling price.

THE ABSOLUTE MINIMUM

Here are the key points to remember from this chapter:

- Many eBay sellers make a good living by selling other people's merchandise on consignment, as an eBay Trading Assistant.
- When you join eBay's Trading Assistants program, you are automatically listed in the Trading Assistants Directory.
- TA's can pick up merchandise from their clients, or open a drop-off location to receive merchandise.
- All serious Trading Assistants have a contract for their clients to sign.
- TA fees range from 10% to 50% of the final selling price.
- A quick way to get started with consignment selling is to buy into an eBay drop-off store franchise.

30

MAKING A LIVING FROM EBAY

Chances are you're just starting out on your online auction adventures—learning how to buy and sell and take advantage of everything eBay has to offer. As you gain more experience, however, you may decide that you're pretty good at the whole thing, and start to wonder what it might take to ramp up your eBay activities. You might even dream about one day making your living from selling goods online.

For tens of thousands of eBay users, making a living from online auctions isn't a dream—it's reality. It's definitely possible to sell enough items to generate a livable income from eBay auctions. It takes a lot of hard work and it's as complex as running any other business; but it can be done.

Let me tell you how.

Becoming an eBay PowerSeller

One of the steps to running your own eBay business—although not a requirement, by any means—is to become an eBay PowerSeller. eBay's 100,000-plus PowerSellers generate enough business to warrant special attention from eBay, in the form of dedicated customer support, premier tools, and the occasional special offer. Plus they get to display that cool PowerSeller logo in all their auction listings.

To become a PowerSeller, you must meet the following qualifications:

- Maintain a consistently high level of eBay sales (see Table 30.1)
- Maintain a minimum of four average monthly total item listings for three straight months
- Have been an active eBay seller for at least 90 days
- Achieve and maintain a minimum feedback rating of 100, 98% positive
- Deliver post-auction messages to successful bidders within three business days of each auction close
- Be an eBay member in good standing and uphold eBay's "community values"—including honesty, timeliness, and mutual respect

The most important point is the first, because it's the most quantifiable. There are five levels in the PowerSeller program; qualification for each level is based on average gross monthly sales, calculated over the past three months of selling activity. Table 30.1 shows the qualifying requirements for each level.

Table 30.1   PowerSeller Requirements, by Level

Level	Requirement (average monthly sales)
Bronze	$1,000
Silver	$3,000
Gold	$10,000
Platinum	$25,000
Titanium	$150,000

That's right, there are some eBay sellers who average $150,000 or more a month. That's almost two million dollars a year in revenues from eBay auctions—no slight accomplishment!

Membership in eBay's PowerSellers program is free. However, you can't apply; PowerSeller status is by invitation only. Each month eBay sends out invitations to sellers who meet the PowerSeller criteria. You become a member by (1) meeting the criteria; (2) receiving an invitation; and (3) responding positively to the invitation.

Want to learn more? Then go to the main PowerSeller's page (pages.ebay.com/services/buyandsell/welcome.html) and read up!

Turning Your Online Auctions into a Real Business

How easy is it to turn your online auction hobby into a profitable business? It's all a matter of volume—and good business planning and management.

Let's consider an example. Caitlin has found a source for iron-on transfers for T-shirts and sweat-shirts. She can buy these transfers for $1 each and (based on her experience and research) can sell them on eBay for an average price of $5. That's four dollars profit for every transfer she sells.

Caitlin has huddled over her copy of Quicken and determined that she needs to generate $30,000 in profit (*not* in revenues!) to make her eBay business worthwhile. Assuming that she works 50 weeks a year (everyone needs a vacation), that means she needs to average $600 in profit each week. At $4 profit per item, she has to sell an average of 150 iron-on transfers a week—each and every week.

> **note**
>
> To keep your PowerSeller status, you have to *maintain* the base sales rate. If your sales drop below these levels, eBay will give you 30 days to bring your account back into compliance; if you don't, your membership in the program will be revoked. (You're free to requalify at a later date, however.)

Because only about half of all eBay auctions end with a sale, Caitlin knows that to sell those 150 items she has to launch 300 auctions each week. That's a lot of work, as you can imagine.

Can Caitlin make a go of it? It depends. Can she physically manage 300 auctions a week? Can she pack and ship 150 items a week? And, more important, can she realistically *sell* 150 items a week—is the market big enough to support that sort of sales volume?

If Caitlin answers yes to all those questions, there's still more planning to be done. To begin with, this example greatly simplifies the costs involved. Caitlin will need to figure eBay's costs for all those auctions—the listing fees for 300 auctions, and the final value fees for 150 completions. If she accepts PayPal payments, she'll need to determine what percentage of her buyers will use PayPal, and what her fees for those transactions will amount to. Assuming that she uses a third-party website to help her launch and manage those auctions, she'll also need to figure those fees into her cost structure.

All totaled, these auction listing and management costs can add up to close to 10% of her revenues. That means increasing her cost per item from $1.00 to $1.50 or more—which reduces her profit per item to just $3.50. With this reduced profit margin, she'll need to sell even more items to hit her profit dollar targets—an extra 20 or so successful auctions each week.

All this needs to be factored in—before Caitlin launches a single auction. And at these volume levels she's definitely running a business, which means reporting the income to the IRS and paying taxes. There's also the matter of *sales taxes*, which she'll need to collect on all sales made to buyers in her home state.

The takeaway here is that making a living from eBay sales is just like running a business, especially in its financial complexities. Anyone contemplating this type of endeavor should do some serious business planning, which should include consulting an accountant or another financial planner.

If the numbers work out, you need to answer one more question: Is this something you'll enjoy doing every day of the week, every week of the year? Even if you can make money at it, managing hundreds of auctions a week can wear down even the best of us. Make sure that you're up to it, and that you'll enjoy it, before you take the leap.

> **note**
>
> Turning your eBay sales into a real business is a major undertaking. If you're serious about making the leap from occasional seller to full-time merchant, check out my companion book, *Making a Living from Your eBay Business* (Que, 2005), available wherever business books are sold.

Maintaining Your Sales Inventory

If you need to be launching several hundred auctions a week, where do you find all those items to list? It's a simple fact that you can't become a PowerSeller by listing onesies and twosies. Instead, you need to find an item you can buy in bulk, and then list multiples of that item week after week.

Although beginning eBayers can find items to sell by haunting flea markets and estate auctions, PowerSellers most likely won't find what they need in those venues. A better strategy is to approach local retailers or wholesalers and offer to buy 10 or 20 (or more) of a particular item. Buy whatever quantity earns you the best price break—as long as you think you can move them.

You can also buy bulk lots of merchandise from online wholesalers and liquidators. We discussed some of these sites in Chapter 14, "Before You Sell: Do Your Homework!" Check out Liquidation.com (www.liquidation.com) and Wholesale411 (www.wholesale411.com) to see what's available, or use Ándale Suppliers (www.andale.com) to hook up with suppliers of specific types of merchandise.

If you're a serious collector, you might have your eBay business right there. When your comics collection numbers in the tens of thousands, or you have thousands of rare coins filed away in your basement, you're ready for power selling—and power buying. Just remember to buy low and sell high, and you'll be in business.

Finally, consider the selling price of the items you want to sell—and the profit you generate on each item. You have to sell a lot more of a $5 item than you do of a $50 item to make the same amount of profit. (Assuming both generate a similar profit percentage.) And, of course, the more items you sell, the more work you have to do. The most successful PowerSellers do it by selling higher-priced, higher-profit items, for which the revenues—and the profits—add up a lot quicker.

Automating Your Auction Activities

Managing hundreds of simultaneous auctions is hard work. Most PowerSellers end up working more than a standard 8-hour day, and more than five days a week. (eBay reports that most of their PowerSellers work anywhere from 10 to 16 hours a day on their auctions!) The time it takes to find new items to sell, photograph them, write detailed item descriptions, post the auctions, send post-auction emails, and pack and ship all those items quickly adds up.

The more auctions you list, the more it behooves you to automate as much of the auction process as possible. For most PowerSellers, that means signing up with one of the big websites that offer bulk listing and post-auction management, such as Ándale (www.andale.com), Auctiva (www.auctiva.com), SpareDollar (www.sparedollar.com), or Vendio (www.vendio.com). Be sure to factor the site's fees into your cost structure, and let them help you manage all your auctions.

You should also try to automate your physical auction activity. That means creating some sort of auction "office" or workspace in your home. This workspace should include everything you need in order to create auction listings (including your digital camera and scanner) and to pack and ship your finished auction items. In addition, you'll need space to store all your excess auction inventory; this may be your basement or garage, or even a rented storage locker.

note

See Chapter 27, "Using Selling Management Software and Services," to learn more about the services offered by these auction management sites.

Automating your processes also means establishing some sort of auction-related schedule. Pick one or two days a week to launch all your auctions; pick one or two days to visit the post office. Stick to your schedule and you'll avoid running around like a chicken with your head cut off; after all, dead chickens aren't known for their business efficiency.

On the subject of shipping, you should try to simplify your packing and shipping activities as much as possible. This means limiting the types of items you sell to just a few so that you can standardize on packaging. It's much easier to stock just one or two different-sized boxes than it is to store a dozen or more sizes. If you sell a limited variety of merchandise, you'll also be able to better estimate your shipping costs ahead of time.

Using Caitlin's iron-on transfer business as an example, this is a great item to sell. She's dealing with a standard-size product that's both flat and light—ideal for shipping in an oversized envelope, at a flat rate. This means she can not only purchase shipping envelopes in bulk, but also purchase postage ahead of time—and eliminate those regular trips to the post office.

Tracking Revenues and Costs

Every business should keep detailed records, and your online auction business is no exception. Whether you use an auction management service that offers report generation, a financial-management program like Quicken or QuickBooks, or your own homemade spreadsheet or database, you need to track what you're doing.

In particular, you want to track unit cost and final selling price for every auction you list. You should also track all your ancillary costs—shipping, PayPal fees, eBay listing and final value fees, and so on. By tracking all your costs and revenues, you can generate an accurate profit and

tip

When you reach this sales volume, you should also investigate the pick-up services offered by many shipping services. Dragging hundreds of items to the post office every week is a *lot* of work—which you want to eliminate, if you can.

"Mike Sez"

Although it's important to keep detailed records regarding your eBay auctions, generating a few reports is no substitute for engaging an accountant—especially when taxes enter into the equation. Remember, any profits you make on your auctions must be reported as income, and you must pay taxes on your income. Unlike in a "real" job in which taxes are deducted from your weekly paycheck, the taxes you owe from your self-run business are paid to the government as quarterly estimates. Trust me, you don't want to handle this tax stuff yourself. It's definitely worth a few bucks to have an accountant handle all your business taxes for you—and he can probably help you find a few extra deductions, besides.

loss statement, and thus determine how much money (if any) you're generating from your online auction activities.

It also helps to track information about the buyers of your auction items—name, shipping address, email address, and so on. The name and shipping address are necessary in case an item gets lost in transit; the email address is necessary not only for auction-related communication but also for promotional purposes—which we'll discuss next.

Promoting Your Online Auctions

If you're running a hundred or more auctions a week, you want to draw attention to your auctions. That might mean splurging for some of eBay's listing enhancements (boldface, gallery, and so on), although these extras typically aren't worth the extra cost. Better to promote your auctions on your personal website, via message board postings, and in all your emails.

Probably the most important type of promotion, however, is word of mouth—based on your good reputation. You want to encourage repeat bidders and drive buyers into your online store (if you have one) for additional sales. That means treating your buyers fairly and with respect, and going the extra mile to ensure their satisfaction. It also means sending previous buyers emails when you have items up for auction that they might be interested in. (Which argues, of course, for keeping comprehensive records of all your eBay auctions.)

THE ABSOLUTE MINIMUM

Here are the key points to remember from this chapter:

- If you're selling more than $1,000 per month, you may be eligible for eBay's PowerSeller program.

- To turn your eBay hobby into a money-making profession, you need to start with some detailed business and financial planning.

- Most PowerSellers specialize in a specific type of item—and buy it in bulk.

- Successful eBay businesses keep detailed records and perform regular analyses of their auction activities.

- The more auctions you list, the more value you'll get from third-party auction management sites and services.

- When you start making a living from your eBay auctions, be sure to engage the services of a qualified accountant—to manage your tax liabilities, if nothing else.

Index